BLACK CHURCH BEGINNINGS

BLACK CHURCH BEGINNINGS

The Long-Hidden Realities of the First Years

Henry H. Mitchell

WILLIAM B. EERDMANS PUBLISHING COMPANY

GRAND RAPIDS, MICHIGAN / CAMBRIDGE, U.K.

© 2004 Wm. B. Eerdmans Publishing Co.
All rights reserved

Wm. B. Eerdmans Publishing Co.
255 Jefferson Ave. S.E., Grand Rapids, Michigan 49503 /
P.O. Box 163, Cambridge CB3 9PU U.K.

Printed in the United States of America

09 08 07 06 05 04   7 6 5 4 3 2 1

Library of Congress Cataloging-in-Publication Data

ISBN 0-8028-2785-3

www.eerdmans.com

*To Second Baptist Church of Columbus, Ohio, founded in 1836,
my home church, where I was baptized in 1925.*

*And to its pastors whose active witness has kept me deeply
interested in Black Church history all my life:*

*James Poindexter and H. H. Mitchell continued the already great
church tradition long before my time.*

*In my childhood and youth, Grandpa Mitchell returned
to join pastors E. W. Moore and C. F. Jenkins in further
extending that tradition and its powerful influence in my life.*

Contents

CONTENTS

Preface

In the introductory course in African American church history at Colgate Rochester Divinity School in 1973, I, the instructor, was accused thus: "You teach Black Church history like it's your own family album." I had mentioned from time to time such data as my growing up in one of the first black Baptist associations (in Ohio); my grandfather's presidency of the Virginia Baptists in 1895 (so that he signed the charter when the National Baptist Convention was organized); and my close personal ties with an early figure at Wilberforce. My answer was, "You're absolutely right, and that's how every one of *you* should view it. It's not abstract data required to pass a course. It's the spiritual history of *our* family. Until you see it this way, you won't even know who you are. Among other handicaps, you'll be the helpless victim of widespread misinformation about our family's faith, as having come from the slave masters."

When students of other races get perfect grades in traditional history courses, they are very likely seeing the material as the spiritual and social history of *their* families, a tale with which they have personal ties. African American students desperately need to see Black Church history the same way. When African American church history gets personal, deficits in ethnic self-esteem are healed, to say nothing of the accurate information and the spiritual growth that are made possible.

African American church history has been approached from many valid angles. Denominational growth, great preachers and leaders, and socio-political dynamics have all been covered, but all of these facets of church life were addressed at a scholarly distance. Such study may stir some needed ethnic pride, but the story must involve the masses and their experience in the life of the congregation for today's members or other readers to profit and grow by identification.

An effort is also made here to avoid the common trend, in local church histories, of recording only such data as membership totals, buildings built or bought, mortgage burnings, and purchases of pews and organs. While examples of the early financial struggles of local churches are vital and require a rightful place in making history more concrete and personally relevant, the main data concern the ministries. Beverly Gray has written an early history of Eden Baptist Church (1824) in the "Peepee Hills" of Southern Ohio, in which a revival is reported. She traces the careers of the saved all over the United States. The history of First African Baptist Church of Philadelphia records two members volunteering to return to slavery for a year, as bond for an enslaved preacher whom their church had called as pastor. He was to earn his purchase price during that year away, and he did. Data like this make a history doubly vivid and literally very personal.

Traditional histories tend to focus on organizational development, socio-economic analysis, external power issues, and great orator-achiever heroes. These are all valid subjects and will be included in digest, with due respect for the excellent research done in earlier histories. But the local congregation's internal structure and struggle into existence, the shape of ministry and ministerial leadership, and the dedicated effort of entire congregations are the main concern of this church history. It is primarily the story of churches as local congregations and spiritual families, and then as members of denominations and other groupings.

The sources consulted in the writing of most church history tend to be from outside the churches themselves, with few if any references to the churches' own records. Where there is discrepancy between public records and previous authors on the one hand, and church records on the other, the church records are taken as definitive. Thus a church reported as begun in 1845, because of incorporation in that year, is here reported as beginning when they first began regular worship in, say, 1836, as stated in the church's own records. Local church reports and published histories are contradicted here only with overriding hard data to the contrary.

It is the purpose of this volume to provide a more accurate introduction to the early history of the Black Church in the United States of America. A great deal hinges on the way one sees this period, but not much attention has been given to it, especially 1619-1800. Much of this is due to the fact that there was so little study done on Africa and blacks in colonial America before 1960, and so little writer participation in the African American churches of the masses.

It has been my intention to place in writing a point of view "from the bottom," as it were — to speak from within the church of the masses, as well as the emergent middle classes. The frequent reference to secondary sources is provided for the use of all who wish to track down original sources and go deeper. However, I maintain that the asterisked data here, from local church records, are themselves primary data. I accept such accounts above all others because it is *their* history, and most of these congregations were gathered in worship long before they had reason to be on record at the courthouses with deeds to property or articles of incorporation.

Another important issue in this work is that of how much white influence prevailed in the formation of the African American church, its worship, and its belief system, and what at the beginning could be validly labeled an experience of conversion to the faith. It is my high expectation that those who hold that black religion was given to African Americans by slave masters will be disabused of this dangerous misreading of the facts of the early religious life of the slaves. With this correction, African Americans can be helped to overcome the cripplingly low view of themselves that has been fed not only by errors of history but by subtle messages from the majority culture even today.

Acknowledgments

At a conference last week, a friend sought to know which source of funding I had used to write this book. He was astounded when my reply was "None." It dawned on me that I did have providentially placed friends, and, more than I had previously sensed, I owed them a great deal of gratitude.

Laity such as Helen B. Giles and Peggy Lee of historic First Baptist Church of Petersburg, Virginia, helped launch the study. Ethel Nichols of Philadelphia was the source of an important case history, as was Mozelle Medcalf at South Point, Ohio, of the historic Providence Baptist Association, who shared the best of their remaining records. Their then Moderator, Pastor Douglas C. Carter of Burlington, shared the 150th anniversary souvenir book. Jerome B. Washington, pastor at Detroit, provided the critically important Louisiana state history, and Cleopatric Lacy, pastor at Griffin, Georgia, supplied crucial sources on schools. Pastor Dennis E. Thomas of historic First African Baptist Church of Richmond, Virginia, provided important materials.

From the world of professional historians I was provided with critically important research by Professors Lewis V. Baldwin and Dennis C. Dickerson, both of Vanderbilt University, and the latter a historian for the African Methodist Episcopal Church. Ms. Beverly Gray of Chillecothe, Ohio, expert historian and retired teacher, offered leads to significant corrections of traditional understandings. Vitally important and graciously generous assistance was rendered by the American

Baptist Historical Society and the Virginia Historical Society. Eddie L. Perry of the American Baptist office and James D. Armstrong of the A.M.E. Zion Historical Society lent a hand as well.

Words fail to provide adequate thanks to Martha Simmons, Co-Editor of the *African American Pulpit* and peerless scholar and editor, who graciously offered her expertise as the professional editor-consultant for this book. Her sharp criticisms repaid me for the red ink I put on her papers years ago, when I was her teacher. However, the quality of my writing is immensely better than it would have been without her. I will always be grateful for her sacrifice, as she also labored towards her Ph.D. and covered all her other responsibilities.

Finally, every imaginable support was given gladly by Ella Pearson Mitchell, my beloved partner for now sixty years. She did everything from the reading of proofs with an eagle eye, to research, to covering for me when deadlines forced me to change other schedules. Above all, she refused to let me be discouraged, always giving abundant emotional and spiritual support. My gratitude is endless.

Abbreviations

*   Asterisks denote material from the brief published histories of the related church group.

\#   Symbol indicates material from archives of the African Methodist Episcopal Church (Dept. of Research and Scholarship, Dennis C. Dickerson, Ph.D., Executive Director); Nicole D. Dickerson is the author of the report on the starting dates of churches.

\>   Date drawn from chronological listings in Mechal Sobel, *Trabelin' On: The Slave Journey to an Afro-Baptist Faith* (Westport, Conn.: Greenwood Press, 1979), pp. 250-356.

Introduction

To the average American, it might seem strange to date this book on African American religion from 1619, the year the soon-to-be-enslaved Africans landed in Jamestown, Virginia. However, the religious faith and practice of the masses of black Americans goes back even earlier than 1619; the continuum starts in Africa. In the words of Bruno Chenu, "More than an imposition by the whites, it was the similarity between the Christian religion and their traditional religion that fostered the passage of the faith of the hated master. And African beliefs still lived beneath visible Christianity."[1] Of course, this is contrary to the widely circulated assumption that Africans were largely stripped of their native culture and religion during or after their voyage to these shores. The truth is that there is much hard evidence proving that Africans retained a great deal of their original cultural heritage. This is especially true of religion, which was much harder to stamp out than visible behaviors such as styles of manual labor. The long-handled hoe of the colonies may have won out over the back-straining short-handled hoe of Africa, but the tenacity of the communally embraced traditional belief system was far greater. It was the people's psychic survival kit.

In the 1960s and 1970s, just when those tenacious, African-rooted cultural influences might have begun to slip into final oblivion by the

---

1. Bruno Chenu, *The Trouble I've Seen* (Valley Forge: Judson Press, 2003), pp. 48-49.

process of slow acculturation, there came a civil rights revolution. It was accompanied by a major African American cultural renaissance. Many rose up in black pride and enthusiastically re-embraced the very African influences they had long been taught to be ashamed of.

In other words, the religious beliefs and practices of the masses of African Americans today are still heavily African. They are part of a living religious stream that began in Africa, not in Europe as so many have supposed. Significant aspects of today's African American religious practice have flowed unbroken throughout the years and are now in a mode of healthy revival. Gayraud S. Wilmore said it thus in his *Black Religion and Black Radicalism:* "notwithstanding elements of white evangelicalism in the mainstream of black faith, there was from the beginning a fusion between a highly developed and pervasive feeling about the essentially spiritual nature of historical experience, flowing from the African traditional background, and a radical secularity related both to religious sensibility and to the experience of slavery and oppression. This fusion accounts for the most significant characteristics of black religion. . . . It is now clear that black religion in North America had roots in Africa and the Caribbean as well as in the Great Awakenings of the eighteenth and nineteenth centuries."[2]

James Melvin Washington stated it more succinctly: "The religious discourse and rituals of slaves were quite African. How could it be otherwise?"[3] Later he stated it in cultural terms: "they did forge a powerful religious tradition whose cultural legacy has greatly enriched American culture, and helped reconstitute African culture [in the United States] in a new guise."[4]

Mechal Sobel's "Vital Statistics and Summary Histories" of the earliest African American congregations is the most complete listing of African American Baptists presently available.[5] Sobel's understanding reflects a viewpoint this book will reinforce:

2. Gayraud S. Wilmore, *Black Religion and Black Radicalism,* 2nd ed. (Maryknoll, N.Y.: Orbis Books, 1983; reissued 1993), pp. 3, 15.

3. James M. Washington, *Frustrated Fellowship* (Macon, Ga.: Mercer U. Press, 1986), p. xiv.

4. Washington, *Frustrated Fellowship,* p. 21.

5. Mechal Sobel, *Trabelin' On: The Slave Journey to an Afro-Baptist Faith* (Westport, Conn.: Greenwood Press, 1979), pp. 257-356.

Africans brought their world views into North America where, in an early phase of slavery, the core understandings, or Sacred Cosmos, at the heart of these world views coalesced into one Neo-African consciousness — basically similar yet already significantly different from West African understandings. Over time, . . . a coherent Afro-Christian faith was created, and its reality was reflected in a vibrant and known institution, a Black Baptist church, the history of which goes back to the 1750s.[6]

Chapter One elaborates and documents these supposedly stripped away African root elements that still surface in African American belief and practice. Chapter Two traces slave population growth and documents the supposedly "silent years" of African American religious history in this country (to 1750). It tracks the all-African traditional set of beliefs and practices as it evolved into Christian beliefs and practices that were also African. Because of the overlap, African beliefs could also be profoundly compatible with Christian faith, and richer for the mutual exchange. Chapter Three records the beginnings, the organization, of the first African American congregations, North and South, 1750 to 1800. Chapter Four details prevailing influences on the interior life of the new congregations. Chapter Five traces the development of new churches from 1801 to 1840. Chapter Six surveys new church development, 1841-1865, and the development of denominational bodies. Chapter Seven chronicles the activities of African American churches in various forms of social activism, including support for the Civil War. Chapter Eight chronicles the role of African American religion in the Reconstruction Era, labeled here the "Golden Age" of the black churches in establishing congregations, family life, education, politics, and economic self-determination. There follows an epilogue dealing with topics not included, and summing up the meaning of this study for the future of the African American church.

This earliest religious history (1619-1750) is the least-known aspect of African American heritage, among African Americans as well as whites. It is also the period most needed, from the perspective of historical accuracy, and for the factual support of African American spiritual self-understanding and ethnic self-esteem. Too long have African

6. Sobel, *Trabelin' On,* p. xvii.

Americans with the advantages of higher education been trained to believe that Christianity among blacks was largely the result of slave masters' efforts to make more docile slaves. So-called "militants" and some intellectuals who claimed to affirm African American self-esteem have scoffed, in error, at the black Christian church. They have ignored the fact that, at its best, the African American church has proven to be the greatest source for motivating self-liberating action, as well as healthy self-pride among African Americans. In addition, no other aspect or agency of the common culture comes close to the vanguard of African American churches in the retention of African influences on black culture. It is healing to the African American psyche and spirit to be assured that a great many of the core beliefs of African American Christians were held by our forbears in Africa and brought with them to America, rather than taught to them from scratch by oppressors. All of these chapters spell out the survival of African influences, and the largely self-directed course of rich African American religious history, as it developed in the earliest decades of the churches.

Chapter 1

The African Roots of the African American Church

The powerful early influence of African traditional religion and culture on the belief and practice of those enslaved in America is easy to find. Yet the opinion of the great African American sociologist E. Franklin Frazier has persisted in one form or another among scholars. Although Frazier acknowledged some African influences, the best-known part of his position is summed up in this quotation from his book, *The Negro Church in America,* written just prior to his death in 1962:

> From what has been pointed out concerning the manner in which the slaves were stripped of their cultural heritage, we may dismiss such speculations as the one that [their Baptist and Methodist worship] was due to their African background.[1]

Frazier was undoubtedly influenced by his mentor at the University of Chicago, Robert E. Park, who said in a 1918 address before the American Sociological Society,

> In fact, there is every reason to believe, it seems to me, that the Negro, when he landed in the United States, left behind him almost everything but his dark complexion and his tropical temperament.

1. E. Franklin Frazier, *The Negro Church in America* (New York: Schocken Books, 1963), p. 8.

It is very difficult to find in the South today anything that can be traced directly back to Africa.[2]

A more recent version of a similar trend of thought can be found in the research of Albert J. Raboteau's *Slave Religion* (1978). He clearly documents important African cultural survivals in places like Brazil, but interprets the data regarding survivals in the United States this way:

> Under British North American slavery, it seems that the African re-ligious heritage was lost. Especially does this appear so when black religion in the United States is compared with the cults of Brazil and the Caribbean.[3]

Raboteau actually entitled the chapter from which this quotation was taken "Death of the Gods," meaning that the specific names of African deities were lost, but even implying that the influence of the African be-lief system died with the names. The correction of this critically impor-tant under-emphasis is essential to African American spiritual self-understanding, so it is heartening to note that Raboteau's *Canaan Land: A Religious History of African Americans,* published in 2001, offers a some-what different perspective: "Thousands of Africans from diverse cul-tures and religious traditions, forcibly transported to America as slaves, retained many African customs even as they converted to Christianity."[4]

Crucial facts have been there all along. Until the latter half of the twentieth century, the data simply had not been collected and inter-preted in a manner sufficiently clear to overcome, in the minds of many, the notion that African Americans were culturally stripped and religiously brainwashed. Thus, for these researchers, the Christianity of the enslaved *had* to be the result of white instruction. Raboteau's earlier examples of black religion, such as the writings of Phillis Wheatley, are far from representative of the "invisible institution" of slave religion and of the majority of the African American churches that flowed from

2. Robert E. Park, in *Journal of Negro History,* 60 vols. (Washington, D.C.: Associ-ated Publishers), vol. 4, p. 116.

3. Albert J. Raboteau, *Slave Religion* (New York: Oxford University Press, 1978), p. 47.

4. Albert J. Raboteau, *Canaan Land: A Religious History of African Americans* (New York: Oxford University Press, 2001), p. ix.

it. The facts set forth in this book spell out the unmistakable case for African religious survivals in general. These facts were obvious long before Frazier wrote, but it took decades of wide-ranging research and actual visits to Africa to crystallize a detailed rebuttal to the earlier work of Frazier and others. Meanwhile, the major outlines of this truth were early perceived by a few, such as the great African American scholar W. E. B. DuBois, the pioneering anthropologist Melville Herskovits, the sociologist George P. Rawick, the African American historian John W. Blassingame, and the tireless researcher Mechal Sobel.

In 1915, even though DuBois had not set foot in Africa, he was still able to offer profound insight into the African roots of black religion. To be sure, his insight is flawed with a few terms and preconceptions that neither he nor we would use if writing today, but it is nevertheless a landmark of insight into the Black Church:

> At first sight it would seem that slavery completely destroyed every vestige of spontaneous movement among the Negroes. This is not strictly true. The vast power of the priest in the African state is well known; his realm alone — the province of religion and medicine — remained largely unaffected by the plantation system. The Negro priest, therefore, early became an important figure on the plantation and found his function as the interpreter of the supernatural, the comforter of the sorrowing, and as the one who expressed, rudely but picturesquely, the longing and disappointment of a stolen people. From such beginnings arose and spread with marvelous rapidity, the Negro church, the first distinctively Negro American social institution. It was not at first by any means a Christian church, but a mere adaptation of those rites of fetish which in America is termed obe worship, or "voodoo-ism." Association and missionary effort soon gave these rites a veneer of Christianity and gradually, after two centuries, the church became Christian, with a simple Calvinistic creed, but with many of the old customs still clinging to the services. It is this historic fact, that the Negro church of to-day bases itself on the sole surviving social institution of the African fatherland, that accounts for its extraordinary growth and vitality.[5]

5. W. E. B. DuBois, *The Negro* (New York: Oxford University Press, 1970), pp. xiii, 113-14.

Evidence for Cultural Survivals

The unmistakable evidence of the survival of African culture among enslaved Africans can be seen in an abundance of ways overlooked by Park and Frazier. The most obvious evidences are the outlawing of the highly complex drumming codes, and the effective practice of African traditional medicine on white patients. The very laws against drumming and medical practice show the existence and popularity of these powerful and sophisticated practices in the culture of the Africans in the colonies.

When whites discovered that enslaved Africans often communicated the latest news to each other days before their masters knew it, they were terrified by the potential for conspiracy.[6] Drums were outlawed even for worship.[7] Along with ritual dancing, drums were declared "sinful." Blacks then used hand clapping and foot patting for their percussion element in worship, having to give up the richer meanings that were once communicated on the drums. However, the complicated polyrhythms of Africa are still quite evident in the foot patting and hand clapping of some African American churches.[8]

The exact power of the original drum codes was made clear to the Martin Luther King Fellows of Colgate Rochester Divinity School in the summer of 1972, in Ewe, Western Nigeria. The town chief, a pharmacy college grad with interests in cultural anthropology, had his chief drummer demonstrate that the drum still could say anything the mouth could say. A member of the tribe was sent to a post over a hundred yards away. Someone then whispered a message in the ear of the chief drummer, who talked with his drum to the person at the distant listening post.

The talking drum held under the arm had soft sides that yielded three different tonal pitches, high, middle, and low, according to the pressure of the arm. This amounted to a "Morse Code" with three signals — a trinaural rather than a binaural system. It required expert

6. John Lovell, Jr., *Black Song: The Forge and the Flame* (New York: Macmillan, 1972), p. 121; John W. Blassingame, *The Slave Community* (New York: Oxford University Press, 1979), p. 35.

7. Miles Mark Fisher, *Negro Slave Songs in the U.S.* (New York: Russell & Russell, 1968), p. 29.

8. Blassingame, *The Slave Community*, pp.22-23.

hearing to distinguish the pitch levels, and a keen mind to decipher the code. The hearer and the drummer must have had both of these most impressive skills. The drummer beat his drum, and the fellow who had been sent away came back and did what the message told him to do, without hesitation. It seemed amazingly simple.

The speaker had whispered this message: "Find the pocket radio and put it in its case," which is exactly what the demonstrator did. The amazed speaker said, "I bet you don't even have a word for 'radio.' What on earth did you tell that brother?" The chief replied, "You're right. We don't have such a word. We told him, 'Find that which speaks to you and you can't speak back, and put him in his house.'" The message was transmitted with ease and brevity, with no audible consonants or vowels or visual promptings. The point was very clear: African drums were at the very least as good as Western Union. The tonality of the drums carried great meaning in African culture. Drum tonality survived in the colonies[9] until as an observable behavior it had to be suppressed by laws enforced by violence.

The medical skills learned by African priest-doctors (*not* "witch doctors") survived much longer than the drum codes, because the practice of these skills was suppressed only among white patients. Kofi Opoku reports that the skills of homeopathic medicine had been originally learned in Africa, alongside African priestcraft, in a minimum of three years of intensive training.[10] On the remote colonial frontiers of Virginia and the Carolinas, these African traditional cures often offered the best medical care available, and they were willingly utilized at first by whites as well as blacks. When it began to be noticed that the life expectancy of particularly harsh masters under treatment was somehow uniformly short, the slave owners outlawed the practice of African traditional medicine on whites. It was permitted among blacks as an effective protection of the health of valuable "property," attesting to its curative powers when such were needed to keep slaves alive and working.

In fact, many of today's so-called home remedies are survivals of an impressive collection of folk medical wisdom from Africa. Near Accra, the King Fellows mentioned above visited Oku Ampofo, a

9. Lovell, *Black Song*, p. 121.

10. Kofi Asare Opoku, *West African Traditional Religion* (Accra and Singapore: FEP International Limited, 1976), pp. 74-76.

British-board certified physician and surgeon who sometimes prescribed European medications. But he preferred pharmaceuticals only when he knew of no African homeopathic (root and herbal) cures that fitted the case. He maintained a dispensary for these traditional African medications as late as 1972. Today, in both Africa and America, black medical professionals are being drawn back to probe the healing powers of that medical culture that was supposedly stripped from their African ancestors.

African American midwives used folk medicine (not "remedies") such as sugar and alum. Today nurses pack bedsores in hospitals with sugar, and men use the alum of styptic pencils to stop bleeding after facial cuts from shaving. In 1925, folklorist Newbell Niles Puckett wrote in his historic piece *Folk Beliefs of the Southern Negro* that the midwives using these substances were "under the impression that it hastens the curative process."[11] Puckett not only affirmed the African origin of the cures; he placed on record the uses to which they were applied.

Perhaps the most impressive example of African medical expertise brought across the Atlantic is to be seen in a reference to early African practices of immunization:

> During the heated dispute about inoculation against small-pox, Cotton Mather, who favored it, interviewed some Negroes of the city and learned that they had brought the practice from Africa. He attempted to set down their answer in their own words, for, as he wrote, "The more plainly, brokenly, and blunderingly, and like Ideots, they tell their story, it will be with reasonable Men but the much more credible." [Mather wrote:] "I had from a Servant of my own, an account of its being practiced in *Africa*. Enquiring of my Negro-man *Onesimus*, who was a pretty Intelligent Fellow, Whether he ever had ye Small Pox; he answered, both, Yes, and No; and then told me, that he had undergone an operation, which had given him something of ye Small-Pox, & would forever preserve him from it. . . ."[12]

11. Newbell N. Puckett, *Folk Beliefs of the Southern Negro* (New York: Negro Universities Press, 1968), p. 333.

12. Letter of July 12, 1716, in the Philosophical Transactions of the Royal Society, printed in *Journal of Negro History,* 60 vols. (Washington, D.C.: Associated Publishers), vol. 24, p. 247.

Another strong evidence of the cultural carryover from Africa was the folktales common among the enslaved. Speaking of the well-known "Tar Baby" tale, Melville Herskovits early (1941) declared, ". . . the tales as found in the New World represent a part of the cultural heritage brought by Africans to this hemisphere."[13] The tales gleaned by people like Joel Chandler Harris from these great African storytellers were unmistakably part of their roots, no matter how many other countries and cultures may have had similar tales.

In addition to the polyrhythms mentioned earlier, the various survivals of musical style from Africa also included call-and-response, spontaneous composition and improvisation, and certain formal dance movements. The latter included songs sung to give rhythmic timing to ease strenuous labor, as well as to invite the spirit in worship. Lawrence Levine declares that slaves used "music in almost every conceivable setting, for almost every possible purpose. . . . Slaves brought the banjo, the musical bow . . . and a number of percussive instruments with them from Africa."[14] Also surviving was the "motor inventory," the anthropological terms for a collection of typical body movements. Whether in worship or elsewhere, they were the same movements, in Accra and in Harlem.[15]

Two other pieces of evidence for survivals were found in the Sea Islands. One was the widely known Gullah dialect, which retains the sounds and grammar of the African Akan language, and such words as "goober" for peanuts. The other was African grammar's inclusion of genderless pronouns. Thus both male *and* female were referred to as "he."[16] It wasn't African ignorance of English; rather it was their native Akan grammar used with English words.

The rhetoric of African "ritual insult," in which one vents anger against an offender, survives in adapted form in African American street culture. It is known as "signifying," and allows for a healing release of the hostility from being offended. Feelings are vented without

---

13. Melvin J. Herskovits, *The Myth of the Negro Past* (Boston: Beacon Press, 1958), pp. 272-73.

14. Lawrence W. Levine, *Black Culture and Black Consciousness* (New York: Oxford University Press, 1977), p. 15.

15. Raboteau, *Slave Religion*, pp. 35-36.

16. Blassingame, *The Slave Community*, p. 29.

permitting response by the offender, who, although in earshot, is presumed to be excluded from the conversation.[17]

A final example of culture that certainly was not stripped was the funeral rites so widely practiced and so obviously brought over from Africa. They included dancing and drinking in all-night ceremonies celebrating the deceased's return "home."[18] There were vestiges of African burial culture in the symbolic figures atop graves in Louisiana as recently as 1979.[19]

Survivals of African Religious Practices

One way to document DuBois's theory of the evolving merger of Christianity with African religion is to observe the various stages of the evolution of black religion in the Caribbean. Cultic groups there range from 90 percent African and 10 percent Christian to the opposite proportion. I personally have taken part in "Shango Baptist" rites (on the island of Trinidad) that were at least 90 percent African. Elements observed included the dance, the sacrifice of chickens and sheep, and trance states (spirit possession). Albert J. Raboteau reports the same, and agrees that the Christian hymns that were sung preliminarily appeared to be a warm-up for the *real* rites. The hymn singing was apparently routine, without much awareness of the meaning of the words, and possibly serving merely as a vehicle for a rhythmic beat. With these only-peripheral elements of Christian hymnody, this group's main worship was overwhelmingly African.[20]

Such a progressive shifting of the mix of elements likely occurred in the first slave communities of the colonies in the late seventeenth and early eighteenth centuries. This was especially true in Virginia and the Carolinas, where larger communities of slaves were concentrated. This early, first-stage African worship, of course, was clandestine and not under white supervision. White reports described early African gatherings as wildly heathen, with not a clue as to the always-present

17. Levine, *Black Culture and Black Consciousness,* pp. 8ff.

18. Blassingame, *The Slave Community,* p. 333.

19. Mechal Sobel, *Trabelin' On: The Slave Journey to an Afro-Baptist Faith* (Westport, Conn.: Greenwood Press, 1979), p. 199.

20. Raboteau, *Slave Religion,* pp. 35-36.

religious significance. Frazier aptly termed this evolving church the "Invisible Institution."[21] From this mostly African stage, as Dubois stated, Africans became more and more Christian through the years. By the 1750s, black worship began to surface as formally recognized (and, to some unofficial extent, self-governing) congregations. The process by which these congregations evolved has only relatively recently been researched. Meanwhile, the "Invisible Institution" and its more African worship continued in secret and unsupervised, but not uninfluenced, until after the Civil War.

One manifestly African religious rite that survived after the Civil War was the "ring shout." One was recorded in the minutes of an 1878 meeting in the Baltimore Conference of the African Methodist Episcopal Church. Although this occurrence was long after the early period being discussed here, it is a clear example of an African religious survival over a period of as much as 150 to 200 years. A.M.E. Bishop Payne objected to the practice, but the presiding elder declared, "Sinners won't get converted unless there is a ring."[22] This shout had been used since the seventeenth century, when Africans had arrived in larger numbers. Somewhere along the way the ring was also adapted to Christian purposes.

This 1878 incident serves in interesting illustration of the earlier mentioned mixtures of African and Euro-Christian rites in the Caribbean. In January of 1974, in Kingston, Jamaica, the King Fellows attended the A.M.E. Zion Annual Conference, just after it had received over 200 new congregations into denominational affiliation. A full ring shout was in progress. These new congregations had belonged to a group called "Zion Revival," whose culture had been about 50 percent African, maybe 25 percent primitive Christian, and 25 percent white-missionary-revival influence, from which they took their name. The union of these congregations with the A.M.E. Zions came about when an A.M.E. Zion missionary helped the Zion Revivals save many of their homes, threatened by newly inflated land values and high taxes. They were extremely grateful. Apparently attracted also by the sharing of the

21. E. Franklin Frazier, *The Negro Church in America* (New York: Schocken Books, 1963), p. 16.

22. *A History of the African Methodist Episcopal Church,* vol. 2, ed. Charles Spencer Smith (New York: Johnson Reprint Company, 1968), pp. 126-27.

name "Zion," they applied for membership and were received into the A.M.E. Zion Conference. They were even willing to be instructed in orthodox Christianity at any point where their practices were contrary to tradition. It was fascinating to observe the A.M.E. Zion *acceptance* of a full-fledged African ring shout in 1974. It had the full permission of the bishop, who actually took part in the ring shout himself. This same process of stages of cultural adaptation no doubt prevailed in the "Invisible Institution" in America, and ring shouts are actually known still to occur in a few black churches across the country.

However, this African ring shout survival was not without opposition. It was suppressed by leaders of official African American church bodies, such as A.M.E. Bishop Daniel A. Payne, who presided over the A.M.E. churches of Maryland and Virginia. Bishop Charles S. Smith recorded Bishop Payne's judgmental reaction to the 1878 Ring Shout mentioned above: Payne's bitter judgment was expressed in words like "corn-field ditties" and "fist and hoof religion."[23] Payne's suppression of African survivals may be responsible, in at least some small measure, for the A.M.E. church's slower early growth in Payne's Second Episcopal District, compared to its much greater growth in states like South Carolina and Georgia, where the African culture was affirmed by A.M.E. bishops like Henry McNeal Turner and others.

African Culture and Early Conversions

The most important question about the early black Christians' "conversions" has to do with exactly what this meant to native African families hastily tutored. The more limited conversion reports available to historians like Carter Woodson were unable to address this issue adequately.[24] The only detail of concrete definition raised in any of these reports had to do with the slaves' ability to read or remember and/or speak and understand what conversion meant in English, *to native speakers of English.* No person who had not learned any African language

23. *A History of the African Methodist Episcopal Church,* vol. 2, pp. 126-27; Raboteau, *Slave Religion,* pp. 66-69.

24. Carter G. Woodson, *The History of the Negro Church* (Washington, D.C.: Associated Publishers, 1972), pp. 4-16.

or worldview could have begun accurately to teach another worldview to an African pupil. Thus, it was virtually impossible that most Africans could have understood conversion.

In fact, one could verify conversions only by the various outward phases reported. That is, a gifted African who easily learned English and memorized things like the Lord's Prayer, the twenty-third Psalm, and the Apostles' Creed was considered converted. There is good reason to believe that one would perform all of this just to please the master — if not in every case, certainly in most. It was as if there were the desperate need for slaves to make the master think they were happy and content. Every slave knew masters believed that discontent slaves were dangerous. Thus one learned to smile regardless.

One can only guess what Church of England conversion in Virginia meant to a mind still operating in an African belief system and frame of reference. No two reports on the Africans' acceptance of the Christian faith were likely to have been based on the exact same African inner understandings. All Anglican (Episcopalian) reports were based on a doctrine of conversion defined as formal statement of belief, recited as memorized. This view prevailed despite the fact that most clergymen in early Virginia were already "non-separating" Puritans who had stayed in the Church of England.[25] This brand of priest, despite official doctrine, had beliefs closer to evangelical revival practice. This, if uncovered, might have been helpful toward more spirit-centered African conversions at an earlier date.

The Africans themselves saw faith and religious commitment as a natural part of their culture, and based on *experience*, accompanied by some aspect of spiritual possession. It is not hard to see how much this view was deeply rooted, since it prevails among the masses of African Americans even today. Seventy-five years ago it was common to hear an African American elderly saint declare, "If you ain't *felt* nothin', you ain't *got* nothin'." In other words, a deeply felt emotional experience was crucial evidence of conversion or salvation.

Slave conversion reports are also undermined by common assumptions that conversion made slaves more docile or profitable. While this docility may have been true in some cases, it was more likely that they submitted to "conversion" because they intended to be seen

---

25. Sobel, *Trabelin' On,* pp. 63-64.

as docile. It thus becomes clear that nothing can be said with *certainty* about any depths of slave conversion in the colonies, from the first arrivals until the spread of the influence of the First Great Awakening. This is a judgment of cultural and existential reality, not theology or doctrine. We do know this much:

1. Conversion was so loaded with the danger of slaves feeling spiritually equal to white masters that a great many slave owners preferred *not* to run the risk. As Sobel put it, "'Indocile' without English or before conversion, and 'haughty' afterwards, the black response to the Anglican religion was not generally a positive one from either the black or white point of view. . . . Local slave owners were not pressing for conversion; quite the contrary."[26] The slowness of slaves to learn the language, or admit that they could speak it, made true conversion even more subject to question.

2. The memorization of Anglican creeds and catechisms was no guarantee of profound grasp or serious belief. But it was surely a sign of monumental memory (characteristic of African culture) and skillful surface conformity, once one had attained some competence in English.

3. Teaching of the faith was focused on children *born* in the colonies, because of language and their openness of mind. Adults were taught along with both white and black children. These adults were not blind to this disrespect. They may well have listened carefully only to sift out what they could learn of the white God who was the center of the power so important in African worldviews. It was out of this initial exposure to God as power that some of the first surface conversions of Africans may have taken place. Christianity was more acceptable than it might have been without the God of power.[27] However, the Anglican faith was resisted by the vast majority of Africans, with or without catechetical instruction. Even the slave children's worldview was influenced by their parents far more than by their Anglican owners and teachers.

26. Sobel, *Trabelin' On,* p. 60.
27. Sobel, *Travelin' On,* p. 62.

In the North there were fewer slaves and fewer efforts to gain converts in the period leading up to the 1750s. Northern African Americans were not gathered in self-sufficient communities of culture, and so were naturally more influenced by the majority culture. The process described by DuBois was primarily confined to the larger slave communities of the plantations in the South. The soul-stirring conversions that came after the First Great Awakening were based on a view of conversion totally different from an Anglican or even a Puritan view. Conversion became a heavily African-influenced merger/adaptation of the new, white conversion, behaviors, and beliefs. The influences flowed both ways and enriched the faith wherever there were large concentrations of African Americans in the South, as well as in large cities like Philadelphia.

Even in the midst of majority cultural pressure in the North, the preference for their own African identity was evident in the choice of the word African, as included in the names of the Methodist denominations cited (African Methodist Episcopal and A.M.E. Zion), and local congregations such as the First African Presbyterian Church and the First African Baptist Church, both of Philadelphia. The natural African cultural preference is also evident in the tales, songs, and dances of old Africa that were joyously passed on in great festivals permitted among the enslaved and the freed in New Hampshire, New York, Pennsylvania, and even Maryland.[28] Similar to modern Mardi Gras, these festivities showed no distinction between sacred and secular. With these festivities, African Americans expressed their culture, whether sacred or secular. African call and response, uninhibited enthusiasm, and freedom of expression prevailed. In both South and North, the greatest reservoir for preserving African cultural survivals was and is the African American church or its earlier secret substitute, the "invisible institution."

Survivals of African Traditional Religion in Black Christianity

The greatest and most obvious survival of African traditional religion in the conversion culture and the general worship of the African Amer-

28. Eileen Southern, *The Music of Black Americans: A History* (New York: Norton, 1971), pp. 49-55.

ican church, then and now, is the tradition of "shouting," or possession by the Holy Spirit. In African traditional religion, devotees were and are possessed by one of several sub-deities, as identified by the priest to fit a person's specific need. In Christianity it is only the Holy Spirit who possesses and causes ecstasy. This is the most significant difference between possession in African traditional religion and possession in Christianity. In both traditions, this experience of shouting, or possession, is the height of the rite, the greatest evidence of the presence of the deity in the service. This presence is emotionally cathartic and healing, as well as known to give guidance for life. In both African traditional religion and Christianity, fellow worshipers treat the possessed with awe and reverence.

African traditional religious survivals are also seen in Spirituals and various cultic rites. The best known of such Spirituals is "Let Us Break Bread Together on Our Knees." The words, "When I fall on my knees, with my face to the rising sun," are likely straight out of Africa. The tone scale, as well as the mentioned call-and-response patterns, are West African also. The folk process of development of the Spirituals is well described by an ex-slave:

> I'd jump up dar and den holler and shout and sing and pat, and dey would all cotch de words and I'd sing it to some old shout song I'd heard from Africa, and dey'd all take it up and keep at it, and keep a-addin' to it, and den it would be a spiritual.[29]

Among African Americans, the immense and immediate popularity of the new Baptist faith, with its baptism by immersion, was a clear throwback to the powerful importance of water rituals in African traditional religion. And the same might be said of communion services, as kin to the ever-present African rite of pouring libation. These rites were obviously influenced by white models but chosen by Africans and adapted to their cultural tastes and existential needs.

Less obvious but deeply ingrained African survivals in the Black Church are such practices as the church's function as literal extended family, and the way the elderly were respected as late as the 1970s. The titles "Brother" and "Sister" (in Christ) are common in churches of all

---

29. Blassingame, *The Slave Community,* pp. 33-34.

ethnic groups, but the African sense of congregation as virtual blood kin is a survival of African villages and towns. They were (and to some lesser extent still are) literal blood-kinship communities. Formal titles like "Mr." and "Mrs." were unknown in traditional communities. Familial titles such as mother or brother were applied to everybody, and many Africans from small communities had no experience with any other way to address people. These titles persisted in the slave communities, so much so that masters copied the same terms of address, no matter what their motives. In other words, slaves were called "Uncle," and the titles "Mr." and "Mrs." were denied them, but the titles were hardly missed in the slave community. They had never wanted or used "Mr." or "Mrs." in the first place. These familial titles fit well in the African American church's nostalgic effort to re-create on these shores the traditional African extended-family community. These same African familial titles survived in African American street culture as well.[30]

The fact that the Black Church is still evolving from African traditional religion is also seen, to some extent, in the way the churches of the masses still resist the removal of the senior members from office, no matter how feeble they may be. (Of course, power is also an issue.) Even the extravagantly flattering speeches of introduction, still often showered on aged deacons and pastors, are traditional praise speeches consciously or unconsciously honoring the office, as opposed to the occupant of the office. The speakers are just fulfilling a ceremonial function still alive and well in African culture as well as the United States.

As DuBois declared in the quotation above, the growth and strength of the Black Church in America stems from the fact that it is a cultural continuation of the "sole surviving social institution of the African fatherland. . . ." Cultures are a group's survival kit — their collection of rules, values, and modes of action for coping with the realities of their existence. This culture took centuries to evolve. It takes generations to change or lose it, even when oppressors attack it by coercive force.

---

30. Elliott Lebou, *Talley's Corner* (Boston: Little, Brown and Co., 1967), pp. 166-67.

African Survivals: Parallel Belief Systems

The most important African survivals of all may very well be in the belief systems, African traditional religious doctrines, as closely related to and merged with the orthodox Christian faith. At some points, the parallels are amazing, as with the omnipotence, justice, omniscience, and providence of God.[31] None of these attributes of God had to be learned first in slavery. And all of these crossover African beliefs survived so amazingly well in America because they served so well to support African American psychic survival under oppression. Of course, these shared beliefs (actual orthodox doctrines) were *not* the same set of biblical beliefs that the white masters selected to teach slaves. Records of Moses and the Exodus were deleted from the working Bible of the masters. Emphasis was placed on texts out of context, like Ephesians 6:5, which urges "Slaves, obey your masters." But slaves knew better.

Meanwhile, a few slaves illegally learned to read the whole Bible, and others just heard the Word and retained it. They then selected the parts that strengthened them and gave them hope. Thus, when they read what Paul said in Galatians 6:7 about people reaping what they sow, this law of identical harvest was easily accepted because it had been previously taught in African traditional religion. In addition, they were especially fond of the part about people who do good reaping in "due season" (6:9). In fact, that theme of due season is still greatly cherished in the African American pulpit, because of the help and hope it still gives oppressed people.

They were also glad to find their ancient African credo in virtually pure form in the Bible. Africans used Bible wisdom selectively to replace the holy wisdom of the homeland, which in its African form had disappeared with the shift of language from their African tongues to English. There are hundreds of African proverbs that declare that we reap what we sow, using a variety of metaphorical images to declare the justice of God. And so too with other doctrines.

African slaves would never have believed this justice doctrine if they had first heard it from a cruel master. Failure to recognize that slaves already had this early depth of spiritual and ethical insight is an insult to the great wisdom of our enslaved foreparents. And they voted

---

31. Raboteau, *Slave Religion,* p. 8.

with their feet when the white preacher or teacher strayed from what they knew was the real gospel truth. The deep conviction that masters were accountable to a just God for disrespecting the personhood of slaves was one reason they kept sane minds and weathered the cruelties. God's guarantee of justice meant that slaves had cosmic significance. One could not abuse them without having to face God's judgment and punishment. The functional support and emotional healing implicit in this doctrine still cause believers to depend on belief for support and to keep faith alive and well throughout African American culture, in both church and street, and still in the midst of oppression.

Surely no master taught slaves the Spiritual of social protest, about too few pairs of shoes issued for one year: "All *God's* chillun gotta shoe." There was no risk involved, since the spiritual was "signifying" about "heaven." They sang "Everybody talkin' 'bout heaven ain't a-goin' there. . . ." It is not difficult to decipher whom these believers in God's justice had in mind, or about whom they were signifying. They finished by promising to flaunt their shoes and shout all over heaven, to protest the fact that they were not allowed to shout in white worship. This song was not otherworldly religion; it was an African-belief-based affirmation about God as just and themselves as significant in God's sight. They eagerly accepted Paul's version of the justice of God, reaping what you sow, because it exactly matched their ancient truth in the metaphor of identical harvest. It retained its significance for the purposes of survival: Africans are not abused and treated unjustly with impunity.

African traditional religion looked up to one omnipotent High God with power to enforce this ultimate justice. Africans were not really polytheistic, as many suppose. Rather, their one distant High God ruled many deputy or intermediary deities, to whom various earthly functions were assigned. Osadolor Imasogie of Nigeria has said that "the phrase 'bureaucratic monotheism' best describes African traditional religion."[32] This is indeed an apt rendition in English.

The African traditional religion "summa theologica" was expressed in what are called "praise names." For Yorubas, "Olodumare" meant "God, the Omnipotent." It is the same as the Old Testament

---

32. Osadolor Imasogie, "African Traditional Religion and the Christian Faith," *Review and Expositor* 70, no. 3 (Summer 1973): 289.

praise name El Shaddai (Gen. 49:25), or the English "The Almighty." The doctrine of omnipotence took on awesome proportions as a means for slaves to cut masters down to proper size in the cosmic scheme, and to establish the eternal hope that God, not masters, was ultimately in charge of human history.

This all-powerful and just God was not to be hoodwinked. One Akan (Ghanaian) praise name was Brekyirihunuade, the Omniscient, "He who sees all, even from behind."[33] The Bible renders it El Roiy, "the God who sees me" (Gen. 16:13). When African Americans sing a gospel song that declares that "God knows how much we can bear," they sing about a God who will see and understand, maintain justice, and keep the load from being too heavy (I Cor. 10:13). That same all-knowing God will say, "Well done!" to the often misunderstood. Here again African religio-cultural roots join biblical belief, which surfaces in both church and street, in song and sermon and ordinary conversation. The church has no monopoly on these profound folk beliefs; the whole ethnic group depends on them.

The most popular doctrine in African traditional religion, however, is the doctrine of the Providence of God. And this, too, is evidenced in African modes. Proverb/laws such as the identical harvest, and praise names such as Olodumare and Brekyirihunuade are supplemented by what might be called proverb/parables. To express divine providence, an Akan from Ghana may say, in powerful metaphor, that "It is God who drives away the flies for the cow who has no tail." Or one may say, "It is the Supreme Being who pounds fufu [fibrous, staple-like hard yams] for the one without arms."[34] All of this is parallel to the Apostle Paul's word about providence — everything working together for good (Rom. 8:28), but that is not where enslaved Africans heard it first. In other words, the providence of God was well established in their worldview and belief system long before they crossed the Atlantic, and it was not hard accurately to translate it into biblical English.

The continuity of the deeply imbedded African belief system added to the continuity of the social institution that, as DuBois said, caused the Christian church to thrive so well among the enslaved. Again, however, continuity or no, they would never have embraced

---

33. Opoku, *West African Traditional Religion*, p. 15.
34. Opoku, *West African Traditional Religion*, p. 28.

Paul's Providence of God if its sole source had been cruel slave master teachers. They were happy to find it in their new corpus of Holy Wisdom, the Bible, as *they* read, memorized, and interpreted it for themselves on their own terms.

There are other doctrines of Old and New Testament origin that are similarly parallel to the African traditional belief system. In fact, all ten of "Aunt Jane's" African American Christian affirmations in the book *Soul Theology* have parallels in African traditional religion.[35] God's grace is not as dominant in African traditional religion as in the Christian gospel, but there are numerous praise names that say much the same thing.[36]

The only major aspects of Christian orthodoxy that were new to Africans were Jesus, hell, and the Bible. A joyous embrace of Jesus Christ came once the enslaved Africans had drawn from the Bible a good picture of Jesus as both Son of God and sharer in their earthly oppression. They identified with Jesus as a means of approach to the High God (2 Cor. 5:19) — what Paul might have called a means of reconciliation to the High God who was known in Africa but believed to be very remote.

This distance wasn't caused by original sin, however. Rather, it was about divine ineffability or transcendence. In Africa, they had viewed the High God in awesome, unapproachable terms, closely parallel to the early Old Testament. The huge chasm between the High God and humanity in African traditional religion was bridged by three intermediary entities: (1) the living dead ancestors; (2) the divinely ordained bureaucracy of sub-deities (for whom earthly shrines were sometimes built); and (3) an orderly, supportive social structure with levels of appeal all the way to the top deity. This structure rose from nuclear family to extended family elders, to village chiefs, to regional chiefs, and eventually to a chief of chiefs, such as the Akans' Ashantahene.[37] No problem was too large to be solved before reaching the highest of these levels, but there was at least the theoretically extreme possibility of having to appeal all the way to High God.

---

35. Nicholas Cooper-Lewter and Henry H. Mitchell, *Soul Theology: The Heart of American Culture* (Nashville: Abingdon Press, 1986).

36. Opoku, *West African Traditional Religion*, pp. 14-18.

37. Opoku, *West African Traditional Religion*, p. 33.

In the colonies, by contrast, this corps of deputy deities and ancestors and the entire ascending social infrastructure were snatched away. Enslaved Africans were not even allowed the security of nuclear families. However, the High God in person was providentially brought near by Jesus. As Roman Catholic Bishop Peter Sarpong of Kumasi, Ghana, declared to the King Fellows in 1972, "The good news for Africans today is not, 'He is risen.' Life after death and the 'living dead' are old hat. The really good news was and is, 'God *with* us — Immanuel!' The gulf is bridged!" This good news, as then received in Africa, had been well received two centuries earlier by Africans in the American colonies. Jesus made God personal and immanent, in an American situation of much greater need for an approachable God than in their motherland of Africa.

The second new aspect found in Christianity was a doctrine of hell. The African traditional belief system included no eternal hell. The tribal belief structure and social system provided punishment in *this* life. If the sin were great enough, one was consigned to what might be called oblivion, or utterly ceasing to be. Worthy lives continued as honored, living-dead ancestors, fed and communed with by the current living souls, who on occasion sought and received guidance from the ancestors.

When enslaved Africans saw cruel masters die what looked like peaceful deaths, their strong belief in the justice of God demanded a place where these sinners could receive the full measure of justice due to them, but not visible here in this life. It appeared their old oblivion must be wrong, and the white folks must be right. There must be a hell in which to give the punishment deserved. Thus evolved the spiritual's word about people who are "talkin' 'bout heav'n" and "ain't a-goin' there."

The third new element added to the existing affirmations was the Bible as the Word of God. The African traditional belief system had an impressive collection of proverbs, tales, songs, and danced meanings by which memory of their holy wisdom had been maintained by oral tradition. In the colonies, original tribes were divided and mixed around, and the dominant language became English. This African treasury of holy wisdom, all of it originally preserved in oral tradition, was slowly dissolved as a body, leaving only a few tales and wise sayings such as might be preserved in *Tales of Uncle Remus.* However, the basic ideas or everyday doctrines survived.

Meanwhile, the African mind was traditionally eclectic, not closed to the beliefs of others. In fact, they were prone to *seek,* as a divine ally, the god of any people "powerful enough to conquer us." In Africa, they had always managed to add such a god into their belief scheme somehow. Thus they took the initiative of seeking to know more of the Bible and the Christian faith of their conquerors. It did not matter that their oppressors withheld some parts of the Word. Most often, they took from the Bible the very parts masters sought to deny them.

On their own they found Moses and Jesus in the Bible. They stood for much that spoke to enslaved Africans' needs. Over time, there evolved a powerful adoption of selected parallel portions of Holy Scriptures as a functional, oral-replacement-in-English for their own revered traditional oral wisdom. Access to scripture was illegal, and whites in some states could be sentenced to prison for the "felony" of teaching a slave to read the Bible.[38] However, African traditional religious culture was very strong on memory, and once slaves heard a reading, they were well on their way to memorizing it. Their embrace of the Bible became so complete that illiterate ex-slaves, as late as the 1930s, were still able easily to recite and accurately interpret large sections of Scripture.

In the current controversies concerning biblical inerrancy, the old African American embrace of the authority of Scripture is a viable and attractive alternative to both extreme positions. In the African American tradition, biblical authority is powerful, but without the cold rigidity of literal print, or bibliolatry. Rather, the Bible's authority is handed down through the ancestors. The way a truth is stated is always in biblical language. But one tends, in African fashion, to offer it as a quote: "My father always said. . . ." A great thinker like Howard Thurman often introduced a powerful truth with, "When I was a boy in Florida, my Grandmother said. . . ." This authority was not abstract and detached, but flowed from the Bible through the powerful witness of the ancestors' real life.

38. Arna Bontemps, ed., *Great Slave Narratives* (Boston: Beacon Press, 1969), pp. 288-89.

Conclusion

In this same mode, it is essential that African Americans, Christian or not, should know their religious roots in Africa. Instead of just as data and fact, this history is a part of our very own self-understanding as persons oppressed in the Americas, and a crucial input as we set our course in life. This does not detract from our ties and commonalities with other Christians, as well as other faiths and cultures. Rather, this cross-cultural "pollination" enriches the experience of all concerned, and gives a strength and integrity to black spirituality, which can become a blessing to the entire world.

Chapter 2

Slave Population and Conversions: The Silent Years of 1619-1750

The first twenty Africans were brought to Jamestown, Virginia, as indentured servants in 1619. Six years later there were only twenty-three in Virginia, and by 1650, there were only 300. The pace increased after that: there were 12,000 Africans in Virginia in 1708, as compared to only 18,000 whites. By 1756 there were 120,156 Africans and 173,316 whites, and in many counties, blacks outnumbered whites.[1] Trends in Virginia were matched in South Carolina, and later in other states.

Unlike slave populations in South America and the West Indies, Africans in the North American colonies early experienced a positive birth rate (more births than deaths). After 1710, the majority of enslaved Africans in the colonies were born there. By the close of the transatlantic slave trade in 1808, there were a half million Africans and African Americans, and by 1860, there were 4.5 million, with almost all of these additions coming by birth, not illegal importation.[2]

This ever-increasing host of bearers of African culture was for the most part not viewed as spiritual beings for half a century. This seemed best to masters, since one widespread rumor had it that if Africans did indeed have souls and became Christians, they would have to be set free

---

1. John Hope Franklin, *From Slavery to Freedom,* 3rd ed. (New York: Alfred A. Knopf, 1967), p. 73.

2. Mechal Sobel, *Trabelin' On: The Slave Journey to an Afro-Baptist Faith* (Westport, Conn.: Greenwood Press, 1979), p. 23.

— manumitted. It took assurances from bishops of the Church of England to convince some masters that the freeing of the soul in Christ did not alter the bondage of the body in any way.[3] A resolution to this exact effect was enacted by the Virginia Assembly in 1667.[4]

The North American colonies thus approached slavery quite differently from the Catholic countries, since the Catholic church had recognized and regulated slavery for centuries. Certainly at least in theory, the Catholic church had more humane rules, such as requiring the honoring of slave marriages because their souls were affirmed and united by the church. Canon Law also decreed the slaves' right to earn some wages on a day off (maybe permitting them to save money and buy their own freedom, or making it possible for them to give in the church's offerings).

The Anglican churchmen of Virginia lacked any such flexibility, even though they had started in 1619 with a more humane system known as indenture. According to this plan, the indentured servants worked off their fares for ship passage to the colonies. This required a long, hard period of years, but not endless slavery.[5] However, this system was completely abolished in practice by 1640. The Virginia Assembly recognized slavery by law in 1661,[6] but even its official recognition that slaves had souls (1667) was a cruel form of justifying the slave system as a means of "saving the souls" of these supposed "heathens."

The truth is that on the issue of not being human, African culture and religious belief were and are far from heathen, as evidenced in the African beliefs reported in Chapter 1. As soon as enough Africans were imported and settled in a single location, they readily recalled and shared the commonalities of their African religious traditions and engaged once again in an adaptation of their already similar worship practices. Records of their being forbidden to gather clearly establish the fact that, regardless of the variety of tribal backgrounds on any given plantation, they did gather and devoutly engage in an African style of common worship.[7]

---

3. Carter G. Woodson, *The History of the Negro Church* (Washington, D.C.: Associated Publishers, 1972), pp. 6, 8.

4. Franklin, *From Slavery to Freedom*, p. 86.

5. Leslie Fishel and Benjamin Quarles, *The Negro American: A Documentary History* (Glenview, Ill.: Scott, Foresman and Company, 1967), p. 19.

6. Fishel and Quarles, *The Negro American*, p. 19.

7. Bruno Chenu, *The Trouble I've Seen* (Valley Forge: Judson Press, 2003), pp. 48-49.

The slave codes against their gatherings were said to be enacted to curb disorderly conduct and profaning of the Sabbath.[8] But these codes were actually for other reasons: (1) for freeing up another day for slaves to labor; (2) for fear of facilitating conspiracy; and (3) for fear of slaves using religious services as covers for hatching rebellion — and that not without cause. In 1687 a mass funeral in the Northern Neck of Virginia was discovered to be a cover for a planned, bloody rebellion.[9] This was only one of many rebellions, and the record of their place in black religion will be discussed in a later chapter. The point to be made here is that this and numberless other religious gatherings of slaves occurred as early as the 1660s, long before there was, if ever, any serious or widespread thought of winning the enslaved to the Christian faith, or of recording anything about their spiritual welfare.

White Religious Influence on Enslaved Africans

The progress of missionary influence among the Africans was late and slow, and managed to reach only a small percentage of the enslaved. Conversion was so loaded with the danger of slaves feeling equal to masters that a great many slave owners preferred not to run the risk.[10]

A group of twenty slaves were baptized into the Anglican Church in South Carolina by 1705, having been under instruction as early as 1695. Woodson also cites a man and woman baptized in 1723 in nearby St. Andrews Parish, and a literate slave under instruction at St. John's Parish. The most important effort in the area was a school to train Negro missionaries, under "Harry and Andrew," African slaves, in Charleston. This instruction ran from 1743 to 1763, when the better of the instructors died.[11]

Mechal Sobel reports catechetical classes as early as 1708, in Kent County, Pennsylvania, with classes offered as early as 1724 in Pettsworth, Virginia. She reports a truly rare and highly motivated exception among Anglican priests in Virginia: "Anthony Gavin, at the

---

8. Fishel and Quarles, *The Negro American,* p. 24.
9. Franklin, *From Slavery to Freedom,* p. 74.
10. Sobel, *Trabelin' On,* pp. 41, 60.
11. Woodson, *The History of the Negro Church,* pp. 6-7.

frontier parish of St. James, Goochland, traveled over 400 miles a year, praying at twelve different places. In his very first year of service, 1737-1738, he baptized 229 whites and 172 blacks."[12]

One is bound to wonder how the 172 blacks processed this experience, since the revivals of the First Great Awakening had not yet blossomed in that area. In North Carolina, more typical groups reported baptized were as small as two or three. Groups as large as "15 to 24 in one month, 40 to 50 in six months and 60 to 70 in a year" were baptized after the urging of bishops. Although one report was "355, including 112 adults" in an eight-year period, there was never any great movement to evangelize slaves in the territories of the Anglican church's influence (Virginia and the Carolinas).[13] Regardless of the admonition of (nonresident) Anglican bishops, masters soon learned that slaves who could read a prayer book, as required, could read anything else they cared to read. This, along with a shortage of priests,[14] meant that no significant number of the enslaved were converted to Christianity by white initiative during the so-called "silent years" from 1619 to 1750.

Still, Africans were not supposed by many masters to have souls to be saved until Bishop Gibson of London wrote a second round of forceful pastoral letters in 1727, over 100 years after the first arrivals. To clear the way for the missionary efforts on behalf of the slaves, he urged quite specifically that becoming converted and baptized would not alter slave status. Souls would be free in Christ, but chains on bodies were unchanged.[15] African-influenced belief and practice was forced underground, to grow on its own initiative and according to its own terms.

The exceptions to this underground evolutionary process came largely *after,* rather than before or during, the First Great Awakening (1730s and 1740s). In the North, where slavery was still practiced during these early years, a relatively few Africans were admitted to white churches. For instance, Carter Woodson reports an interesting assortment of missionary efforts and conversions in Eastern Pennsylvania. In 1672 and 1679, George Fox, a Quaker, urged instruction of Negroes and

12. Sobel, *Trabelin' On,* p. 62.
13. Woodson, *The History of the Negro Church,* p. 8.
14. Sobel, *Trabelin' On,* p. 60.
15. Woodson, *The History of the Negro Church,* p. 6.

Indians. In 1712, at Chester, Pennsylvania, laudable efforts were made to "train up the Negroes in the knowledge of religion." In the same year, at nearby Philadelphia, twelve adult Negroes were baptized after admirably answering examinations from memory. In 1704, in New York City, Elias Neau (died 1722) established a catechizing school for Negro slaves. In 1714, in Albany, among the slaves there was a great "forwardness to embrace Christianity." However, these conversions continued to emphasize *instruction*. Even the Quaker emphasis on inner experience was not carried over into Quaker outreach to Africans, whose culture had some strong parallels to Quaker inward religious experience.

Conspicuously absent from this report so far is New England, more recently known to be a center of abolitionism and concern for African Americans. It is odd, indeed, to note that salvation for blacks during this earlier period was not considered wise in Puritan territory, for the simple reason that church and state were still united there until the early 1800s. Thus, to baptize blacks into membership in the Congregational church meant voting-power citizenship in the state, for which Negroes were not yet considered "ready."

Notwithstanding this regional resistance to blacks voting, the newly developing free-church Baptists in Newton, Rhode Island, baptized an African named Quassey in 1743, and some eighteen Africans were baptized into the First Baptist Church in Providence in 1762. Because Rhode Island did not follow the church/state pattern of the rest of New England, Baptist church membership was not tantamount to being registered to vote. In 1771, the First Baptist Church of Boston received some blacks as members. But here, again, Baptists were not officially "established" (and therefore supported by taxation in Massachusetts), and thus did not have to be granted the right to vote.

There was in the North no record of anything comparable to the widespread underground African cultic observances of the Southern plantations. It was out of these invisible institutions that the Southern churches of the vast masses of African Americans grew. (Many urban churches of the North were and are still of this same culture, but this came after the migrations from the South beginning in the early twentieth century.)

In the 1700s, the closest Northern parallels were the already mentioned African secular celebrations, which were encouraged and historically recorded because whites saw them as very entertaining and not as truly religious or conspiratorial. They were not done in secret, of course.[16] As was previously mentioned, these gatherings were roughly comparable to the contemporary Mardi Gras in New Orleans.

The Nature of the Numbers

It was not until 1701 that the Society for the Propagation of the Gospel in Foreign Parts (SPG) was organized in London. One of its chief goals was to reach the "heathen" Africans and Natives in the American colonies. Their first successful missionary, Rev. Samuel Thomas, had already begun instruction as early as 1695, at Goose Creek, north of Charleston, South Carolina.[17] It was there that some of the very first recorded Christian converts were baptized into the Church of England. By 1705 Thomas reported twenty communicants, and 1,000 under instruction. By 1723, in North Carolina, there were larger numbers of baptisms (60-70 in a year), and one worker reported that two slaves had actually memorized the Lord's Prayer, the Apostles' Creed, and the Ten Commandments.[18] Mission work was begun in locations from Pennsylvania (1712) to Georgia (1751).

But these conversions were a tiny percentage of the total slave population, and the conversions were hardly credible or valid, by definition. Conversion was based on English language skill and successful rote memorization of such Christian standards as the Lord's Prayer and Psalm 23. No black convert to Anglican Christianity was required to testify to a soul-stirring experience. It is hard for a modern African American believer to escape the deep suspicion that the vast majority of the "converts" were actually only the ones who learned best how to work the system.

Add the fact that these reports cover seventy-five years *after* the earliest arrival of Africans, and fifty years after arrival of any larger groups of Africans. It becomes obvious that there were much earlier religious gatherings among the African slaves. These outlawed gather-

---

16. Eileen Southern, *The Music of Black Americans: A History* (New York: Norton, 1971), pp. 53-55.

17. Woodson, *The History of the Negro Church,* pp. 6-7.

18. Woodson, *The History of the Negro Church,* pp. 8-9.

ings were, as DuBois said, independent, underground, and based virtually entirely at first on African culture. The religion of the African American masses even today is on a continuum that starts in these indigenous gatherings far more than in the masters' thinly veiled instructional attempts to develop a more obedient, dependable work force. Even during the second seventy-five years, 1700-1775, the written records (SPG reports) showed comparatively tiny results until the fallout from the First Great Awakening. As James Melvin Washington put it, "Only a few slaves in these two British colonies [Virginia and Carolina] or anywhere else in the New World freely joined churches before the 1770s."[19]

Carter G. Woodson culled from SPG correspondence representative samples of African conversions, baptisms, and worship attendance.[20] The greatest number of reports were from the North, because there was less resistance to the SPG there. The total slave populations in the North were comparatively much smaller than in the South, although the *percentage* of culturally vulnerable house servants or free associates converted would have been much larger in the North. These reports are typical of the period covered in this chapter. *Then* followed reports of revivals and missionary efforts beginning in the mid 1700s. The 1770s records of organized black church groups follow one hundred fifty years *after* Africans arrived in this country. What happened in the mostly silent century just after arrival is the first topic of this chapter's exercise in research, using meager primary sources and working by inference from later slave testimony, cultural parallels, and white source data recorded for entirely different purposes.

For instance, the fact that Africans could gather at all at first, on their own African traditional religious terms, without the cultural interference of being monitored, is explained by the fact that they were classified as property, along with the cattle. In the minds of most masters, slaves were conveniently believed not to have redeemable souls. When it was conceded that Africans did in fact possess spiritual souls (and minds), the bondage of their physical bodies was not sufficiently secure for recognition of souls to be really popular with masters. Since

19. James M. Washington, *Frustrated Fellowship* (Macon, Ga.: Mercer University Press, 1986), p. 8.
20. Woodson, *The History of the Negro Church,* pp. 9-15; cf. Chaps. I, II.

acknowledgment of souls did not have any force of law, the baptisms at Goose Creek in 1723 were the exception, not the rule, and who knows just how much of what blacks thought of as real "religion" was involved?

Masters bent on getting every possible farthing from their chattel were ill inclined to teach slaves to read dangerous literature such as Bibles and prayer books. This highlights the fact that the early African rites of worship mentioned by DuBois had a whole 130 years to adapt and evolve on their own initiative without any significant effort by whites to win them to Christian faith and practice. The fact that these African rites existed at all is documented by the fact that assemblies of slaves had to be outlawed, along with their drums. So the fact that their rites and beliefs included increasing adaptations of Christianity is due very largely to the slaves' own initiative, not to missionary labor for the most part.

This little known freedom of Africans to go their own way religiously was further enhanced by the great shortage of priests in the major slave areas of Virginia and the Carolinas — to say nothing of the quality of the few clergy who did come. The comparison between an appointment in England and one in Virginia easily reveals why so very few priests wished voluntarily to go to the colonies. The parishes in England had sanctuaries built many generations earlier, and long since paid for. The members of the parishes resided in fairly densely populated neighborhoods, joined by developed roads. Pastoral calls were not difficult. Further, most British parishes owned lands and had what amounted to substantial endowment income. Beyond all this was the fact that the Church of England was "established," which meant that public taxes were expected to be levied to support the Church of England, much like our public schools. Thus the priest in England had a comfortable dwelling and income, even if the congregation failed either to worship in goodly numbers or to contribute at all generously.

Virginia parishes were the opposite in many ways. Membership was spread over wider areas, less densely populated, and connected by what could hardly be called roads. Parishioners were kept busy developing a wilderness into productive plantations, and they were far from rich in almost all cases. Colonists resisted taxes levied for the support of the priests and churches, and there were neither historic church buildings nor endowment incomes from earlier centuries. The slave masters had to be *begged* for both pastoral salary and construction costs. This gave the laity unprecedented power over the clergy, a fact the laity cherished. They actually succeeded in preventing the assignment of a bishop to the colonies. These Anglican lay colonists desired no higher authorities from the homeland once they had tasted their new-found clout.

Virginia planters rebelled against the legislature's levy to pay a priest an annual salary of "16,000 pounds of tobacco, plus house and glebe [an assigned plot of land]." When His Majesty declared null and void a law allowing cash instead of tobacco, the clergy tried to reverse this ruling in the court of Hanover County. The planters were defended in court by Patrick Henry in his first case. Among Henry's passionate pleadings were references to the clergy as "lazy and greedy parsons." The clergy lost the case, being assigned damages limited to only one penny. The demise of the established Anglican church was not far off.[21]

Thus it was like being sent to Siberia for a priest to be sent to a parish in the colonies of the South, and there weren't any Church of England congregations in early Puritan New England or Dutch Reformed New York. In these early years, the priests sent to appointments across the Atlantic were often virtually sentenced, sometimes even threatened with being defrocked if they refused to go. Thus, as Edwin Gaustad said, "Clergy were scarce and often of poor quality . . . remedies, however appropriate, proved beyond the means or the will of seventeenth-century [lay] Virginians."[22]

Patrick Henry's critical words regarding the priests were not nearly as strong as those of Deveraux Jarrett, himself a fiery, powerful preaching, loyal Anglican priest and evangelist. A few years before the Methodists broke away from the Anglicans in 1784, Jarrett wrote to John Wesley:

> Virginia . . . has long groaned through a want of faithful ministers of the gospel. . . . We have ninety-five parishes in the Colony, and . . . I know of but one clergy of the Church of England who appears to

21. Holland N. McTyeire, *A History of Methodism* (Nashville: Southern Methodist Publishing House, 1887), pp. 251-53.

22. Edwin S. Gaustad, *Documentary History of Religion in America* (Grand Rapids: Eerdmans, 1986), p. 98.

have the power and spirit of vital religion. . . . Cannot you send us a minister of the Church of England, to be stationed in that one vacant parish I mentioned?[23]

We know of no response to this plea, but we do know that the existent shortage left no personnel or program for reaching African slaves. Neither was the SPG able to send more than a tiny corps of highly motivated missionaries to reach the Africans and the Native Americans. One pastor was so burdened with the great needs of his white parishioners that he could see no need to be concerned about the blacks.[24]

In the 1840s, as abolitionist activities grew fiercer, there arose a movement to reverse the anti-missionary reaction to Nat Turner's Rebellion, and actually bring Christian teaching to the slaves on a broad scale. Bishop Meade and the Virginia Episcopalians, the Presbyterians, Methodists, and Baptists adopted strong resolutions concerning the instruction of the slaves. But ten years later, it was the unanimous judgment of all the church bodies concerned that they had accomplished close to nothing. Thus, once again, the enslaved Africans had free rein to develop their own faith, at least underground.[25]

Positive Contributing Factors

The fact that Christianity took root at all among African Americans from 1619 to 1750 is not due in any appreciable measure to missions. The three major contributing factors are widely overlooked. First is the open, eclectic character of African traditional religion. The typical West African town was also a faith community, but it had no missionary ambitions. It was assumed that where another tribe's belief system was different, its version was equally valid for its people. Thus it was all right for several different Yoruba subgroups to believe that God made the first man in *their* town. They were further open concerning others'

---

23. McTyeire, *A History of Methodism,* p. 318.

24. Sobel, *Trabelin' On,* p. 60.

25. *Journal of Negro History,* 60 vols. (Washington, D.C.: Associated Publishers), vol. 16, pp. 212-17.

beliefs when their own tribe or nation lost at war. They had an eclectic desire to include in some way the god strong enough to give victory to their conquerors and over their own gods. Enslaved Africans were thus *anxious* to learn of the white man's God and Bible. Second, they were even more anxious when they found (often stole) and interpreted the Bible for themselves. There were the parallels between African traditional religion and the Old Testament mentioned in Chapter One, and there were the powerful liberators named Moses and Jesus. There was no docility in their part of *this* book. Third, and more visible and easy to date, is the impact of the commonality between the expressive culture of Africa and the unprecedented (for whites) free expressiveness and emotion of the First Great Awakening.

The Character of Early Underground Religion

Despite the fact that some slaves were allowed to attend slave masters' churches, and some were even required to attend, practically all plantations of any size had their own secret and unmonitored services of worship.[26] The very fact that these meetings had to be secret accounts for the great scarcity of data concerning them. They were so secret that only certain of the Africans themselves, the ones who could be trusted, were invited. One's own children might not be told the time and place and character of what was going on.

Most writings about the "invisible institution" had to be written after Emancipation, years later, by individual freed slaves. Thus one only gets personal glimpses of what went on at various places. One slave master may have been fairly easy on the brush-arbor gatherings, while another might have been on constant watch. Some were so oppressive and prone to whip the determined secret worshipers that devout, saintly slaves died of the cruel beatings. Other masters were known to look the other way when slaves worshipped, so long as there were no rebellious side effects.

The typical clandestine congregation had a pastor. Some were approved by the master. When this happened, the messages in the approved and monitored services were different from those in the "invisi-

26. Thomas Weber, *Education in the Slave Quarters* (New York: Norton, 1978), p. 191.

ble institution." Other pastors were unofficial and persecuted for having too much respect and influence among the field "hands."[27]

The ministry of the people's preachers was very important to the enslaved. Their needs for guidance and comfort were immense. The awesome importance of this spiritual and emotional support can be seen by the fact that the time to engage in worship was taken from the already too-brief free times away from field work. Work time already ran from sun-up to sundown. Time for worship was taken from the brief period left for the personal needs of sanitation, sleep, food, and child rearing. This spiritual nurture must have been highly treasured indeed to motivate the sacrifice of such limited and precious free time.

One evidence of the basically African character of worship in the early years was the inverted pot or kettle so common in African tradition *and later slave lore.* In America it was used supposedly to control sound and keep masters from knowing of these forbidden secret services of prayer and praise. The practice is so widely known today because many ex-slave narratives of the 1930s still reported in generous detail these clandestine antebellum prayer and praise gatherings. Mrs. Sutton, a former slave, explained it this way:

> Lot of them would want to have meetings in the week, but the white people wouldn't let them have meetings, but they would get a big ole wash kettle and put it right outside the door, and turn it bottom upwards to get the sound, then they would go in the house and sing and pray, and the kettle would ketch the sound. I s'pose they would kinda have it propped up so the sound would get under it.[28]

This sound blocker was not failure-proof, however, and slaves did get caught and whipped from time to time.[29] Nevertheless, this tradition, with its manifest African roots, was well remembered long after these meetings had evolved into fully traditional Christian midweek prayer services. The underground sermons were greatly enjoyed, and the

27. Weber, *Education in the Slave Quarters,* p. 192.

28. George P. Rawick, *The American Slave: A Composite Autobiography* (Westport, Conn.: Greenwood Press, 1972), Series 1, p. 40.

29. Rawick, *The American Slave,* Series 1, pp. 39-40.

sermons ordered by the master officially for approved worship were not held against most approved preachers. The appreciation accorded the men of God was not only for their biblical wisdom; a great deal of it had to do with the sense in which the pastor's approach confirmed divine affirmation of their being and identity, using the culture of their roots.

The idea that ex-slave memory of nineteenth-century gatherings collected in the twentieth century can be used to document clandestine worship as early as the eighteenth and nineteenth centuries merits some further explanation. The theory of African continuity in slave culture and evolving religious practice is far more plausible than the strange idea that the evolving clandestine Christianity of the enslaved was somehow taught by the very whites who feared and outlawed the meetings. Why would an underground worship include biblical material unless the enslaved themselves carefully selected it? The supposedly silent years cease to be literally silent because of the undeniable cultural continuity and the self-willed inclusion of more and more selected elements of Christian faith. These elements were chosen from their own reading of the stolen Bible, and some aspects were later included from the attractive elements of the First Great Awakening.

African traditional worship had emphasized singing long before it had evolved into recognizable Christian hymnody, and African worship was never at a loss for songs for the occasion. African traditional religion had always used songs for teaching history and character. The pattern was to compose songs on the spot. Some of these songs gained wider use as spirituals, but in their original form were simply first sung in one location. Miles Mark Fisher has traced these folk creations.[30] His sources, again, tend to be from the latter part of the eighteenth and early nineteenth century, but the very existence of the songs testifies to the earlier singing tradition of the "silent years," of which Fisher's recorded songs are the inevitable descendants.

The evolving percentages of African traditional religion and orthodox Christianity mentioned in Chapter One are useful for envisioning the process of acculturation, but this percentage model is misleading in at least one way. It may imply erroneously that there was less of African traditional religion when more of Christianity was introduced.

---

30. Miles Mark Fisher, *Negro Slave Songs in the U.S.* (New York: Russell & Russell, 1968), pp. 1-26.

This is not actually what happened. In the early worship of the slaves there was almost *no* conscious jettisoning of major aspects of the best of former African belief and practice. Rather, there seems to have been a flow in which self-selected biblical concepts amounted to spontaneous translations of traditional African beliefs into Christian English. This was neither the purging of major portions of African traditional religion nor the radical conversion away from their indigenous faith.

African sub-deities were renamed in Roman Catholic territories such as Louisiana to conform in function with established saints.[31] Indeed, devotees of authentic voodoo (which is identical to Yoruba traditional religion) were often required to be in good and regular standing in the Roman Catholic Church (and given full funeral rites in both traditions).

Among the slaves in the Protestant colonies, a different process prevailed. Without white priests to direct the underground flow of faith, the African mindset simply responded to bits of the Bible as they themselves were able to find and interpret them, based on their own pre-established and compatible traditional belief system as well as their needs. God's attributes of omnipotence, omniscience, justice, and providence mentioned in Chapter One are examples of this overlap. The commonalities of African traditional religion with orthodox Old Testament Christianity were easily drawn to the surface, with or without conscious rational comparison.

Equally influential, if not more so, would have been the African centrality of spirit possession. In African traditional religion there were several sub-deity/spirits, now conflated to become the one Holy Spirit. The creative adjustment of titles was easy. The shouts and possessions of the Great Awakenings validated Christianity in African eyes at least as much as it validated African emotional expression in white eyes, especially at this point. Traditional African worship is at its highest when one is possessed by the spirit of a particular sub-deity. The transition that had to be made was from many possessing deities (one at a time) to a single Holy Spirit as possessor. It was that (Holy) Spirit who caused many a black Christian to get "happy" and shout in holy ecstasy. The healing once gained through a traditional priest's proper di-

---

31. Albert J. Raboteau, *Slave Religion* (New York: Oxford University Press, 1978), pp. 76-80.

agnostic choice of a particular possessing spirit was eventually achieved by the one God, the Holy Spirit. Even the three-in-one trinity of the Godhead was easy to envision, since this sort of fluidity among aspects of the deity was also common in Africa.[32] Thus what DuBois called the "extraordinary growth" of the Christian church among enslaved Africans was greatly enhanced when the third person of the Trinity, the Holy Spirit, broke out of the mold of the literate, formal, structured Anglican liturgy and "got loose" in the radically new "dispensation" of the Great Awakenings.

The spontaneous expressiveness fostered by the preaching of George Whitefield and others in the First Great Awakening led to an enormous increase of African public commitment to the Christian faith. The ecstasy experienced in traditional slave worship could now be publicly affirmed as authentically Christian at the same time. An example of Whitefield's impact on enslaved Africans comes from an ex-slave, a pioneer African author named Gustavus Vassa, who had been baptized in the Anglican Church in England while still young. He wrote after hearing Whitefield:

> When I got into the church I saw this pious man exhorting the people with the greatest fervor and earnestness, and sweating as much as I ever did while in slavery on Montserrat beach. . . . I was very much struck and impressed with this; I thought it strange that I had never seen divines exert themselves in this manner before.[33]

Vassa reported elsewhere that he had been deeply moved and made to feel a nostalgic connection with his African home and roots.

Vernon Loggins, author of the book from which this quotation is taken, goes on to say:

> The Christianity which Whitefield and his predecessors preached in America brought to the Negro a religion which he could understand, and which could stir him to self-expression. He responded to it with enthusiasm.

---

32. Rawick, *The American Slave*, Series I, p. 48.

33. Vernon Loggins, *The Negro Author: His Development in America to 1900* (Port Washington, N.Y.: Kennikat Press, 1964), p. 4.

Loggins's work was seeking the source of Vassa's inspiration as an author, but he also gave the cause for a major shift of blacks towards enthusiastic *public* commitment to the Christian faith. Further, the impact of Whitefield and others caused greater interest in the salvation of both enslaved and freed Africans. The result is that more and more records of this new kind of Christian conversion experience for blacks began to surface in the aftermath of the First Great Awakening.

In fact, this revival's direct influence on blacks in the *South,* as well as whites there, continued long after it had died among whites in the North. This influence is directly traceable, in one typical instance, from New England all the way to the beginning of one of the earliest formed independent black Baptist churches, at Silver Bluff, South Carolina, between 1773 and 1775.[34]

The point is that this worship and preaching tradition was neither learned nor invented from scratch on these shores. Its roots went back to Africa and the silent years of early slavery, an African cultus evolving more and more into a bicultural pattern, one that remained authentically African even as it became more like the new Christian revival mode.

A Tracer of Cultural Compatibility

We can see a trail of cultural compatibility beginning with two 1745 conversions under Whitefield, in Connecticut, a trail running to the white church in Kiokee, Georgia, where, George Leile, the founder of the Silver Bluff church, was converted. The trail is well marked.[35] Shubal Stearns (1706-1771) and his sister's husband, Daniel Marshall (1706-1784), were the Whitefield converts. In 1751, they decided to become Baptists and soon felt the call to head south, where the First Great Awakening was in bloom. After fruitful labors in revivals and church starts in Virginia and North Carolina, Daniel Marshall launched several Baptist congregations around Kiokee, Georgia, near Augusta. George Leile, a slave born in Virginia in 1750, was converted in

---

34. Woodson, *The History of the Negro Church,* pp. 35-36.

35. *Eerdmans' Handbook to Christianity in America* (Grand Rapids: Eerdmans, 1983), p. 119.

1772, in the Buckhead Creek Baptist Church, where his master was a member.[36] He was soon ordained to do missionary work among the slaves along the Savannah River, where he organized the Silver Bluff church. The Revolutionary War intervened, and various segments of the church membership went in several directions. Leile went from a launch of a budding congregation in the Savannah area to Kingston, Jamaica, and began even more work there.

This tracing shows in some detail the providential flow of the compatibility of Great Awakening preaching with African traditional religion. The clue is hidden in a variety of records. Ben Franklin, no serious churchman by any account, reported that Whitefield had a voice such that "one could not help being pleased with the discourse, a pleasure of much the same kind with that received from an excellent piece of music."[37] This tonality was duplicated among many who admired and followed Whitefield in their preaching. Stearns, the greater preacher of the two missionaries, was in this tradition. Morgan Edwards said Stearns's voice was musical and strong.[38] Sydney Ahlstrom reported a "holy whine" as characteristic of the early Baptists of the South, who "encouraged all the *extremer* forms of religious expression."[39]

The best-known characteristic of the African American masses' preaching even today is a style called "whooping," a relative of chanting, but not mistaken for chanting by the African American masses. It has a distinctive African twist. It is the cultural residue from the tonality of African languages, as mentioned in Chapter One, in connection with the tonal talking of drums. The point here is that the "extremer" expressions and "holy whine" of white revivalism were so parallel to African tonality that blacks didn't have to hide their culture any longer. Nor did they need to fear that the true believers of any race would call it pagan and unfit to be used in the worship of God.

The power of this tonality can be described as somewhat resembling the appeal of European liturgical chant, combined with the dramatic impact of operatic singing. Add to this the moving power and healing personal affirmation of cultural nostalgia, which prevails in

36. Washington, *Frustrated Fellowship*, p. 9.

37. Sydney E. Ahlstrom, *A Religious History of the American People*, vol. 1 (Garden City, N.Y.: Image Books, 1975), p. 111.

38. *Eerdmans' Handbook to Christianity in America*, p. 119.

39. Ahlstrom, *A Religious History of the American People*, vol. 1, p. 393.

many places even today. Thus the formal conversion of Africans was emotional enough, but probably more for traditional recall and nostalgic identification than for the typical Puritanical "sorrow for sin" of white converts.

It must be remembered that emphasis on sin was a product of Western Christianity, and came new to the African belief system when encountered in America. Even so, there was a strong African parallel to the period of "seeking" and being under conviction, prior to full conversion. Liele reports that his conversion took "five or six months" of spiritual labor.[40] However, the white preachers' attempts at inducing guilt over such things as taking meat from white masters had not succeeded among the vast majority of slaves, who felt entitled to sufficient nourishment to support their labors.

It is altogether obvious that commonality of belief, Whitefield's dramatic vividness and emotional expressiveness, and his homiletic tonality all combined to make formally acceptable to enslaved Africans a Christian faith already in progress underground. The culture of the Great Awakening was used by God not so much to "save" thousands as to legitimate their African ways of expressing the Christian faith, which they had already independently begun to seek and interpret for themselves.

The Truth about African Traditional Religion and Superstition

Before elaborating on the "Jesus element" in this compatibility between Christianity and African traditional religion, it is helpful to review the relationship between African American Christianity and the common stereotypes of African American voodoo and conjure. How could the reports of positive black Christianity offered here be true, if the African culture out of which they came was as superstitious as is commonly assumed? Considering the great spread of such stereotypes as dominant in slave culture, the question of a close relationship of these stereotypes to African traditional religion and to African American religion is legitimate. In other words, how did historians like Newbell Puckett record

40. Sobel, *Trabelin' On,* pp. 104-5.

so much superstition and miss all of this positive, healthy traditional religion and Christian belief among the enslaved Africans?

The African end of the answer did not come to light until a radical awakening to the biases of missionaries in Asia. It came from an exhaustive study called *Rethinking Missions: A Laymen's Inquiry After 100 Years.*[41] "Foreign missionaries" were pressed to repent of their misrepresentation of indigenous cultures as "pagan." For reasons unknown, the study didn't include Africa, but the findings applied most appropriately. It had to be faced that African traditional religion was, in many ways, a fitting, Old-Testament-type parallel preparation for receiving Christ.

Peter Sarpong, Roman Catholic Bishop of Kumasi, in Yoruba land (Western Nigeria), told the Martin Luther King Fellows in 1972 that missionaries had hidden the Old Testament in many cases, because they knew very well that the Africans would say, in effect, "What's new about Christianity? We've had that all along." He referred not only to the parallels between the Africans' "living dead" and the Christians' "eternal life"; he saw also every major Old Testament characteristic of God paralleled in African religion. African culture had some superstitions, he agreed, but so did Europe and America, and the African superstitions were no more dominant than those of Europe. *All* people have superstitions, just as all races have myths. He made it plain that most Africans no more believe God to be an idol image than Americans believe God to be a statue in a Roman Catholic station of the cross. All have simply found it easier to sense the presence of God in these shrines. The point is that in its more virulent forms, animistic superstition, or worship of natural objects, is resorted to largely, though not exclusively, by the unlearned and utterly powerless and oppressed, both of European and of African descent. The supposed charms and curses of the lowest levels of voodoo are not characteristic of mainline Yoruba traditional religion, for instance. A search of a huge marketplace in Ibadan, Nigeria, finally yielded a tiny table selling amulets, curses, and charms. That one dealer may have amounted to one tenth of one percent, or less, of the total mass of small retailers in that vast market.

There has remained a corner of superstition in the minds of *all*

---

41. *Rethinking Missions: A Laymen's Inquiry After 100 Years* (New York: Harper, 1932).

races of Americans, including African Americans. A classic example of the latter occurred in 1945 when a California pastor from Louisiana was discovered "dusting" the communion table and the four corners of the sanctuary. His purpose had been to gain protection from the critics of his personal life. His resort to witchcraft was not forgiven. Members refused to receive the communion he had prepared and dismissed him summarily. This reaction was largely righteous indignation, but undoubtedly it included some hidden fear and superstition also.

Many still see voodoo as dominant. Mechal Sobel makes the mistake many others make when she says, "Voodoo actively permeated all of slave life." But she is far closer to the truth when she says, in response to another scholar's error, "However, it now seems much more likely that blacks created their own style of English and their own style of Christianity and that both preserved the African ethos to a significant degree. . . . It is important to look for African meanings given to European terms."[42]

Centuries-old superstition, as well as lofty and equally ancient beliefs, practices, and religious ecstasy, all combine to establish that there was afoot in the early slave communities a providentially used process of dynamic religious adaptation. It issued in an emergent African American faith community that was and still is quite traditional in many ways, and at the same time deeply, richly Christian, with touches of white influence in the superstitions as well as in the faith.

The Appeal of Jesus

In Chapter One we saw three elements of established Christianity that were new to Africans, the most important of which was Jesus. The basis of Jesus' appeal is the way in which he compensates for African traditional religion's emphasis on the transcendence of the High God, as seen also in the Old Testament. Such distance almost amounted to alienation, except that the void in Africa was filled by the ancestors, along with a "bureaucracy" of sub-deities mediating between High God and humankind. A stable social structure also fed their belief system. In America, all this was gone, and the lesser divinities were replaced, as

42. Sobel, *Trabelin' On*, pp. 41, 45.

a body, by Jesus of Nazareth. With him there developed an amazingly intimate relationship.

What was stated in English theological terminology as the immanence of God was made concrete and vivid in the person of Jesus, seen as fully human and trusted as an aspect of the Trinity. The appeal was not in terms of abstract belief, however, so much as in relationship to Jesus in a mystical, personal way far more at home in African traditional religion than in Western culture. African openness to Christianity was not from the overestimated influence of missionaries; rather, it was the reality of Jesus in the experience of the enslaved. This arose out of the relevance of an oppressed, fellow-suffering God figure. This aspect of the Son of God is expressed in the spiritual genius and personal intimacy of the Christmas Spiritual "Sweet Little Jesus Boy":

Sweet little Jesus boy, they made you be born in a manger.
Sweet little Jesus boy, they didn't know who you was.

The world treat you mean, Lawd; treat me mean too,
But that's how things is down here; they don't know who you is.

This closeness to Jesus is most manifest in the plaintive question, "Were you there when they crucified my Lord? . . . Oh, sometimes it causes me to tremble." The most benevolent of the teachings permitted to slaves could not have been responsible for such an empowering intimacy with the Son of God. It was the insight given by the Holy Spirit to those who read or heard and then memorized the New Testament for themselves.

This seemingly sentimental image of a baby in a manger, however, is not to be confused with a faith without teeth. They sang other spirituals with words like "Ride on, King Jesus; no man can hinder Thee." Of this sweet little one-time infant, they declared, "He is King of Kings; He is Lord of Lords. Jesus Christ, the first and last; no man works like Him." They sang their liberationist desire to know: "Didn't my Lord deliver Daniel? Then why not ev-er-y man?" These were not distant ideas; they were sung with zest and sincere enthusiasm, born of specific certainty and personal identification.

They saw Jesus' reign in concrete terms such as a Day of Judgment, a day to be literally celebrated, because their oppressors would get their just due: "Sinners will be runnin' in that Great Day. . . . And the righteous will be marchin' in that Great Day." The justice of God was not to be feared, as unsuccessfully taught by their cruel tutors. God's justice was their guarantee that they could not be violated and brutalized with impunity; their personhood was sacred in the divine scheme of things under God. They sang of Judgment Day in genuine joy: "In-a Dat Great Gettin'-Up Mornin', Fare Ye Well."

They foresaw the day when the preachers would fold their Bibles because the last soul would be converted. The final end in the hands of an all-powerful and just God was celebrated still further: "My Lord, What a Morning!" This Lord they loved so much was coming back, to wake the nations underground. Obviously this was a new theological concept for Africans, but once they found it in Christian teachings, they radically adapted it for themselves. The end time and heaven as taught to them by the slave establishment still had them as servants in heaven. But the Revelation (7:9) they read about had every kindred and people and tongue on an equal footing.

Too long have Spirituals been interpreted as compensatory, something too close to an opiate for the people. James H. Cone, father of African American theology, rightly declares that it is time to read Spirituals as serious theology, serving real needs.[43] Without abstract speculation, and grounded in existential experience, these Africans in America had a consistent and firm belief system. Jesus was so important because he symbolized and lived out the guarantees of personhood and ultimate justice. Whatever they sang of heaven was only social-protest shorthand for what ought also to be true here on earth. They sang also of the end-time supreme court for the judging of sinners, chief of whom were cruel masters and bosses.

The central theme of personhood or "somebodiness" is all the more impressive when one realizes, with Cone, that "Slave catechisms were written to insure that the message of black inferiority and divinely ordained white domination would be instilled in the slaves."[44] The fact that this indoctrination failed in many cases can only be traceable to roots in African traditional religion, and the way these roots empow-

---

43. James H. Cone, *The Spirituals and the Blues* (New York: Seabury Press, 1972), p. 19.

44. Cone, *The Spirituals and the Blues*, p. 23.

ered authentic and accurate interpretation of the Bible. It is not possible to date the full emergence of these beliefs in the form of Spirituals, but it is certain that this ability to overcome attempted indoctrination can arise only out of the continuity and integrity of African roots and the guidance of God. And these go back to whenever an enslaved African left home, and whenever these first-generation, unwilling immigrants lived long enough to pass their belief base on to their children. This was done with great power, even though it was transmitted much more by contact than by any formal teaching.

Thus the "silent years" were not really silent, and they are at least as important as any other period. Indeed, all other periods are based on these years. It is high time that we gave proper credit to the enslaved forebears, and stopped assuming that during this period their souls were vacuums waiting to be filled by the oppressors. These ancestors are worthy of the highest praise for the magnificent continuity of their great culture and faith, which they accomplished against the greatest of odds.

Chapter 3

The Very First Black Congregations: 1750-1800

The powerful and lasting impact of the colonies-wide revivals called the First Great Awakening and the Second Great Awakening caused an enormous increase in Africans, both enslaved and freed, making public confessions and formal commitments to the Christian faith. At first the trickle of only a few slave converts had simply been absorbed into the established white congregations. But the Great Awakenings brought an authentic religious experience to thousands. This was bound to generate additional desire among whites and blacks for separate worship in separate congregations. White church members were not nearly as happy as their black colleagues were with the spontaneity and free expressiveness of Great Awakening–style worship. And these churches, especially in the South, were often culturally overwhelmed in worship with sizeable and irrepressible majorities of non-voting black members.[1]

Robert Ryland, the sympathetic white pastor of Richmond's First African Baptist Church, tactfully described the problem thus: "And the instructions of the pulpit could not be always adapted especially to their [blacks'] wants. . . . The interests of both, therefore, imperatively demanded their permanent separation." A severe shortage of seating

---

1. C. Eric Lincoln and Lawrence H. Mamiya, *The Black Church in the African American Experience* (Durham: Duke University Press, 1990), pp. 24-25.

space only added to the white church's problems of contrast with the African culture of worship.[2]

The Stages of Separation and Independence

The processes by which African Americans achieved separation and a measure of self-governance varied from church to church, city to city, and region to region, with major significance given to the ratio of white to black or slave to free. No single example can be said to be completely typical, but the First Baptist Church of Richmond is a fairly good numerical example of the simple problems of overwhelming racial proportion and the overcrowding of space.

Founded in 1780, the First Baptist Church of Richmond had the following proportions of black and white in the following years: 1800, 150 black and 50 white; 1838, 1,600 black and 350 white.[3] In 1841 the 387 white members sold their building to the 1,708 black members (mostly slaves)[4] for $6,500, half the appraised value. Thus was the renamed First African Baptist Church set apart. However, behind this neat division of members and manifestly fair transaction of business was a complex set of considerations that raised many issues affecting the early formation of all African American Christian churches.

For instance, in 1849, the property title had to be vested in the new trustees of the new First African Baptist Church of Richmond, and these trustees had to be elected by the church's black members from the separating minority of *whites*.[5] Members of the "Supervising Committee" had to be appointed by the Baptist Association, and also came from three white congregations. This white committee chose as first pastor of the separated black congregation Dr. Robert Ryland, President of Richmond College. This appointment was supposedly subject to the church's approval. He served First African Baptist Church with remarkable commitment and excellent pastoral insights and relations until 1865.[6]

---

2. Thomas Ryland, *History of the First African Baptist Church* (self-published), p. 248.

3. Mechal Sobel, *Trabelin' On: The Slave Journey to an Afro-Baptist Faith* (Westport, Conn.: Greenwood Press, 1979), p. 208.

4. Ryland, *History of the First African Baptist Church*, p. 247.

5. From the brief published history of the church group.

6. Ryland, *History of the First African Baptist Church*, p. 249.

The church chose thirty male members as deacons to serve as lay leaders under Ryland. While he was zealous about Bible training, he carefully avoided preaching openly against slavery and having his pastorate terminated by law. He was equally careful not to preach *for* slavery. He clearly merited the trust placed in him, given the limitations under which he was forced to labor. John Jasper, the famous black preacher, was among the sixty-five converts included in the church's first baptism, and Lott Carey, the pioneer missionary, came to town from the country and joined this congregation.

However, even if white Baptists had sought to grant full black independence, the 1838 Virginia Legislature denied permission for any independent black church. Sobel sums up the resulting comparison of black church independence patterns in Virginia and Georgia thus: "Whereas white Baptists in Georgia sought to infiltrate and dominate black churches, those in Virginia . . . chose [as required by law after the Nat Turner Rebellion] to maintain black churches as branches,"[7] which they supervised and carefully controlled.

With complications such as this, the independence of the historic black churches cannot be precisely defined and dated. Even when there are dependable records, any objective level of black independence is impossible to establish, because of the inescapable white dominance and what Sobel rightly terms the "sub-rosa autonomy" and ingenuity of the African Americans. The evolving processes of independence can best be understood by introductory studies of specific churches that illustrate types of development. The gamut runs from black congregations heavily dominated by white sponsors to those who found subtle, creative ways to assert their underground independence and follow their own wills as black congregations. This self-determination applied particularly to finance, choice of deacons and local preachers (not ordained or allowed in the pulpit), and ingenious gatherings other than formal worship, baptism, and communion. Prayers by these gifted laity were often akin to sermons in tone and length.

It must be understood that prior to 1800 *no* church, North or South, evolved without some form of white denominational recognition, trusteeship of land title, and/or certification to the government by respected whites that the Blacks involved would cause the slave sys-

7. Sobel, *Trabelin' On,* p. 205.

tem no trouble. Ol' Captain's Church, begun in 1786 in Lexington, Kentucky, is the only known exception.

Another example, near the opposite end of the spectrum, involved the First African Baptist Church of New Orleans, founded in 1817 as a mixed congregation which became "African," with an African American pastor, in 1826. Their history reports persecution in the late 1830s, when it was against the law to hold any public gatherings, and leaders were often punished to the "full extent of the law." Even when permission was finally obtained, the terms were cruel. They could only meet two hours, from 3:00 to 5:00 P.M. on Sundays, and that under the watchful eye of a white police officer, whom they had to pay the exorbitant fee of two dollars per hour. They could all be jailed if their service overran the rule by one minute.[8] This experience was not unique in the slave states.

Despite firm formal commitments to Baptist doctrines and the polity of congregational autonomy, white Baptist "influence" over blacks unavoidably functioned as arbitrary authority. For African American congregations, the polity in actual practice was more akin to Presbyterianism. Whether whites exited mixed congregations and formed their own, or whites invited the blacks to exit and form their own separate congregation, the black group was always thought of as the white church's mission, subordinate to the sponsoring church. This arrangement was inevitable because of the legal requirement for white sponsors and guarantors. Without such, the government prohibited blacks from gathering for mass worship at all.

In most cases the separation of congregations was supposedly amicable, but in every case the black congregation had no choice but to accept "assistance" and continued supervision of a pastoral nature. This was true in both the North and the South in the early years, and continued in the South right up to the Civil War. In the South, white "official" pastors were discharged the minute the Union troops took possession. In the North, the presence of whites faded as the assistance always needed by new congregations was replaced by African American mutual assistance.

---

8. From the brief published history of the church group.

The Emergence of Black Pulpit Genius

This early supervision included appointment of white preachers in almost all cases, if only for the monthly service of holy communion, as with Bethel African Methodist Episcopal Church in Philadelphia. Black exhorters were considered incapable of serving as full pastors, and were denied full ordination. This arbitrarily low appraisal of black preachers prevailed despite the impressive effectiveness of some black preachers. It gave white churches an excuse for trying to maintain tight control over Black churches. There were, however, striking exceptions to this trend. When a black preacher was more gifted than available whites, and was badly enough needed, he might serve, at least for a few years, as the founder and functioning full pastor of a mixed congregation.

Henry Evans (1740-1810) preached so effectively to whites and blacks that he was permitted to found a Methodist church in 1790, in Fayetteville, North Carolina. He stayed there until his death in 1810, but as *assistant* to (later bishop) William Capers.[9]

"Black Harry" Hosier (1750-1806), Methodist Bishop Asbury's coachman, was widely reputed to be a far better preacher and orator than the bishop. He drew larger crowds and helped greatly in establishing churches.[10] Yet Asbury ordained this brilliant but untrained preacher as a deacon only. (Asbury himself was not formally trained either. He had come to the colonies in 1771 as a young lay preacher, to help supervise the new movement. He was selected as Wesley's main assistant in 1772. He was ordained deacon, then elder, and then both appointed and elected bishop in 1784, when American Methodists became a formally organized denomination.)[11]

In 1795, Josiah Bishop, in Portsmouth, Virginia, was given the cash to buy his freedom by the (mostly white) Court Street Baptist Church (organized 1789), so he could be their preacher.[12] Mechal Sobel states that he was a full pastor to both blacks and whites from 1792 to

9. William J. Walls, *The African Methodist Episcopal Zion Church* (Charlotte, N.C.: A.M.E. Zion Publishing House, 1885, 1974), pp. 24-26.

10. Carter G. Woodson, *The History of the Negro Church* (Washington, D.C.: Associated Publishers, 1972), pp. 48-49.

11. Holland N. McTyeire, *A History of Methodism* (Nashville: Southern Methodist Publishing House, 1887), pp. 280, 297, 348.

12. Woodson, *The History of the Negro Church*, p. 46.

1802,[13] but the facts of this are still in dispute. Debates over how much leadership whites actually needed and accepted from blacks are typical of this kind of racial arrangement. Nobody denies, however, that Josiah Bishop's powerful preaching unified the whites who had been severely divided previously. They were blessed for years by Bishop's ministry.

Also in Virginia was an African known as Uncle Jack, who was purchased free, given a farm, and licensed to preach. He served effectively for forty years, beginning in 1792. He seems not to have been a pastor, but more of a roving revivalist under whose preaching many, both white and black, were saved.[14]

Further examples of African Americans preaching to mixed audiences range widely. Lemuel Haynes (1753-1833), a black Congregationalist, served white churches in New Hampshire, Vermont, and New York.[15] John Chavis (1763-1838), a black Presbyterian, studied at Princeton, and tutored and preached to whites and blacks in Virginia and North Carolina.[16] Joseph Willis (1758-1854), a free black native of South Carolina, founded (1805) the first Baptist church of any race west of the Mississippi. Often operating at his own expense, he was effective with whites and blacks, and organized in Louisiana the first five churches, which he then organized into the Louisiana Baptist Association in 1818.[17]

The Separation of Black and White Congregations

The inevitable desire of mixed churches to separate by race came to a head with the organization of black churches in the last half of the eighteenth century. Before dealing with the actual places and denominations of some of the new black congregations, it is important to be clear about the basis for division. It was not just plain and simple racial antipathy or prejudice. It was also the differences in the three "c's" of class, culture, and control.

13. Sobel, *Trabelin' On*, p. 302.
14. Woodson, *The History of the Negro Church*, pp. 46-47.
15. Woodson, *The History of the Negro Church*, pp. 52-56.
16. Woodson, *The History of the Negro Church*, pp. 58-59.
17. *Encyclopedia of African American Religions*, ed. Larry G. Murphy et al. (New York: Garland Publishing, Inc., 1993), p. 845; Woodson, *The History of the Negro Church*, p. 74.

The class factor evolved as the white Baptists and Methodists, both North and South, engaged in social and economic upward mobility. As members of newer, less respectable religious movements, these believers needed and welcomed black members. Once the hard labor and frugal lifestyles of the whites had paid off in an elevation of their class status, these whites became uncomfortable with their black members. The cruel eviction of the blacks in St. George's Methodist Church in 1787, only three years after they were organized into a denomination (and less than three years after blacks had sacrificed to help complete their building), is a classic instance of what was more a class issue than a culture or color issue.

The issue of the culture of worship was illustrated above concerning First African Baptist Church in Richmond. As white Baptists became more affluent and socially respectable, they were embarrassed by the emotional freedom they once cherished. What for blacks had been a worshipful affirmation of their ancient culture became for white Baptists and Methodists a brief interlude in a longer Western history of a culture of formality in worship.

Still more important was the refusal of whites to share organizational power or control with African Americans, whether slave or free. This power issue is illustrated by the white Baptists at Portsmouth mentioned above. Pastor Bishop's pulpit gifts transcended white culture, under the uniting influence of the new worship of the First Great Awakening. Yet their "union" dissolved as soon as black "members" sought the right to vote in true Baptist equality. The African Americans of this strong congregation later withdrew their request when they saw that simply asking to vote was causing their outright exclusion from membership. They grew faint of heart and asked to be received back into the "fellowship" on the old, voteless basis.

Bishop himself went northward and served in early African American churches at Baltimore and New York City, where he seems to have been the first pastor of the famous Abyssinian Baptist Church. The members he left behind did not form a fully separated African American congregation (Zion, Portsmouth) with a black pastor until 1865, the close of the Civil War.

These same three major issues of class, culture, and control, and especially the latter two, confront and hinder every effort of different races to worship and work together, even now. From the outset, these two factors bore heavily on the terms of actual "independence" (or lack of it) prevailing in the very first African American churches in the South, and later in the North. The sample histories later presented here, of the First African Baptist Churches of Savannah, of Norfolk, and of Philadelphia, will bear this out. The crucial issue of control at times rendered bitter even the otherwise heroic educational efforts of white denominations in the South after the Civil War. Even in the post–World War II era, the greatest challenge facing ethnically or racially "transitional" congregations has been, and still is, how to settle the issues of culture and control. In other words, the ones who provide the financial resources tend to insist on control, but those who provide the participants want equality of vote, regardless of how much they can or cannot give.

The Determination of Which Black Church Came First

The question of control forces a variety of definitions as to what might constitute a fully separated and "independent" congregation of African Americans. Thus it is difficult to declare exactly when the "first" church of such supposedly independent African Americans began, since there is always some question as to whose "independence" was greater, as well as who met for worship first. Added to that is the challenge of assessing *continuous* existence, and how that may be defined. Then there is the question of how independent a black church can be considered when legally compelled to have a white pastor. In fact, a spirited debate still goes on as to which was the first *independent* black church in the United States. In this historical treatment of churches prior to 1800, the listing sequence is based on each church's arbitrary claim of beginning, or date of first meeting, regardless of continuity of existence.

When congregations achieved true independence from significant white domination is manifestly beyond verification. Once we get past the very first churches, the ones described here include primarily the surviving churches begun between 1800 and 1840 and reported in available sources. Those reported in some detail were chosen as *examples* of the historical processes by which they finally attained considerable independence and continued existence. As to which was *the* first, congregations making the claim will have to settle for being classified simply as *one* of the very first four or five African American congregations in the United States.

At this point it must be understood that records vary as between local church histories and presumably scholarly works. In most cases it will appear that this work gives preference to histories published by churches, with exceptions noted and reasons given. It will be found, however, that utterly unresolved conflicts remain here.

The very first formally established African American churches to be mentioned in any history met not in Lunenburg (now Mecklenburg) County, Virginia, in 1758, according to Mechal Sobel,[18] but in Prince George County in 1756, according to church records. Sobel reports that the Bluestone Church in Lunenburg County had white preachers under the influence of Shubal Stearns. Their names were Philip Mulkey and William Murphey, and they preached to the slaves on the plantation of William Byrd III (Sobel, pp. 102, 196). These slave members were, of course, subject to sale and were soon "scattered" when Byrd came upon hard times.

Later, in 1772-74, this church was reconstituted on the same plantation, with another white pastor. At that time four blacks were "ordained" (Sobel, p. 296). Sobel believes these same Lunenburg "congregants later served as the nucleus for the Petersburg [Colored] Baptist congregation which moved to town in 1820" (Sobel, p. 102). Sobel's summary shows John Benn, an African American, as *pastor* (Sobel, p. 296). This church's own records agree on 1820 and Pastor Benn, but their congregation is reported as moving just across the river from Prince George County (*not* Mecklenburg County) to the city of Petersburg, after their meeting house on another estate burned down.

Sobel's report of this church starting in Lunenburg County, therefore, appears to be in serious error. She has transferred names and dates from the Bluestone Church to what became the First Colored Church of Petersburg, also started in 1774. The *Petersburg* record of the church simply crossing the river is far more plausible for the relocation of a church of slaves than a move of 90 miles or more east, from Mecklenburg County. If the Bluestone Church was resurrected and re-

---

18. Sobel, *Trabelin' On*, p. 250. Subsequent references to this book will be given parenthetically in the text.

located at all, it would have had to be to nearby Chase City or Keysville, in the County of Mecklenburg, near the western border of Virginia, not near Petersburg to the east.

Since this "First Colored Church" of Petersburg claims their original worship was also on a plantation of Col. William Byrd III, the two reports could both be true as to the names of the plantation owner and the preachers. Byrd did in fact own lands in both places. But the Prince George property, from which the Petersburg church purports to have come, was tiny compared to the 3,821 acres in Lunenburg (later Mecklenburg) County.[19] The names of the preachers who first preached in Bluestone, Philip Mulkey and William Murphey (Sobel, p. 296), bear strong resemblance to the names in the church's own record: "In 1756 Elders William Murphy, Phillips, and Mackey preached to scattered members of the New Lights [opponents of the Calvinistic doctrine of predestination]. In 1758 and 1759, arrangements were made to organize the members into a church; however, they remained scattered until 1774. . . . This organization was moved to Petersburg after the meeting house was destroyed by fire." It is at least conceivable that the same men preached both in Lunenburg County, which Byrd represented in the Virginia Assembly, *and* also in Prince George, across the river from Petersburg. But the records of this much smaller plantation are scant and unclear. It is not enough to know that William Byrd III started out as one of the richest men in Virginia, and that he appeared to have been generous in general, and unusually open to preaching to slaves. This would explain the same white preachers serving in both places, but even the ownership of the "359 acres on both sides of Reedy Creek" in Prince George County is documented in a limited way,[20] and offers too small a land holding to need enough slaves for even a very small congregation.

There seems also to be no record of such a *church* (1774-1820) for Africans in Prince George County. In fact, across the James River from Petersburg, the earliest "colored" church of which this author has found *record* was in Charles City County, just north of Prince George County, and twelve miles from Petersburg. It was the Elam Baptist Church of Charles City (Ruthville), founded in 1810(!), according to

19. Library of Virginia.
20. Library Of Virginia.

church records, with, reportedly, the gracious aid of a Colored Church in Petersburg (which must have been the racially mixed Gillfield Church, which was founded in 1788 and became all-black in 1803. "First" Colored Baptist had not moved to Petersburg until 1820). Elam records suggest that perhaps ten of the founding members had formerly rowed twelve miles to worship in a Petersburg church.

Elam Church had both slave and free members, and they published a copy of a deed that conveyed to the church its site, from two of its free members, Abram and Susanna Brown. This gift was recorded December 17, 1818. Elam's records indicate that Abram Brown was the son of William Brown, a member of the First Colored Church at Petersburg.[21] The gratitude for help from the Petersburg Church, which is expressed in the Elam history, plus the recorded date of the deed to the property, place in question the exact name of the county of origin and the 1820 date of relocation of Petersburg's "First" Colored Church.

The puzzle is somewhat resolved by the fact that Sobel attributes the Elam founders who had held membership in Petersburg to the Gillfield or *Second* African Church there (Sobel, p. 300). The Elam history reports 1809 revivals, out of which the church started in 1810. One of the three preachers was a "Sampson" (*Elam Baptist Church History,* p. 12). This suspiciously resembles the "Sampson White" who served Gillfield in 1837 (Sobel, p. 206). This could readily support Sobel's Gillfield source of the members, but if it is "Second African," and was founded in 1788, how could "First Colored" not arrive in Petersburg until 1820 and still be "first"? Nevertheless, the Elam record (*Elam Baptist Church History,* p. 9) states that the help came from Petersburg's *First* Colored church.

These varying claims are published here in the hope that the data will be found and shared, with which to establish an accurate record of black church beginnings in the State of Virginia.

The Elam record adds to its earliest history a common distinction between slave and free members. The Elam church's history, in speaking of friendly whites, just casually mentions "mingling and comingling of negroes and slaves" (*Elam Baptist Church History,* p. 17). The

---

21. Elam Baptist Church, *History of Elam Baptist Church,* p. 11. Subsequent references to this brief history will be given parenthetically in the text.

Elam history clearly favors the escape of slaves to freedom in the North, and it was only late in the era of slavery that local white powers succeeded in forcing the slave members out of Elam, into a separate congregation. Many only dropped out, however, returning to Elam after emancipation in 1865 (*Elam Baptist Church History*, p. 17).

However, one does have to wonder at this congregation's license to exist with no mentioned direct recognition or approval by white Baptists except its admission into the Dover Association in 1813. One wonders also at its land title in the name of its own trustees, a gift of free blacks who held title. However, their first three fully recognized pastors were white (1813-1865). Of the third, a Rev. J. H. Christian, the official history states, "The members seem to have been well satisfied with his service, which was nominally nothing, as he only came to be in place according to the law, as the gathering together of any number of colored persons . . . was an unlawful assembly unless certain white persons were present" (*Elam Baptist Church History*, p. 20).

Likewise, because of the laws enacted after the Nat Turner Rebellion in 1831, the First Petersburg church was forced back to selecting or being assigned white pastors in 1840 and 1858. Only after the Civil War were they truly independent, beginning an unbroken line of African American pastors. In 1865, Elam church called its first African American pastor since 1813. *No* white pastor was asked to stay after the Civil War. The black licentiates (sometimes called "floor preachers"), who had done the real preaching all along, were once again called to the pulpit as the official pastors.

The African American church most commonly written of as the "first" nominally independent black congregation was at Silver Bluff, near Aiken, South Carolina, twelve miles from Augusta, Georgia. They first met somewhere between 1773 and 1775 (probably 1774). Their exact place of meeting is the subject of some confusion, since the cornerstone on an old chapel at Silver Bluff reads that this building's congregation was founded in 1750, twenty-three years before the first black congregation. Lincoln and Mamiya mistook this chapel for the first chapel of the Silver Bluff Church.[22]

The issue may be settled in Walter H. Brooks' well-deserved praise

22. C. Eric Lincoln and Lawrence H. Mamiya, *The Black Church in the African American Experience* (Durham: Duke University Press, 1990), pp. 23, 428.

for "George Galphin — Patron of the Silver Bluff Church": "A master less humane, less considerate of the happiness and moral weal of his dependents, less tolerant in spirit, would never have consented to the establishment of a Negro church on his estate. . . . It was he who provided the Silver Bluff Church with a house of worship, by suffering his mill to be used in that capacity. And it was he who gave the little flock a baptistry, by placing his mill-stream at their disposal."[23] The chapel building dated 1750 was *not* a mill building situated on a mill stream, so it couldn't have been the meeting place for this "first" black church.

As with all churches to be discussed, this Silver Bluff church's "independence" concerned only certain inner affairs. The members *and* the building were owned by whites, and whites again governed ordinations. Even so, the Silver Bluff congregation had more autonomy than the Virginians did, with records indicating a tone more of respected advice than arbitrary authority. They also made some autonomous major decisions, including such things as moves to Savannah, during their period of freedom under the brief rule of the British.

Silver Bluff's founding preacher was George Liele, who was freed by Henry Sharp, a white Baptist deacon, to preach to the slaves up and down the Savannah River. Among his converts was David George, who became Silver Bluff's first full-time pastor. Seeking to retain the freedom under the British, David George led fifty members to Savannah in 1778, where Liele already served as first pastor at First African Baptist Church, launched in 1775. In 1782 David George led a group of his former members to Nova Scotia, along with the retreating British. George Liele did the same, fleeing to Jamaica to remain free under the British. This left the Savannah church without a pastor from 1782 to 1788, when Andrew Bryan was ordained. Since this original nucleus had been pro-British, and had come to Savannah from Silver Bluff to keep the emancipation promised by the British, the Savannah church suffered great persecution after the British were driven out. But this struggling African American congregation held on and maintained continuity. Thus First African Baptist Church in Savannah claims to be *the* direct descendant from the Silver Bluff Church, and the oldest black Baptist church in the United States in some form of "continuous" existence. First Afri-

23. *Journal of Negro History,* 60 vols. (Washington, D.C.: Associated Publishers), vol. 7 (1922), p. 181.

can of Savannah officially adopted May 20, 1775, the year of Liele's ordination, as their date of beginning.[24] The Springfield Baptist Church of Augusta, which was much closer to Silver Bluff, also claims to be the direct descendant of the Silver Bluff church, but neither offshoot was literally continuous. When Jesse Peter (who also used the name Jesse Galphin) elected not to flee with Liele and the British, nor with the George group to Nova Scotia, he returned to Silver Bluff (1788), and to the status of being Galphin's slave. He had been ordained and now was allowed time to resurrect the Silver Bluff Church, where he remained until 1791 (Sobel, p. 314). With sixty members at the time, this Silver Bluff congregation then vanished from recorded history, and a new congregation suddenly appeared twelve miles away at Augusta.

Walter H. Brooks's exhaustive research, published in 1922, convinced him, a proud Virginian, that the Silver Bluff Church in South Carolina had the most viable claim to the independence and continuity which would, in his view, define it as "the oldest Negro Baptist Church in this country."[25]

Once again, the issue of being first in history is not as verifiable or important as the issues of culture and control. The first African American church in the North may have preceded all these Virginia, Georgia, and South Carolina Baptist churches in historical time and control. This will be discussed a little later. Meanwhile, as we saw in the previous chapter, there is a "Tracer of Cultural Compatibility" describing the direct flow to Georgia of the powerful, dramatic, image-laden, and tonal preaching style of George Whitefield. As already noted, his revival's new rites and expressive style were profoundly compatible with African culture.

The newly converted George Liele, having first heard Christian preaching from these new white models, no doubt embraced the "holy whine" (tonality) of Marshall and Stearns.[26] Liele in turn passed this African-resonant model on to David George, Jesse Peter, and the succeeding preachers at these first African American churches. Their enhancement of the imagery and tonality of Marshall and Stearns was

---

24. From the brief published history of the church group, pp. 20-21.

25. *Journal of Negro History*, vol. 7 (1922), pp. 2, 172.

26. Sydney E. Ahlstrom, *A Religious History of the American People*, vol. 1 (Garden City, N.Y.: Image Books, 1975), p. 393.

doubtless to the delight of both ethnic groups in this area. Here as perhaps nowhere else was a cultural commonality between black and white which may explain, at least in part, the uncommon measure of self-determination accorded the original church at Silver Bluff and both of the succeeding churches at Savannah (in the early days) and Augusta and environs.

In addition to what this cultural bond could have contributed to the lesser level of white control enjoyed by these black preachers and congregations, Brooks documents an unusually warm and gracious spirit in the Galphins and, at first, the (white) Baptist association. Even so, however, the word independent can hardly be taken literally. After all, the buildings were on loaned land, and title to church sites finally purchased had to be held by law in trust by white trustees. True, this legal arrangement was at least better than the borrowed mill at Silver Bluff, or the rice barn near Savannah that was so generously provided by Jonathan Bryan and used for three years rent free.[27] The point is that culture shared didn't have nearly enough influence to bring about anything close to complete church independence for African Americans.

In 1788, Andrew Bryan, a protege of Liele, was ordained and called to the First African Baptist Church of Savannah. Two years later, Jonathan Bryan sold Andrew Bryan his freedom at a bargain.[28] The ordination, of course, was still under the control of a white-dominated "Association" of churches. Above all, preachers at First African of Savannah dared not openly oppose slavery in any way, as was the case at Richmond's First African Baptist Church.

Even so, there is on record a sample of amazingly daring preaching by Andrew Bryan's nephew and successor, Andrew Marshall. Charles Lyell, a British traveler, who was also greatly impressed with the congregation's singing and ad lib prayers, reported of Marshall: "He also . . . told them they were to look to the future of rewards and punishments in which God would deal impartially with 'the poor and the rich, the black man and the white.'"[29]

This preaching is all the more daring and indicative of indepen-

27. From the brief published history of the church group, pp. 35-38.
28. From the brief published history of the church group, p. 37.
29. Leslie Fishel and Benjamin Quarles, *The Negro American: A Documentary History* (Glenview, Ill.: Scott, Foresman and Company, 1967), p. 136.

dence of spirit in the light of the oppression that followed the exit of the British. In the church's published history the following quote appears:

> Individuals were punished by their masters. . . . They were often waylaid and severely flogged on their way to and from their humble meetings. But none of these things moved them! Indeed, the severer the persecution, the more resolutely did these saints rely upon God and stick to their worship. Finally one day their humble shepherd and about fifty of his followers were seized in the public square and so severely beaten that their blood ran down and puddled on the ground about them. But . . . Andrew, already inhumanly cut, . . . with uplifted hands cried to his persecutors: "If you would stop me from preaching, cut off my head! For I am willing not only to be whipped, but would freely suffer death for the cause of the Lord Jesus."[30]

False accusations were leveled, and the parishioners were jailed and their meetinghouse taken from them. It was at this point that Jonathan Bryan interceded for what he saw as literal martyrs, had them released, and provided his rice barn for their worship. They finally received a judge's order to be allowed to worship in daylight, and the church flourished.

However, Andrew Marshall, the next pastor, had to face false charges of accepting bricks from unauthorized slaves,[31] and had to be cleared by whites. He was later charged with holding Campbellite doctrine unacceptable to the Baptist association, who directed the church to discharge its pastor. Significantly, the church independently ignored the ruling and was excluded from the Sunbury association from 1832 to 1837. On their return to full fellowship in the association, they reported 1,810 members.[32] They had lost 155 members to a split, and suffered the loss of hundreds of slaves forced to worship nearer their plantations.

---

30. From the brief published history of the church group, p. 34.
31. From the brief published history of the church group, p. 46.
32. From the brief published history of the church group, pp. 50, 73; Sobel, *Trabelin' On*, p. 321.

They had started in 1832 with 2,795 members, and returned to 2,296 by 1841.

All of this history suggests an evolving level of independence not yet complete, but close to it, with dependence on supportive white assistance only at points where the ungodly oppression of other whites had to be neutralized. Also, much of the assistance granted was only proper as between sister churches in a family of churches (such as a certifying denomination) regardless of race. Whether first or second or third in the historical sequence, this story of First African in Savannah reflects in general another level and type of the struggle of black churches for ecclesiastical freedom in the South.

Other Black Congregations in the South, 1750-1800

The following list includes black Baptist churches not previously noted as contending for "historic first" and established south of the Mason-Dixon line prior to 1800. In addition, there are a historically significant number of what later became African Methodist Episcopal (A.M.E.) and A.M.E. Zion churches, when these denominations were formed in 1816 and 1820. Most of the Baptist churches here are shown as sequentially listed by Sobel, who notes the date when churches were first gathered in worship, legally incorporated, separated from whites and enabled to call a black pastor, or accepted into predominantly white associations of Baptist churches. The beginning dates of the A.M.E. churches are as shown in a recently researched list graciously provided by the Department of Research and Scholarship of the African Methodist Episcopal Church, prepared by Nicole D. Dickerson (#). For A.M.E. churches, sources other than Dickerson are specifically noted. Where Sobel's dates are used for local Baptist churches, the mark > is used. Asterisks (*) denote where local church sources were used.

1764   The first Methodist society organized in the colonies was at Sam's Creek, Frederick (now Carroll) County, Maryland, about thirty miles northwest of Baltimore. John Wesley had preached there as early as 1758. One of the founding "twelve or fifteen per-

33. McTyeire, *A History of Methodism,* pp. 253-54.

sons" in the Sam's Creek Society, meeting in the cabin of the Strawbridges,[33] was a slave named Anne Sweitzer, "Aunt Annie."

1772#   Emanuel Church was born in Portsmouth, Virginia, with A.M.E. affiliation coming later.

1776>   Williamsburg (Virginia) African or First Colored Baptist is among the black Baptist churches with a claim of being among the very first. It had white pastors in 1849 and 1859, but its first pastors were black, including Gowan Pamphlet, perhaps the best known of the early black preachers. All members were black, many of them free. The church was accepted into the Dover Baptist Association in 1793, and had 750 members in 1830.[34]

1777#   Ebenezer, a group of black Methodists, came together in Bohemia Manor, Maryland.

1779>   Welsh Neck Colored Baptist Church, Darlington County, South Carolina, separated from a white congregation, but always had a white pastor even after that, until 1865.

178?   Evans Metropolitan A.M.E. Zion Church of Fayetteville, North Carolina, descended from one of four preaching stations to which Henry Evans fled while still under persecution, and before he was finally accepted and protected in the founding of the First Methodist Church of Fayetteville, in 1790. The white Methodists intentionally omitted any mention in their records of the existence of such black Methodist societies, especially in the South. However, the Evans group met continually, first in the home of sister "Dicey Hammons, grandmother of Bishop Thomas H. Lomax, who later pastored the church and built the first brick structure on that site." The church was taken into the A.M.E. Zions in 1866.[35]

1781   The oldest black Catholic community in the United States was established in St. Augustine, Florida, by escaped slaves.

1782>   A Negro Baptist Church was founded at King and Queen County, Virginia.

1785#   The Bethel Church (later A.M.E.) of Baltimore first met for worship.

---

34. *Journal of Negro History,* 60 vols. (Washington, D.C.: Associated Publishers), vol. 16, p. 203.

35. Walls, *The African Methodist Episcopal Zion Church,* pp. 24-26.

1786#   The Mt. Gilboa Church (later A.M.E.) first met in Catonsville, Maryland, near Baltimore.

1786>   Sobel lists Pleasant Green Missionary Baptist Church (first known as Ol' Captain's Baptist Church), Lexington, Kentucky, as begun in 1786. However, the church uses the date of 1790 (local church history, p. 36). "Brother Captain" (Peter Duerett) was a hired-out slave, but his preaching reached hundreds. As a slave he was never ordained by the white Elkhorn association, but in 1810 "Captain" was given a kind of tacit, handshake approval of his baptisms, recognizing his powerful witness. His church's land title was also held by slaves, with no white trustees (church history, pp. 37-40). It is to be noted that one of Captain's assistants, another ex-slave named Loudin (London) Ferrill, led most of Captain's members to form First African Baptist, a willingly subordinate branch of (white) First Baptist Church in 1820.[36] By 1861 it had become the largest church in the Elkhorn association (Sobel, p. 336). Nevertheless, Pleasant Green was the oldest black Baptist congregation west of the Alleghenies (church history, p. 36). This church still has expanded facilities and programs at its first location.

1786   Tate's Creek African, Madison County, Kentucky, was established.[37]

1789>   Court Street Baptist Church, Portsmouth, Virginia, was actually white dominated (and not a black church as such). It is mentioned in some detail above, and is shown here in connection with this date because Josiah Bishop served as pastor from 1792 to 1802.

1790#   The St. Paul Church (later A.M.E.) of Lexington, Kentucky, first gathered for worship.

1790>   Pettsworth or Wares Church began in Gloucester County, Virginia, with a mixed race congregation and a white pastor. Its second pastor was William Lemon, an African American who served from 1797 to 1832, the year after the Nat Turner insurrection. The church had 57 white and 1,057 black members in 1852

---

36. Lewis G. Jordan, *Negro Baptist History, U.S.A., 1750-1930* (Nashville: Townsend Press, 1930, 1995), p. 94.

37. Jordan, *Negro Baptist History*, p. 94.

when it was dissolved, and the members were received into other churches.

1790> Uncle Jack's (Black) Baptist Church first met in Nottaway County, Virginia in 1790 and was closed after the Nat Turner revolt. A native of Africa, Jack was brought to Virginia at age seven and converted at age forty. He was tutored by his master's children and noted for "perfect mastery" of the English language, a rare accomplishment often overlooked in histories. He was said by authorities to have wonderful "acquaintance" with Scriptures, and his interpretation of the Bible was respected and sought by the most intelligent whites as well as blacks. However, after the Nat Turner rebellion, he consented to cease preaching and agreed that this law might be justified, since most black preachers knew so little and preached so poorly.[38]

1794# Bethel A.M.E. church of Baltimore was legally organized after much preparatory meeting, beginning in 1785. (Note: The generally recognized "Mother Bethel Church" of the whole A.M.E. Church, at Philadelphia, was actually granted legal power to organize or incorporate three weeks *later* than the Baltimore church in the same year.

1797* Gillfield, or Second African of Petersburg, was originally a mixed church with white pastor, and blacks who were mostly free. (Sobel dates beginning at 1788; see Sobel, p. 300.) Blacks formed a separate congregation in 1803, after whites withdrew, but their pastor was white. Sampson White was the only official African American pastor in Virginia after Nat Turner. White served Gillfield one year, 1837. Later prominent in black Baptist history in the North, he was pastor of Abyssinian Baptist Church in New York City.[39]

1798 The St. Stephen Methodist Church, later A.M.E., was begun in Wilmington, North Carolina.

1799 The Mt. Moriah Methodist Church, later A.M.E., was launched in Annapolis, Maryland.

---

38. *Journal of Negro History*, 60 vols. (Washington, D.C.: Associated Publishers), vol. 16, pp. 184-85.

39. Jordan, *Negro Baptist History*, p. 373; James M. Washington, *Frustrated Fellowship* (Macon, Ga.: Mercer University Press, 1986), pp. 23, 41.

1790s?   Quinn Chapel (name chosen after they became A.M.E.) began in Frederick, Maryland.

1800   The Trinity Methodist Church (later A.M.E.) was launched in Ridgely, Maryland.

1800*   The First Baptist Church of Norfolk ("Bute Street") was formed when its black and white members ceased crossing over the Elizabeth River to worship at Court Street Baptist Church in Portsmouth. In 1816, 26 white members withdrew to form the Cumberland Baptist Church, but the 252 remaining contained a few whites. When blacks bought the Bute Street property in 1830, ten trustees were free blacks and four were white, as was Rev. James Mitchell, who served before the split in 1816 until a year before his death in 1849. The church's history reads, "With Mitchell as their nominal head, the church became a viable, independent organization run almost entirely by blacks. The clerk was black and so was a majority of the trustees. They carried on the weekly business of the church, paid the minister's salary, and disciplined wayward members" (church history, p. 3).

Black Congregations in the North: 1750-1800

The claim of primacy among African American congregations in the North is commonly granted to the withdrawing African members of St. George's Methodist Episcopal Church, the followers of Richard Allen and Absalom Jones in Philadelphia. The Bethel A.M.E., and indeed the whole A.M.E. denomination, affirms 1787, the date of withdrawal, as their beginning date. In fact, the vote for the Free African Society to become a church was not taken until 1792, when only Allen voted Methodist, leaving A.M.E. historic continuity solely in Allen.[40] He did draw a congregation together, and Bethel finally became a legal corporation in 1794.

However, in the North, as in the South, the issue of who was first is heavily clouded with complex issues. One challenge to Bethel's pri-

---

40. Richard Allen, *The Life Experience and Gospel Labors of Rt. Rev. Richard Allen,* ed. George A. Singleton (Nashville: Abingdon Press, 1960), p. 29.

macy came from the membership of the Free African Society, those who had withdrawn from mixed St. George's Methodist Episcopal Church. The original members had all voted to become St. Thomas African *Episcopal* Church. Richard Allen had been associated with them from the beginning in 1787, but he considered Methodism far more appropriate for blacks. He therefore declined the African Society's offer to make him their Episcopal priest, and they elected Absalom Jones. Thus St. Thomas African Episcopal Church lays claim to being literally the first congregation of African Americans in the North, since they were the nucleus that withdrew. The same members are recorded as having met as a Methodist society or class as early as 1767. This undermines Allen's claim to Bethel's having literal roots and continuity in the society's many meetings held between 1787 and 1794. Allen's considered choice of Methodism forced him to start almost from scratch to form a strong congregation.

There is a further complication in the record concerning primacy of first meetings, since the A.M.E. archives record black Methodists as gathering a year earlier, in 1766, in Brooklyn, in a racially mixed congregation in the open air. This group, out of which came "The African Wesleyan Methodist Episcopal Church" of Brooklyn, first met in open air services, with sermons by a sea captain converted under John Wesley. The congregation consisted of "twenty-three whites and twelve blacks" in 1794, when they purchased the land on which they had been meeting, and moved into their first building. They bore the name Sands Street Wesleyan Methodist Episcopal Church, and the Methodist records of 1795 show them as a recognized station: "Slaves and free Blacks were allowed to worship in Sands Street Church, even though they had to sit in the gallery."[41] The church increased to 1500 members and had to build again in 1810, taking the name of First Methodist Church of Brooklyn. Great increases in blacks in the next seven years brought tensions, and the whites voted to charge blacks ten dollars per quarter for sitting in the gallery. Blacks voted to withdraw in 1817, to form an African Methodist church, and asked Bishop Richard Allen to send them a preacher. They were finally legally incorporated in 1818.

However, many of the criteria mentioned regarding literal "independence" among the earliest churches in the South, all Baptist, were

---

41. From the brief published history of the church group, pp. 14-15.

irrelevant to St. Thomas and Bethel. *No* Episcopal congregation is without the long-established governance of a bishop in the "apostolic succession." As of 1816, when the A.M.E. churches became a denomination with bishops, Bethel came under similar governance. After that, any serious Bethel claim to independence had to be ethnic, hinging on the fact that the bishop, Richard Allen, was black, not white, and was their pastor.

Again, St. Thomas's independence was equal to that of any white Episcopal church, except that Absalom Jones was not accorded equal voting privileges with white priests in the Episcopal gatherings. Presumably it was because he had not learned the Greek and Hebrew languages required of all priests.[42] While this appears to be a type of the old denial of shared control once again, St. Thomas Church had and has strong claim to being first in the North, based on both this "equal" status in the denomination and on congregational continuity.

The Free African Society was born as the result of an incident in the St. George's Church in 1787, just three years after the formation of the Methodist Episcopal denomination. Allen had attempted to form a black Methodist congregation, but even his loyal black followers had discouraged it. Instead, their sacrificial gifts had greatly supported the construction of the sanctuary of the mostly white St. George's Methodist Episcopal Church. Yet as soon as the building could be used, blacks were relegated to the upper balcony, and ordered off their knees when they dared to pray in an unassigned part of the balcony. The blacks, led by Allen and Absalom Jones, withdrew, promising never to return, and formed the Free African Society,[43] out of which grew the St. Thomas and Bethel churches.

Probably modeled on an African tradition, this society engaged in advocacy for the race, but, more importantly, in mutual assistance and fraternal, lodge-like fellowship. They also provided worship for the members in a building they acquired. When they decided to become a church, they retained their building as the sanctuary for what now became a "Protestant Episcopal" congregation. Allen was left holding title to a lot he had acquired at the request of the society.[44] Allen felt

42. From the brief published history of the church group.
43. Allen, *The Life Experience and Gospel Labors of Rt. Rev. Richard Allen,* pp. 25-26.
44. Allen, *The Life Experience and Gospel Labors of Rt. Rev. Richard Allen,* pp. 28-30.

called to establish there a new Methodist church for blacks. Under the guise of assisting him, a white member of St. George's drew up incorporation papers that vested land title and complete corporate control in the white Methodist conference. It was not until this legal trick was reversed in court, with the help of prominent whites, that Mother Bethel finally became its own independent congregation in 1794.[45]

In 1796, the black Methodists of New York City first met, with the permission and good wishes of Bishop Francis Asbury, who allowed them to "hold such meetings in the intervals of the regular preaching hours of the white church."[46] Asbury was not always on hand, however, and the white Methodists of the John Street Church later engaged in the same kinds of subterfuge as the whites of St. George's in Philadelphia to maintain control of black church properties and church life. Notwithstanding delays due to fears because of the Gabriel Prosser revolt in Virginia as well as to internal problems, Zion sprang free with the formation of their own corporation on February 16, 1801, choosing the name of African Methodist Episcopal Zion Church. April 8 of the same year they managed to get title to some land. In 1806, Asbury ordained three deacons, including James Varick, who later became the first A.M.E. Zion bishop.[47]

The break with the John Street church had as its basis a matter concerning the burial ground, along with the typical reticence to ordain and give full recognition and hearing to African Americans. "For the most part, the church leaders were free, although quite a number of the members were still slaves. They were possessed of unusual intellect and manifold skills," according to historian William Walls.[48] They fitted their house of worship with pulpit, seats, and gallery. Their strong pride and courage, plus impressive skills for cooperation among a team of leaders, enabled them to move swiftly to incorporation in 1801. By the time they met to organize a denomination, in 1820, there were six churches in the group. The name Zion was not added to their title until 1848.

Other black churches in the North before 1800:

---

45. Allen, *The Life Experience and Gospel Labors of Rt. Rev. Richard Allen*, pp. 24-41.
46. Walls, *The African Methodist Episcopal Zion Church*, p. 51.
47. Walls, *The African Methodist Episcopal Zion Church*, pp. 56-65.
48. Walls, *The African Methodist Episcopal Zion Church*, pp. 45, 46.

1714   The first Lutheran services held in North America were held by a congregation named Zion, in a town now known as Oldwick, New Jersey, in the home of two free African Americans, Aree and Jora Van Guinea.

1792# Trinity Church at Gouldtown, New Jersey, and Mt. Pisgah Church at what is now Lawnside, New Jersey, both later A.M.E., were begun. The latter was a mixed race church for twenty-five or more years before a black majority voted to become African Methodist and join with the new denomination.

1795# Bethel Church at Providence, Rhode Island, was begun, later uniting with the A.M.E. denomination.

1800# Mt. Zion at Kresson, New Jersey, and Bethel in Pennsauken, New Jersey, were established. They later became A.M.E. churches.

Chapter 4

Trends Impacting the Early Black Churches up to 1900

So far, we have dealt with such issues as the internal realities behind the statistics of slave conversion, the levels of white influence in the establishment and organization of the separated ("independent") African American churches, and the details of the claims as to which church came first. It is time now to look at least briefly into such concerns as caste and class inside the African American churches, North and South; the black relationship to upward mobility among white Baptists and Methodists; language skills and literacy in a congregation's worship and internal power structures; the roles of laity in the initiation of the proliferation of small churches, as compared to larger urban churches; the placement or distribution of the ministers of various levels of skill and preparation; the careful scrutiny of the conversion experiences and later moral and ethical behavior of members; and the treatment accorded women.

An often-overlooked issue in the early black congregation was the uncomfortable distinction between slave, ex-slave, and freeborn members. It must be kept in mind that all three of the Black denominations (African Methodist Episcopal, African Methodist Episcopal Zion, and Baptist) and many of the earliest churches of the nineteenth century were founded *before* slavery was completely abolished in the Northern states. In 1780, Pennsylvania began to abolish slavery by providing that no Negro born after 1780 could be held in bondage past age twenty-eight. Meanwhile, they were to be treated as apprentices or indentured servants.[1] So a person born after 1800 could still be a slave for a significant part of his or her adult life in a society where few lived past their forties.

Churches in the North especially were prone to avoid electing deacons who were not yet free. And there was constant awareness of class distinctions even though the churches of the North tended to be strongly anti-slavery, and active in the Underground Railroad. Yet black-on-black paternalism by the freed was not uncommon in many circles, even among some active abolitionists. In a history of African American Episcopalians written by Father George F. Brag in 1922, class distinctions were clearly *affirmed* among African Americans, all the way back to the very beginning of organized congregations.[2]

Further driving a wedge within the race was the fact that even when congregations insisted on being inclusive, white owners of slaves were adamantly opposed. Apparently they feared that contact between the enslaved and the free would arouse dangerous ambitions among the former. Some masters refused to allow their slaves to attend worship with free African Americans. Such was the case after First African Baptist Church of Savannah was temporarily expelled from the Sunbury Association. Hundreds of enslaved members were ordered withdrawn from the church before it could be readmitted to the association in 1837.[3] The Elam Baptist Church in Charles City, Virginia, with many free members, was strongly committed to keeping its enslaved members. But it was finally forced to dismiss all slaves or risk being closed down. The whites organized a separate slave congregation, with a second white preacher and building. Many of the dismissed slaves simply dropped out for years, returning to Elam after the Civil War.[4] The evidence is abundant that class and caste, or slave status, created many problems in the life of the churches in the late eighteenth and early nineteenth centuries, both North and South.

Another necessary, functional distinction had to do with basic fluency in English and the simple ability to read the Bible. Leadership

1. John Hope Franklin, *From Slavery to Freedom*, 3rd ed. (New York: Alfred A. Knopf, 1967), pp. 140-41.

2. *Journal of Negro History*, 60 vols. (Washington, D.C.: Associated Publishers), vol. 8, p. 108.

3. First Baptist, Savannah, local church history, p. 73.

4. Elam Baptist Church, *History of Elam Baptist Church*, p. 17.

in worship made it mandatory that at least one member, preferably the preacher, be able to read. The need for written records made literacy even more essential. A classic example of the scarcity of literate recorders of the churches' business is found in the history of the first sessions of the African Methodist Episcopal Church. Almost no records of the first session (1816) were preserved, for want of a literate recording secretary. In the Annual Conference of 1818, they were compelled to use, as writing clerk, fifteen-year-old Richard Allen, Jr. "Here we find the minutes replete with the details of every transaction entered into. . . . He was neither a member of the Annual Conference nor a member of the Church. . . . It is supposed that he was employed as the Secretary, because he was the best scholar that the Conference could obtain. . . . Better have a boy who can do a thing as it ought to be done, than a man who cannot."[5]

The historic development of whole denominations and of many great churches must be understood to have been conceived and executed by a generation of leaders almost all of whom had been legally and forcibly denied the privilege of learning to read. The incorporation papers of church after church were signed with X's. A typical example is the incorporation documents of the First African Baptist Church of Chillicothe, Ohio, founded in 1824. Its non-writing, abolitionist founders soon changed the name to First Anti-Slavery Baptist Church.

But charismatic preachers of the gospel and lay leaders in prayer were not likely to be deterred or disrespected because of illiteracy. This was not at all due at first to a form of anti-intellectualism. Rather it was a combination of cultural factors. One was the fact that their residual African culture included awesomely impressive memory, enabling preachers to hear Bible stories a very few times and then recall them accurately. Thus preparation in meditation was possible without written resources. Emphasis could be placed on gifted imagery, as opposed to abstractions and print. The earlier preachers made the Bible come alive, so that it became more important to be artistically articulate and biblically accurate than to be literate or justified in print.

In addition to the obvious influences of enslavement versus freedom, and lingual and literary skills, there was a set of sub-classes or dis-

---

5. *History of the African Methodist Episcopal Church,* vol. 1, ed. Daniel A. Payne (New York: Arno & The New York Times, 1969), p. 16.

tinctions related to social conditions. It may come as a surprise, for instance, that freed slaves in the North constituted a kind of upper group, harder working than freeborn Northerners. This fact was uncovered by a detailed analysis of blacks in Philadelphia in the early 1800s. Former slaves had on average higher incomes, larger families, a higher percentage of two-parent family groups, and greater church activity. The studies included both manumitted ex-slaves and those who had bought their freedom, but there was no census or other record of escapees by the Underground Railroad, as a master from the South might still be searching for them.[6] One might be bound to conclude that ex-slaves with courage, cunning, ambition, and ability enough to gain their freedom were a special group, if not a caste.

The same initiative that set them free, however it was accomplished, was adequate to move them to leadership in the black community. This finding was something of a trophy for the Quakers and others who did this meticulous study. They covered both their own censuses and the regular federal censuses, between which they did their own. Their goal was to prove African Americans worthy of voting and participating fully in American democracy. They proved their point, but it took a constitutional amendment to gain the vote for African Americans.

On the other hand, the Philadelphia study indicated that the poorest of the black population were less prone to be at ease in established middle-class churches. In between, there was a range of substratification. The details of the study included a family-by-family notation of specific neighborhoods and congregations. Entire denominations tended to include a grouping or caste, from "upper class" Episcopalians and Presbyterians to a spread of Methodist and Baptist churches across the range of socio-economic position. Of 2,776 households studied, 73 percent were Methodists, 9 percent were Baptists, 7 percent were Presbyterians, 7 percent were Episcopalians, and 3 percent were Catholics. Eleven percent of the Methodists were ex-slave, as were 30 percent of the Baptists.[7]

Since Baptists predominated in the South, where local church autonomy prevailed, the ex-slaves escaping north included a higher per-

---

6. Philadelphia Society History Project, pp. 7-10.
7. Philadelphia Society History Project, p. 16.

centage of Baptists. On the other hand, the centralized leadership, itinerant clergy, and written guidelines of the Methodists (A.M.E., A.M.E.Z. and black Methodist Episcopalians) made possible their reaching of a much larger percentage of the African American population of Philadelphia overall. The greater proliferation of small congregations among the Methodists in smaller towns occurred for the same reasons.

The churches discussed in previous chapters tended to be larger, assuming seventy-five members or more, located in larger cities like Philadelphia, Norfolk, and Savannah. But the majority of A.M.E. churches were small, located in smaller cities or towns, and serving very small African American populations. The isolated position of these small churches necessitated some form of community in which to nourish besieged identity and engage in mutual support.

While there was a tiny minority of sympathetic and supportive Quakers, the white majority in these small communities was less than kind to the indentured servants left over from slavery. They were also prone to restrict employment of the free to the typical servant roles, and to less skilled crafts. When indentures ended, these virtual ex-slaves were transitioned into free society through almshouses, whose attention to social and spiritual needs contributed almost nothing. The African American predicament in these small towns made the importance of these small churches "impossible to overestimate."[8]

A typical such church was the Bethel A.M.E. Church located in Reading, Pennsylvania. In 1820, near the time of the first black meetings for worship, the white population was 4,242, mostly German, and the black population was 90. Relatively near the border of the slave state of Maryland, this town's news often included notice of runaway slaves and indentured servants, but there were only a minority of whites sympathetic to the abolitionist cause. The Bethel Church of Reading seems to have been an actual "station" on the Underground Railroad, as were many such A.M.E. churches on known routes North.[9]

This Reading congregation met first as early as 1820 under Presbyterian auspices, and split from that congregation to form an A.M.E. congregation in 1834. The initiative for this move was no doubt partly

8. Richard G. Johnson, *They All Stand Fair: A Social History of Bethel AME Church* (Reading, Pa.: self-published, 1980), p. 9.

9. Johnson, *They All Stand Fair,* pp. 91-92.

stirred up by A.M.E. itinerants from neighboring counties, but mainly it was the desire of the laity for their own community life and their own kind of preaching. There is evidence that the majority of the action was by a nucleus of ten black laymen.[10] Four of these ten laymen went to the Philadelphia Conference of 1835 "to request pastoral attention."[11] In other words, it was laity who took the initiative to press the bishop to assign them to a circuit and send them a pastor. This kind of scenario was duplicated many times in the small towns of the Northeast and Midwest in the first half of the nineteenth century.

The title of this Reading church's history, *They All Stand Fair: A Social History of Bethel A.M.E. Church, Reading, Pennsylvania,* attracts attention to still another issue in these early churches: the careful scrutiny of conversion experiences, and of moral and ethical behavior. The title comes from a phrase used in the regular quarterly conferences, at which all members were in effect examined. Those found acceptable "stood fair."[12] The first trial of a Bethel member involved a charge of illegitimate paternity. The seriousness of the tiny church's judicial process is seen in the wording of the report of the committee of judges, where one did not in fact stand fair: "We the committee to examine the case of John Henson after due deliberation do find an award of guilt against him of immoral conduct."[13] Bethel, Reading, had only thirty members after twelve years.[14] Yet their internal power struggles tended all too often to exclude members who were not immoral, but who were not "in love and charity" (agreement) with the members and/or the pastor.[15] Whatever the charges, they were admonished to repentance, or excluded from the fellowship. Later on, the excluded were often received back into the fellowship after some form of reconciliation. And membership in such churches was so important in those days that one endured the embarrassment and was glad to be received back into fellowship.

The Baptists were likewise strict, expelling from the membership those whom they called "backsliders." Churches tended, however, to reclaim and restore back nearly as many as they excluded. Underlying this

10. Johnson, *They All Stand Fair,* p. 22.
11. Johnson, *They All Stand Fair,* p. 17.
12. Johnson, *They All Stand Fair,* p. 20.
13. Johnson, *They All Stand Fair,* p. 32.
14. Johnson, *They All Stand Fair,* p. 53.
15. Johnson, *They All Stand Fair,* p. 43.

cycle were spot conversions and untrained leadership, with no follow-up instruction in the Christian life.[16]

Bethel's requests to the bishop for a pastor merit some attention. Eventually they were briefly given by appointment the services of one of their own resident members, Sam Murray, one of the founding lay leaders who was later ordained. But most of the early history involved other pastors, who served a circuit of churches and traveled by horseback. The size and support of these small churches did not attract the small supply of genuinely talented clergy, so the fact that these churches survived is in large measure attributable to the loyalty and dire need of the laity. The fact that two later bishops of great stature (Wayman and Payne) were ordained at the same time as Sam Murray made Bethel, Reading, proud. But the attention given to Bethel and other small churches by major leaders in quarterly meetings, to say nothing of Sunday worship, appears to have been very scant.[17] What is true of Bethel, Reading, would be even more true of the churches in areas still further removed from the major urban centers of the Eastern Seaboard.

In view of this great shortage of talent, the treatment of women in the pulpits of the early African American churches is odd indeed. Although black women have been known to preach for some 200 years,[18] the word church still subtly implies male pastoral leadership in the minds of too many people. In the early churches of the three major African American denominations (A.M.E., A.M.E.Z., and Baptist), none accepted a female pastor. Despite the staunch and early stand of the African American churches for justice, in professional placement of black women, "equality is still the exception and not the rule."[19] For this work to give due coverage to women, both laity and clergy, it was necessary to treat them individually, in much the same manner as the chronological listing here of congregations, with fuller treatment for special dates and issues.

The A.M.E. churches have recently formally embraced equality with the election of a female bishop, but their original position is illustrated

16. *Journal of Negro History,* vol. 16, pp. 202-10.

17. Johnson, *They All Stand Fair,* pp. 21-24.

18. Bettye Collier-Thomas, *Daughters of Thunder* (San Francisco: Jossey-Bass, 1998), p. 37.

19. *Encyclopedia of African American Religions,* ed. Larry G. Murphy et al. (New York: Garland Publishing, 1993), p. 847.

by the story of the treatment accorded Jarena Lee in the 1820s. Lee, widow of an A.M.E. pastor, first felt called to preach in 1811, the same year she was married. When she sought advice from Richard Allen, then only a local pastor, his response was that the rules of Methodism simply did not call for women as preachers. In 1818, a year after her husband's death, Bishop (as of 1816) Allen gave her permission to hold prayer meetings and no more in her own house. Then, in 1819, in a worship service at Bethel A.M.E. in Philadelphia, with Bishop Allen in the audience, a preacher started to deliver his sermon and then suddenly floundered. Lee, on impulse, sprang to the pulpit and preached a creditable sermon from the biblical text originally chosen by the faltering speaker.

As she returned to her seat, she feared the worst. But to her surprise, "The Bishop rose up in the assembly, and related that I had called upon him eight years before, asking to be permitted to preach, and that he had put me off; but that he now as much believed that I was called to that work as any of the preachers present."[20] The irony of this story is that Bishop Allen, the rebel against white Methodist tyranny at St. George's Church, was now willing meekly to submit to white Methodist rules on women preaching. And this despite the fact that Jarena Lee was probably a better preacher than two-thirds or more of those whom Allen had ordained and whom he needed so badly in his many pastorless churches. This woman was an able reader and writer, and a powerful preacher. She was also a compassionate pastor, but nobody will ever know what a great contribution she could have made to the needy ranks of A.M.E. clergy, and to the A.M.E. church as a whole, between 1820 and 1840 or 1850. Nor can it be known how the Black Church might have grown if the large numbers saved under the passionate preaching of African American women in Holiness camp meetings in the nineteenth century had instead been won to the fledgling churches of African Americans up North.

1808   "Elizabeth" (1766-1858) became the first recorded African American woman preacher. She was set free in 1796 and became a "preaching woman" in 1808 at Baltimore.

1821   Zilpha Elaw (1790-1850s), who was born free near Philadelphia and grew up as a Quaker after her mother died, was called to

20. Collier-Thomas, *Daughters of Thunder*, pp. 44-45.

preach in 1821. She risked enslavement by preaching in the South. She preached in camp meetings, and across the Northeast, as well as in London, where she may have died in the early 1850s. She received no known recognition by any denominational body.

1830   Rebecca Cox Jackson (1795-1871) joined the Shakers as itinerant preacher. She founded and led Shaker family groups of African Americans and women in Philadelphia, which lasted two decades after her death in 1871.[21]

184?   Julia A. J. Foote (1823-1901) was born in 1823, in Schenectady, New York, as the fourth child of ex-slaves. In 184?, in Boston, she openly confessed her call. For more than fifty years she served as itinerant evangelist and a Methodist-Holiness preacher, from California to Canada and the Northeast. In 1895, she became the first female ordained deacon in the A.M.E. Zion Church, and in 1899, shortly before her death, she was ordained the second female full itinerant. It was a historic Methodist first, but in 2003, the only female Methodist bishops were A.M.E. and United Methodist. Meanwhile, the fruitful half-century of labor Julia Foote gave to independent preaching, largely among Holiness groups, could have been a great blessing to the A.M.E. Zions in needy places like Ohio.

1870   Amanda Berry Smith (1837-1915) was born a slave in Maryland in 1837, but her father soon bought her freedom. Converted to the Methodist Episcopal Church in 1856, in York, Pennsylvania, she saw visions of herself as an evangelist and taught herself to read and write. In 1870 she began her evangelistic work and built up a national following by preaching in churches, revivals, and camp meetings. She spent years in England, Africa, and India, and was noted not only for her Holiness doctrine, but for her feminist advocacy and concerns for social reform. Her main denominational connections were Methodist Episcopal and A.M.E., but she was never ordained by either denomination. She established a home for African American orphans in Chicago, where she retired in 1890.[22]

---

21. Collier-Thomas, *Daughters of Thunder,* p. 48.
22. Collier-Thomas, *Daughters of Thunder,* pp. 48-53.

1872   Harriet A. Baker (1829-1913) was born free at Havre de Grace, Maryland. She first felt called to preach in 1872, but her church did not authorize her until 1874. Leaving her husband and three children, she traveled from 1874 to 1889. Preaching solely to whites in Brownstown, Pennsylvania, in a three-week revival, she witnessed the conversion of seventy-two persons. In 1889, she was appointed to the A.M.E. church at Lebanon, Pennsylvania. In 1897 she settled in Allentown with the title of Evangelist. There she established the Bethel Mission and drew audiences from as far away as New England.[23]

1881   Sarah Ann Hughes began her ministry as an evangelist of the A.M.E. Church in 1881, and was appointed to a church in Fayetteville, North Carolina, in 1882. This rare appointment was in recognition of her fine preaching skills. However, the furor over her assignment continued, and she was defrocked in 1887, a move ratified by the 1888 General Conference.[24]

1895   Mary Julia Small (1850-1945) was born Mary Blair in Murfreesboro, Tennessee. In 1873 she married John Bryan Small, later a bishop of the A.M.E.Z. Church. In 1895 she was ordained deacon, and in 1898 she was the first woman ordained itinerant pastor. However, there is no record of her holding a charge, although she was quite active in missionary work and other ministries.[25]

1898   Florence Spearing Randolph (1866-1951) was born in Charleston, South Carolina, and graduated from Avery Normal Institute. Called to ministry in 1898, and opposed by family and clergy, she was ordained deacon in 1901 and elder in 1903. Her last charge was the Wallace Chapel A.M.E.Z. Church of Summit, New Jersey, where she served from 1925 until her retirement in 1946.[26]

In addition to these women clergy, there was a host of eloquent women of faith whose charisma, activism, and dedication were of criti-

23. Collier-Thomas, *Daughters of Thunder,* pp. 71-72.
24. Collier-Thomas, *Daughters of Thunder,* pp. 26-27.
25. Collier-Thomas, *Daughters of Thunder,* pp. 91-93.
26. Collier-Thomas, *Daughters of Thunder,* pp. 101-5.

cal importance to the advancement of African American churches and communities. Their gifts were given further expression and usefulness in civic organizations such as the National Association of Colored Women, founded in 1896.

Chapter 5

The Spread of the African American Churches, 1801-1840

This brings us to the chronological coverage of the first era of intense African American Church growth, with a descriptive treatment of historically prominent churches established during the first forty years of the nineteenth century. In addition, in the timelines in the appendixes, many representative historic examples of small churches in small communities are listed, along with the other historic and often larger churches. Because the North and South offered radically different conditions for establishing churches, the two geographic areas are treated separately.

African American Church Growth in the North

As the African American presence in the North slowly increased, and legalized slavery died out there (as late as 1827 in the State of New York), the number of African Americans in white churches increased also. It was natural that they should grow restless for both the culture and control of their own free worship, and for the leadership of their own clergy and lay officers. Some white congregations responded to this need with what were initially styled as "black branches," with a level of self-governance that was well above the authority whites permitted in the South. Obviously, one key factor was the Northern advantage of having African American members who, as wage earners, controlled their own incomes. They were also homeowners in many cases. As the African American population grew in numbers and power, and the people learned the language and culture, the time came inevitably for them to own and control their own churches, with or without the "blessing" of whites.

For leadership they frequently called on African American pastors from the South, who had earlier gained the best of "on-the-job" training and experience in larger churches. It was not too difficult to get some of them to gravitate to the freer climate of the Northern cities, despite the much smaller memberships of the churches. There, over time, they could shape once-small African American sub-groups within white congregations into strong, vibrant, African American-culture urban churches. In the smaller towns of the North, with occasional helpful visits from itinerant clergy, laity, as previously noted, labored to organize much-needed small churches as refuges of mutual emotional, material, and spiritual support. Their churches were havens of mutual acceptance — places to "be somebody." This they did on their own, oftentimes, even though white congregations had sought to provide for African American needs with African American branches. The tiny African American community's need was for more than worship; they had a cultural nostalgia and social need for church as extended family. This was to serve in the place of the traditional African society, which was a literally extended, blood-kin tribal structure. No white-controlled "branch" could serve this function.

In Philadelphia, alongside the St. Thomas African Episcopal Church and the Bethel A.M.E. Church, whose beginnings have already been described, there was also the First African Baptist Church. It was formed in 1809, based on amicable letters of dismissal for thirteen African American members from the (white) First Baptist Church, "for the purpose of forming the First African Baptist Church of Philadelphia."[1] When they were admitted to the Philadelphia Baptist Association, the ordained whites appointed to serve communion on first Sundays were thought of as a helpful convenience more than as overseers. A lay preacher from Savannah, Henry Cunningham, was "in charge" from 1809 to 1813, being assisted once a month by white clergy sup-

---

1. *Official History of the First African Baptist Church,* p. 11.

plied by the Association.[2] His assigned colleague, John King, a white member from Virginia, was ordained in 1818, and served as pastor until 1832. (One is prone to wonder why they didn't just ordain Cunningham, who had had experience in the very first churches, down in Savannah.) The key records of pastoral leadership are somewhat confusing until 1832, when James Burrows, a slave from Northampton County, Virginia, was called as pastor. In order to secure his services, two members served in his stead as slaves in Virginia, until Burrows could earn or gather enough to buy his freedom. The desire for their own pastoral leadership must have been desperate for two members to take the awesome risk of accepting slave status in Virginia for a whole year in order to free their pastor. During Burrows's twelve-year pastorate, 1832-1844, the membership grew from 60 to 252, and a Sunday School was organized.[3]

This church's search for a pastor once again illustrates the precarious shortage of pastors among Northern African American churches, especially among Baptists. It explains why the names of pastors drawn from larger Baptist churches in the South will appear on the following lists of newer and initially much smaller Northern churches. This does not explain why three of the first four African American women preachers went apparently unnoticed by African American Methodist and Baptist churches in that same Philadelphia area.

Jarena Lee (1783-185?) was joined in time and place to Zilpha Elaw (1790-1850s), and Rebecca Cox Jackson (1795-1871), but neither of these two was ever accepted by either Baptists or Methodists. Zilpha Elaw, raised a Quaker and called to preach at age thirty-one, risked preaching in the South and in England, as well as across the Northeast. But, while preaching to Holiness camp meeting audiences, she was never denominationally recognized. Rebecca Cox Jackson was a feminist Holiness activist preacher when she joined the Shakers at age thirty-five. In 1857, she founded a Shaker family group of women and African Americans, but was very critical of the A.M.E. pastors and churches.[4]

---

2. *Official History of the First African Baptist Church,* p. 15.

3. *Official History of the First African Baptist Church,* p. 21.

4. Bettye Collier-Thomas, *Daughters of Thunder* (San Francisco: Jossey-Bass, 1998), pp. 46-48.

The Holiness movement that developed as part of the Second Great Awakening seems not to have drawn African American congregations, even though it accepted the preaching of African American women. But independent black Methodist churches founded prior to the A.M.E.'s organizing conference in 1816 gladly embraced African Methodist affiliation. The following chronological list includes African American churches of all denominations:

1802# Mt. Pisgah Church was founded in Salem, New Jersey, and was later represented by Reuben Cuff as one of the five churches founding the African Methodist Episcopal Church in 1816. He was later ordained and appointed in 1822 to the Salem Circuit.[5]

1805 Joy Street Baptist Church, Boston, was founded by Thomas Paul, born and educated in New Hampshire. He launched the independent African American church movement, and led in the building of the first edifice entirely constructed by African American craftsmen.[6]

1807 John Gloucester founded First African Presbyterian Church, Philadelphia. Trained for ministry while still a slave in Tennessee, he was brought to Philadelphia for the purpose of starting a Presbyterian church for Africans. His early efforts included street preaching as early as six o'clock on Sunday mornings. His congregation consisted of twenty-two members in 1807 when the church was organized, but his gifts as a preacher soon won him a larger following. There were 123 members when the church was accepted into the presbytery in 1811. Gloucester had returned to Tennessee for full ordination in 1810, and again in 1819, to purchase his wife and four children for $1,500. He had traveled far and wide, including England, to raise the money. His church had 300 members when he died in 1822, but he had had to devote much of his time to raise much of his budget among the white Presbyterians. When his health failed, he recommended his son Jeremiah to be his successor.

5. *History of the African Methodist Episcopal Church,* vol. 1, ed. Daniel A. Payne (New York: Arno & The New York Times, 1969), pp. 13, 34.
6. *Encyclopedia of African American Religions,* ed. Larry G. Murphy et al. (New York: Garland Publishing, Inc., 1993), p. 574.

When the church did not agree, Jeremiah organized Second African Presbyterian Church with 75 members from First African in 1824. John's son Stephen founded Central Presbyterian Church in Philadelphia in 1844, and son James founded Siloam Presbyterian Church in Brooklyn in 1849.[7]

1807   Macedonia Baptist Church, founding member of Providence Association, was founded at Burlington, Lawrence County, Ohio, near Ironton on the Ohio River, opposite the slave state of Kentucky. According to all available records, this was the first African American church west of Pennsylvania, or in the original states of the Northwest Territory: Ohio, Indiana, Illinois, Michigan, Wisconsin, and part of Minnesota.[8]

1808#   Bethel A.M.E. Church of Pittsburgh was founded. This is still a leading A.M.E. church of that city. It was the base from which was launched the churching of the Northwest Territory.

1808   New York City's Abyssinian Baptist Church was founded by Thomas Paul on the request of First Baptist Church, which dismissed sixteen African Americans "honorably." Paul, a great abolitionist orator and preacher, then returned to the Joy Street Church in Boston. He was followed at Abyssinian in 1810 by Josiah Bishop. Four pastors later, this church called Sampson White, formerly of Gillfield, Petersburg.[9] They sent south for pastors twice in their earlier history.

1809*   First African Baptist Church was founded at Philadelphia.

1809#   Union (A.M.E.) Church of Allentown, Pennsylvania, was founded. The African American Methodist church there now is A.M.E. Zion.

1813   Macedonia Baptist Church was organized at South Point, Ohio, in the Providence Association.[10]

1814   African Asbury A.M.E. Zion Church was begun in New York City.[11]

---

7. *Encyclopedia of African American Religions*, pp. 301-2.

8. Beverley Graves, Chillicothe, Ohio, history website.

9. *Encyclopedia of African American Religions*, pp. 574-75; Carter G. Woodson, *The History of the Negro Church* (Washington, D.C.: Associated Publishers, 1972), pp. 76-77.

10. Providence Missionary Baptist Association 150th Anniversary Souvenir, 1984.

11. William J. Walls, *The African Methodist Episcopal Zion Church* (Charlotte, N.C.: A.M.E. Zion Publishing House, 1885, 1974), p. 68.

1816   St. Philip's (African) Episcopal Church was organized in New York City.[12]

1818   James Varick (later bishop) organized John Wesley Church in New Haven, Connecticut, with thirty-five members. This congregation became a founding member of the African Methodist Episcopal Zion denomination. It later changed its name to Varick Memorial A.M.E.Z. Church.[13]

1818   An African Methodist Society was organized in the Williamsburg section of Brooklyn. It later united with the A.M.E.Z. denomination and took the name of Varick Memorial A.M.E. Zion Church.[14]

1818   First African Baptist Church was founded in St. Louis, Missouri, as a Sunday School for Colored people, where they were taught to read the Bible. It grew so rapidly that they became a separate branch under supervision of the white church in 1822, and an independent church in 1826. Members had to have certificates from their masters in order to attend.[15]

1818#   John Gee A.M.E. Church was established on the Ohio River at Gallipolis.

1819   Union Baptist Church was established at Blackfork, Lawrence County, on the Ohio River. It was a charter member of the Providence Association.[16]

1819>   Salem or Wood River Baptist Church, Illinois, was organized by James E. Welsh, a white missionary, with funding from a white congregation in Salem, Massachusetts. The second black Baptist association was organized there.[17]

1820   Wesley A.M.E. Zion Church was organized in Philadelphia.[18]

1821 or 1822   Nathaniel Paul founded Hamilton Street Baptist Church, Albany, New York, where he also founded the Wilberforce

---

12. *Encyclopedia of African American Religions,* p. lxiii.

13. Walls, *The African Methodist Episcopal Zion Church,* p. 91.

14. Walls, *The African Methodist Episcopal Zion Church,* p. 74.

15. Lewis G. Jordan, *Negro Baptist History, U.S.A., 1750-1930* (Nashville: Townsend Press, 1930, 1995), p. 89.

16. Providence Missionary Baptist Association 150th Anniversary Souvenir, 1984.

17. Mechal Sobel, *Trabelin' On: The Slave Journey to an Afro-Baptist Faith* (Westport, Conn.: Greenwood Press, 1979), p. 280.

18. Walls, *The African Methodist Episcopal Zion Church,* p. 69.

School for Black Children. He was a brother of Thomas Paul, and a native of New Hampshire. An abolitionist orator, he lived later in Canada and England.[19]

1821   Samuel Cornish established the first African American Presbyterian church in New York City.[20]

1822   The first A.M.E. Zion congregation was established in Providence, Rhode Island, by Leven Smith.[21]

1823#   Quinn Memorial A.M.E. Church was established in Steubenville, on the Ohio River.

1823   Blockley African Baptist Church of West Philadelphia was constituted. It is still in West Philadelphia and known as Monumental Baptist Church. It was served by J. H. Jackson, later President of the National Baptist Convention, U.S.A., Inc., for 29 years.

1824#   Allen A.M.E. Church was established in Cincinnati, Ohio.

1824*   First Baptist Church, Chillicothe, Ohio, was actually founded in 1824. It is listed by Sobel as beginning circa 1845. Oddly enough, in 1845, with 181 members, this church was the eighth largest African American Baptist church in the North, according to this same Sobel source.[22] As previously noted, this church once used the name "First Anti-Slavery Baptist Church."

1824   Another one of the earliest African American Baptist churches in Ohio and the entire Northwest Territory was the Eden Baptist Church, founded in 1824 in Ross County, Ohio, eighteen miles from Chillicothe. This church was probably the result of the labor of the same Rev. Nickens who founded First Baptist Chillicothe in that same year.[23]

1825>   Ebenezer Baptist Church, New York City, was founded in 1825. From 1832 to 1836, their white pastor left for mission work in the West. This church had a Missionary Society, Sunday School, and Temperance Society.

1826#   St. Paul A.M.E. Church was established in Zanesville, Ohio.

---

19. Sobel, *Trabelin' On*, p. 262; *Encyclopedia of African American Religions*, p. 573.
20. *Encyclopedia of African American Religions*, pp. 212ff.
21. Walls, *The African Methodist Episcopal Zion Church*, p. 128.
22. Sobel, *Trabelin' On*, p. 215.
23. Local church history, and Beverley Graves, Chillicothe, Ohio, history website.

1827>   Union Colored Baptist Church, Cincinnati, was founded with members from First Baptist by Charles B. Satchell, who later founded churches in New Orleans, Sacramento, and San Francisco. He was also a national leader in the American Baptist Free Mission Society, a racially mixed, strongly abolitionist de facto denomination, and critical of American Baptist Home Mission Society as insufficiently anti-slavery.[24]

1828#   Quinn Chapel A.M.E. Church was established in Wilmington, Ohio.

1829   Dixwell Avenue Congregational Church, the first African American Congregational church, was founded at New Haven, Connecticut.[25]

1831#   Bethel A.M.E. Church was established in Buffalo, New York.

1831   Bethel A.M.E. Church was established in Reading, Pennsylvania.[26]

1832>   Zion Baptist Church, New York City, grew out of Abyssinian. Like many others, membership dropped sharply (1848-1851) after the Fugitive Slave Act, with many members fleeing to Canada.

1832>   Union Baptist Church of Philadelphia was founded, not listed as coming from First African. First leader was a licensed minister from Gillfield in Petersburg. Succeeded in 1851 by Sampson White, also from Gillfield and later at Abyssinian in New York.

1833   Paint Creek Regular Baptist Church was organized in Gallipolis, on the Ohio, and became a charter member of the Providence Baptist Association.[27]

1833#   Charles Street A.M.E. Church was established in Boston, Massachusetts.

1833   An African Relief Society in Hartford, Connecticut, divided in 1833, and out of it came two African American churches, one Congregational and one Methodist, the latter becoming in

24. James M. Washington, *Frustrated Fellowship* (Macon, Ga.: Mercer University Press, 1986), pp. 43, 58.

25. *Journal of Negro History,* 60 vols. (Washington, D.C.: Associated Publishers), vol. 7, p. 15.

26. Richard G. Johnson, *They All Stand Fair: A Social History of Bethel AME Church* (Reading, Pa.: self-published, 1980).

27. Providence Missionary Baptist Association 150th Anniversary Souvenir, 1984.

1836 what is now known as Metropolitan A.M.E. Zion Church of Hartford.[28]

1833# United A.M.E. Church was established in Xenia, Ohio.

1834* Allen A.M.E. Church was founded in Jamaica, Long Island. Starting as a tiny rural congregation, it has grown to a mega-church with more than sixty ministries for economic development, housing, education, street, prison, and health ministries, counseling, and other services. Their pastor at the turn of the twenty-first century, Floyd Flake, served several terms in the United States Congress.

1835> Zion Baptist Church, Cincinnati, was constituted of members from Union Baptist Church.

1836# Bethel A.M.E. Church was established in Indianapolis, Indiana.

1836 Second Baptist Church, Columbus, Ohio, was founded with white help and African American members from First Baptist. Sobel lists this church as 1847, but it is this author's home church, known to have been organized in 1836, eleven years before incorporation in 1847.

1837> First Baptist Church of Hartford, Connecticut, colored branch, organized in 1837, and withdrew outright in 1839 after meeting mostly separately, but resenting segregation whenever they met with white members.

1837# Allen Chapel A.M.E. Church was established in Portsmouth, Ohio.

1837# An A.M.E. church was established in Rochester, New York. It was defunct for a period, but was reestablished in the 1950s under the name Baber Chapel.

1837# Allen A.M.E. Church was established in Terre Haute, Indiana.

1837> The Colored Baptist Church of Upper Alton, Illinois, was organized by John Livingston, who became the first African American pastor ordained in Illinois.

1838 Seventeen African American Methodists withdrew from Boston's white Methodists and petitioned the A.M.E. Zion connection for leadership. By October 1840 they had 140 mem-

---

28. Walls, *The African Methodist Episcopal Zion Church*, p. 128.

bers. They are now known as Columbus Avenue A.M.E. Zion Church.[29]

1839>   Jacksonville Baptist Church was one of the five African American churches organized in Illinois by John Livingston.

1839   The Nineteenth Street Baptist Church of Washington, D.C., was founded. Their pastor for sixty-five years was Walter H. Brooks, cited above in the comment on the first Baptist church.[30]

1840#   Payne Chapel A.M.E. Church was established in Hamilton, Ohio.

1840>   Meeting Street Baptist Church, Providence, became Baptist from non-denominational. They were given help by Moses Brown, a Quaker, who contributed the lot for a building.

1840>   Second Independent (Twelfth Street) Baptist was organized in Boston when forty members withdrew from Joy Street. When their first pastor died, they called Leonard Grimes, well known for his work with the Underground Railroad and Baptist affairs.

Appendix I includes the above, together with a comprehensive listing of all African American churches in the North. A few small churches may have been lost from earlier records, but the image of two amazingly expansionist African Methodist denominations is very clear. This growth is all the more remarkable in light of the fact that they had to start from scratch in development and ordination of pastors. The A.M.E. Zion churches had better relations with the John Street Church than with the Methodist Conference as a whole, and did receive some assistance with ordination.[31] But both connections moved swiftly and largely independently during this period, not waiting for white official approvals and an adequate supply of ordinations, but seeking such certification if it could be had.

The A.M.E.Z. denomination covered a smaller area, with no churches south of the District of Columbia or west of Pittsburgh. Superintendent Christopher Rush's 1843 report of the vigorous A.M.E.Z.

29. Walls, *The African Methodist Episcopal Zion Church*, p. 129.

30. Jordan, *Negro Baptist History*, p. 25; Woodson, *The History of the Negro Church*, p. 196.

31. David H. Bradley, *A History of the A.M.E.Z. Church, 1796-1872* (Nashville: Parthenon Press, 1956, 1972), vol. I, pp. 105-6.

expansion, giving a list of some forty-five locations, is to be found in Appendix II.[32] James Varick had also borne the title "superintendent," and the title bishop was not used until 1868. The success of all three groups, including the less numerous Baptists, is monumental, considering the resources with which they had to work.

African American Church Growth in the South

The growth of African American congregations in the South was greater despite the rigid resistance and legal restrictions. The African American population of the South was simply greater than the African American population in the North until the huge population migrations beginning in the early 1900s. The larger numbers also resulted in greater strength and stability of African American communities in the South. Sobel reports that in 1860 there were at least 130 African American Baptist churches in the South, and only 75 in the North. On the other hand, there were 329 white Methodist supervised missions for African Americans in the South and none in the North, with 89 A.M.E. churches in the South and 192 churches in the North.[33] The A.M.E. Zion denomination had three churches in the South and 49 in the North in 1860.

It is logical to assume that there was, among white Baptists of the South, a flood of African American mission churches parallel to the 329 missions of the white Methodists mentioned above, and that these Methodist missions became C.M.E. churches after the Civil War. It is also probable that most of the 130 African American Baptist churches reported above were from missions, approved if not outright sponsored by whites. The white Baptist church mentioned below, at Beaufort, South Carolina, is illustrative: "Prior to 1841, Huspah [an African American church] was one of many missions of Beaufort Baptist Church."[34]

It is also highly probable that these 130 churches reported are only the tip of the iceberg of sponsored and uncounted African American churches. Even further, the fact is that the disapproved brush arbor

---

32. Bradley, *A History of the A.M.E.Z. Church*, vol. 1, p. 104.

33. Sobel, *Trabelin' On*, p. 322; Payne, ed., *History of the African Methodist Episcopal Church*, vol. 1, pp. 414-18.

34. Sobel, *Trabelin' On*, p. 312.

churches in slave settings are not in the statistics anywhere. So these approved but unpopular African American missions were likely far outnumbered by the thousands of secret worship cells that surfaced and became organized Baptist churches after the Civil War. One dared keep no official written records of these clandestine congregations because so much risk was involved.

Then there were the parallels to Harry Cowan, who succeeded in starting five churches in North Carolina before the Nat Turner rebellion caused them to be closed. In the light of the fact that he is recorded to have organized thirty-seven churches *after* the Civil War, including at least one of his original five, one can only surmise that he went underground in the interim, and that these thirty-seven were actually begun during that period after the rebellion. They would be among the ones mentioned earlier as "surfacing."

Methodists, white and black, were already structured to require records, whereas Baptist autonomy did little to enhance even the record-keeping of whites. One is dependent on scant, circumstantial hints of African American "church" life, but Harry Cowan likely was not unique.[35]

One influence on the probably larger number of Southern African American Baptist congregations not recorded was the previously mentioned relative *freedom* of African American Baptist churches in Georgia, specifically the Sunbury Association. When it was organized in 1818, six of eighteen men in the founding meeting were African American. By 1834, there were eight black churches and only seven white churches. In places where there was no Sunbury arrangement, and Georgia's relative freedom of African American church self-direction still existed, many isolated churches stayed off all records.

Of course, the Sunbury Association wasn't all that it seemed. African American delegates had equal voting rights, but that changed rapidly. In fact, even the hard facts were misleading, what with one African American congregation numbering 1,834, and all white congregations being very small. African Americans took a back seat, voted timidly, and spoke only to answer questions.[36] Even so, this was a cut above the general status accorded African Americans in other sections of the South.

35. Sobel, *Trabelin' On,* p. 311.
36. Sobel, *Trabelin' On,* p. 358.

The limitations on freedom were not applicable to the internal affairs of local African American churches. Whites had influence there only when invited to help settle differences. The result was a Baptist pattern of local autonomy that encouraged African American initiative in organizing far more churches than were officially listed and approved: "By 1840, there were six 'African' churches in the Sunbury Association, with a total of 3,987 members. In all, the association then comprised 5,314 blacks [including those in white churches] and 537 whites."[37]

In Mobile, Alabama, with no apparent influence of a white association, the Stone Street Baptist Church was constituted in 1806. In 1840, they were reported to have 150 members, a fine house of worship, and some excellent licensed preachers. It was ironic, yet practical, that after all this accomplishment, they attached themselves as a branch to the later established white "First" Baptist Church, which met in the Stone Street building until they could get a building of their own. When the African American church came under attack from city officials, it was staunchly defended by white ministers.[38]

In addition to the Southern churches already described, both in Chapter Three and this chapter, the following are from records known to this author, with still more in the comprehensive list in Appendix III:

1802   The Sharp Street (now United) Methodist Church was organized in Baltimore. Daniel Coker left this church to help form Baltimore's Bethel, and the A.M.E. denomination.

1802>   The Second Colored Baptist Church of Savannah was organized by 200 ex-members of First African Baptist Church. As house servants on their "own hire," they were thought of as "African American elite."

1803>   Great Ogechee Colored Church was organized for slaves 14 miles south of Savannah.

1803   The Colored Baptist Society of Alexandria, Virginia, was established, later becoming known as the Alfred Street Baptist Church. Today it is a large congregation with many ministries.

37. Sobel, *Trabelin' On*, p. 359.
38. Sobel, *Trabelin' On*, p. 353.

1805   The Ezion Methodist Episcopal Church was formed when some forty African Americans withdrew from the predominantly white Asbury Methodist Episcopal Church of Wilmington, Delaware. Under Peter Spencer and William Anderson, they completed their separation from white Methodism in 1813, when they were incorporated at Dover as the African Union Church. Loosely affiliated with small congregations in New York and Pennsylvania, they laid claim to being the first African American denomination.[39]

1806>   Stone Street Baptist Church was organized in Mobile.

1810*   The Elam Church of Charles City, Virginia, was organized.

1812   Calvary Baptist Church at Bayou Chicot, Louisiana, was founded by Father Joseph Willis.[40] This was the first Baptist church in the state, and he founded many more churches, and the Louisiana Baptist Association, though he was not ordained until 1813.

1812*   March 8, 1812, fourteen slaves and nine of their owners gathered at the statehouse and organized Raleigh Baptist Church, later known as First Baptist Church. All were admitted by letter from Cool Springs Baptist Church, ten miles to the south. In 1823, Joseph, a slave, was appointed to officiate at the Lord's Supper, for members of his race, and fully ordained African Americans could preach in the sanctuary when white members were not using it. All of this restriction stood with no voice for African Americans even though the membership in 1826 was 70 percent African American. It was not until 1868 that the two races became two congregations, and First Baptist Church, Colored, was formed. A year earlier, the African Americans had already bought a lot for a new building.

1817#   Emanuel A.M.E. Church was founded in Charleston, South Carolina, with Morris Brown as pastor. They had withdrawn from a white-controlled Methodist mission, having heard of the formation of the A.M.E. denomination. Because a great

---

39. Lewis V. Baldwin, *Invisible Strands of African Methodism* (Metuchen, N.J.: Scarecrow Press, 1983), pp. 2-3.

40. William Hicks, *History of Louisiana Negro Baptists from 1804 to 1914* (Nashville: National Baptist Publishing Board, 1914), p. 19.

many of the participants in the Denmark Vesey Revolt of 1822 were African Methodist Episcopal, Emanuel Church was closed until after the Civil War. Morris Brown, away on church business at the time of the insurrection, was not exposed. But he was forced to leave town immediately on his return. He later became the second bishop of the A.M.E. Church.[41]

1820#   Metropolitan A.M.E. Church was founded in Washington, D.C. This is the same church in which President Bill Clinton's Inaugural Prayer Service was held in 1996.

1821*   The African Church of Manchester, Virginia, was founded by free African Americans, and was never part of any white congregation. Although an African American merchant donated their land, the trustees signing the deed to their land had to be prominent white citizens of Manchester. From 1821 to 1835 their pastors were African American, referred to as "worship leaders." As a result of the Nat Turner rebellion, the church was closed for eight months in 1835, and from then to 1865, they were compelled by Virginia law to have white pastors. Since 1910 they have been known as First Baptist Church, South Richmond, and have had only five pastors in 135 years, three of whom served a total of 128 of those years.[42]

1821>   Second African Baptist Church of Richmond was begun under Second Baptist Church (white), but members were not formally released to a separate congregation until 1846, with the African American congregation still under the supervision of the sponsoring congregation.

1830>   First Colored Baptist Church of Washington, D.C., first met in a school room and later an old building, both belonging to First Baptist Church (white), which resisted formation of a separate African American church and opposed its acceptance into the Philadelphia Baptist Association. In 1840 they were accepted, after Sampson White, formerly of Gillfield Baptist Church in Petersburg, was called as their first pastor.[43]

41. Gayraud S. Wilmore, *Black Religion and Black Radicalism,* 2nd ed. (Maryknoll, N.Y.: Orbis Books, 1983), p. 83.

42. Local church history, vol. 2, pp. i-iii.

43. Jordan, *Negro Baptist History,* p. 25; Woodson, *The History of the Negro Church,* p. 96.

1830> Harry Cowan (African American) set up five churches in Rowan and Davidson Counties, North Carolina. They were all closed after the Nat Turner rebellion. After the Civil War, Cowan organized another thirty-seven churches.[44]

1834> A mixed Baptist church organized in Darien, Georgia, in 1834, and had all African American members by 1841. At the beginning of the Civil War, it had 900 black and 23 white members.

1836> First Colored Baptist Church of Baltimore was organized in 1836, with an African American pastor, an ex-slave from Virginia, who served them until he died in 1861. The church's charter stipulated that only freemen could be trustees.

1838> First African Baptist Church of Richmond, Virginia, paid First Baptist Church of Richmond 6,500 dollars for its old building, and a "new separate black congregation was organized under white control." At the time of this nominal separation, the mixed First Baptist Church had 356 white and 1600 African American members. Some of the African Americans in this "new" congregation also came from the Second Baptist Church (white), and both First and Second Baptist Churches decided not to accept any more African American members, "except in rare cases."[45]

1839> Bell Baptist Church of Norfolk (later Bank Street Baptist) was formed in protest over the refusal of Bute Street, or First Baptist of Norfolk, to dismiss its white pastor after charges had been filed against him.

1840> The Huspah mission in the vicinity of Beaufort, South Carolina, was one of five missions of the First Baptist Church (white) operating near Beaufort. In 1841, 251 African Americans members were moved into a church and given a supply preacher.[46]

The rate of increases shown here only boomed further in the years leading up to the Civil War, as we will see in the next chapter.

---

44. Sobel, *Trabelin' On*, p. 311.
45. Sobel, *Trabelin' On*, pp. 304-5.
46. Sobel, *Trabelin' On*, p. 312.

Chapter 6

African American Church Expansion, 1841-1865, and Denominational Bodies

The twenty-five years following 1840 were even more productive of new African American congregations than the previous forty had been. Whereas the churches begun prior to 1800 were essentially self-generated, and the churches born between 1801 and 1840 were partially so, the churches that started after 1841 were much more the result of initiatives of denominations established within that prior period. The substance of this chapter, then, consists of patterns of the denomination-sponsored spread of the churches from 1841 to 1865, after which will be covered the histories of how these denominational bodies began from 1816 up to 1870, and how they developed.

The sources for the composite statistics presented here are the same as the sources used in Chapters Three and Five, except for the C.M.E. churches (founded as the Colored Methodist Episcopal denomination, now known as Christian Methodist Episcopal). The emphasis in this chapter is on the total number of churches and the conditions of establishment in the various locations. The reports vary according to denominational records available, with the A.M.E. archives providing by far the most specific listings. These facts facilitate analysis, with the A.M.E. churches serving as credible samples of trends among *all* the African American churches.

The various regional locations have great importance because of specific details in each. The churches of the South are divided between the border states that did not secede from the Union, and the rest of the South. The former include the District of Columbia, Missouri, Kentucky, Tennessee, Delaware, Maryland, and what became West Virginia (which split from Virginia in 1861 and became a state in 1863). The states of the North are differentiated as to East, Midwest, and West. As in previous listings, and for the same reasons, larger cities are distinguished from smaller cities and towns.

The African Methodist Episcopal Church's archives list sixteen churches founded up to 1800, five of them in cities, and virtually all of them becoming A.M.E. sometime after 1816. They list ninety-three churches founded between 1801 and 1840, twenty-seven of them in cities. In the period 1841-1865, they list a remarkable growth of 116 new churches, 34 of them in cities. The great majority of the churches counted are obviously in smaller cities and towns. This trend prevails in all the denominations — the whole country was less urban and more rural in the nineteenth century.

The regional distribution of the 116 A.M.E. churches was as follows: 42 in the East; 29 in the border states; 27 in the Midwest; 16 in the South; and two in the West. Of the sixteen churches started in the South between 1841 and 1865, only four were founded prior to the Civil War: in New Orleans, Louisiana; Raleigh, North Carolina; Hillsborough, North Carolina; and Mobile, Alabama. In these cities, two of them seaports, the atmosphere was somewhat freer, and the proportion of free African Americans was much greater than in most Southern communities. In the prior period of 1801-1840, six of fourteen churches started in the South and the border states were water accessible: Wilmington, North Carolina; Richmond, Virginia (James River); Charleston, South Carolina; St. Louis, Missouri; Louisville, Kentucky; and Norfolk, Virginia. And all three pre-1800 Southern cities were likewise seaport or sea accessible: Portsmouth and Chesapeake, Virginia, and Baltimore, Maryland. In all of these cities with access to shipping, the existence of more "free Negroes" facilitated the earlier establishment of strong African American churches, despite all the serious legal restraints and handicaps heaped on free Negroes.

An analysis of the areas reached in this period of 1841 to 1865 reveals other factors. For instance, only two of the 116 were in the West: San Francisco (1852) and Oakland (1858). The actual flow of gold in the Gold Rush was waning, but these churches were established to reach African Americans who had sought greater freedom as well as riches in

California. These churches were started by A.M.E. missionaries. In addition, African American Baptist missionary Charles Satchell started churches in San Francisco and Marysville in the same year, 1852. The latter church was located nearer the gold fields.

Of the 116 churches founded by A.M.E.'s between 1841 and 1865, 27 churches were founded in the Midwest, a region moving out of the pioneer status. Only six of these were city churches, and several of those six cities had yet to develop fully. African Americans born in the Northwest Territory were never legally enslaved, but many others were escapees, especially on the route of the Underground Railroad in Ohio. Thus, churches on the Ohio River were poised to assist escaping slaves from just across the river. If they had adequate proof of their freedom, many just remained in places like Burlington, Gallipolis, Steubenville, Ironton, Marietta, Portsmouth, Cincinnati, and Hamilton. Many other A.M.E. churches were founded a little further north, but still in Southern Ohio.

One other source of African Americans in the Midwest was the notable percentage of biracial freed slaves. Many of them had been set free by masters who happened also to be their natural fathers.

The slightly greater success in planting churches in the border states is due in part to the much larger (than the North) African population base from which to draw, and to their greater freedom for church activity than in the deeper South. In cities like Baltimore, slaves were hired out to serve on a more humane work schedule than was common on plantations. There were also a much larger number of free African Americans, even though this number was still small and the treatment extended to the free was still very abusive. That is to say nothing of the treatment given Maryland's slaves, which was what drove so many great souls such as Harriet Tubman and Frederick Douglass to risk their lives in their successful attempts to escape.

The forty-two churches organized in the East from 1841 to 1865 were of course due to the growing base of African Americans in the North, and to their growing freedom. Thirty-three of these churches were in the smaller cities and towns of the Northeast, primarily Pennsylvania, New Jersey, and New York. The fact that so many of these smaller churches still survive and serve is evidence of how much they were needed in smaller communities, so long as there was a base of African American population. Churches in the larger cities, however, were not nearly as large as leading churches in the large urban centers of today. The largest of city churches then were still small enough to serve as extended-family congregations, with mutual support networks and a mostly walking-distance membership. These new (1841-1865) churches were also much more the result of denominational sponsorship than earlier churches. The A.M.E. denomination had now had more than twenty-five years to grow and develop strength for sponsorship.

As noted in the previous chapter, it is not possible to do a similarly detailed analysis of the growth of A.M.E. Zions or Baptists for this same period, 1841-1865. However, Bishop Rush's careful summary of growth (forty-five churches) of the A.M.E. Zions to 1843 appears in Appendix II. And his detailed commentary on conference growth will be included in the section on denominational growth as such that follows in this chapter. For the C.M.E.'s the starting point of church growth is not available, but the records of the Methodist Church, South, show a total of 207,766 slave members in 1860. This number had dwindled down to 78,742 by 1870, when the Colored Methodist Episcopal Church was organized.[1]

The Denominations

The preceding statistics on the spread of African American churches are indicative of three patterns of church beginning. One is the pattern of local initiative, with requests for formal recognition, affiliation, and pastoral service after denominations had been organized. Prior to 1816, all churches classified as Methodist were locally launched. And even after a Baptist denominational body began in 1839, most of their church starts fell into this category of self-generation, since mission support was so voluntary and limited (as opposed to the Methodist hierarchy's power to levy a virtual tax for support for missionary extension).

The second pattern of church beginnings came about when newly formed denominations sent forth missionaries (by whatever title) to unchurched communities to establish an African American congregation. This "unchurched" condition wasn't exactly literal, however, since there were white-sponsored churches for African Americans in some of

---

1. Holland N. McTyeire, *A History of Methodism* (Nashville: Southern Methodist Publishing House, 1887), p. 670.

the towns classified as "unchurched." This white-sponsored type constituted a third pattern of church beginnings. But, as was the case at Reading, Pennsylvania, "real" churches for African Americans dared not be sponsored by whites, since this meant that whites also ruled them. What whites saw as kind supervision African Americans saw as tyranny. And this difference of opinion continues in missionary work even now. The racism of white sponsors may be subtly reflected in the fact that churches in this third category were not included in the statistics reported.

The issue of sponsorship looms so large because whites saw their paternalism, at worst, as greatly needed, while the African American churches came into being as outright protests against cruel abuse and gross discrimination (such as the poorest seats, and receipt of the sacraments only after whites). The treatment accorded Richard Allen and Absalom Jones in the balcony of St. George's Methodist Church may not have been typical in its threat of violence, but this basic attitude towards African Americans was common. Once white Methodists and Baptists ceased to need African American support to get congregations started and sanctuaries built, and once they began their upward climb from a lower-class fringe movement to respectability, they wanted the socio-ethnic lines clearly drawn.

However, it would be a mistake to think of the African American churches as bodies of protest only. There was also a clear sense of need for spiritual and social ministries, to African American communities and families. African American denominations saw themselves as meeting a religious need far too great to be served by any single congregation. Their church-starting role was far more than protesting against poor and segregated seating, plus communion only after the white folks had been served; it was even more than the crusade for liberation and against slavery.

The first of these African American denominations is almost universally considered to be the African Methodist Episcopal Church. They are commonly referred to as the A.M.E.'s and known historically as the followers of Richard Allen. The one conceivable exception to this widespread assumption of A.M.E. primacy historically is the Union Church of Africans, a group in Wilmington, Delaware, led by Peter Spencer, a layman at the time. He was invited to the A.M.E. organizing meeting in Baltimore, in 1816. But he saw his church to be as much the seed of a denomination as Allen's Bethel in Philadelphia. As he attended he envisioned a cooperative movement, with himself in shared leadership with Allen. As it turned out, Spencer resented what he saw as Allen's domination. He and Allen also disagreed over critical issues. This ended the dream of cooperation, and Spencer's name appeared in none of the minutes of the conferences after 1816.[2]

The issues over which they parted were structural, not doctrinal. Spencer pointedly would have avoided the name "Episcopal," because he was staunchly opposed to the episcopacy, the rule of bishops. He further opposed presiding elders, and all clergy for him were to be local, not itinerating. They were also to serve without stated salaries. In September 1813 Spencer's ex-members of Ezion (African) Church organized themselves as a "conference," and had five churches somehow associated with them by April 1816, when the A.M.E.'s began.

So it is altogether proper to report Spencer's unifying intent at the 1816 meeting, but the loosely linked Union of African Churches he founded hardly had sufficiently firm structure to be said to predate the A.M.E.'s. It does still exist, but its growth has been severely stunted. A laity of limited gifts, without regular guidance from a hierarchy, led to many poor decisions. The poor prospects of a volunteer career did not draw gifted clergy. Nor did it draw leaders to replace the first three charismatic founding leaders: Spencer at Wilmington, Anderson at Philadelphia, and Barney at New York City.[3]

Their most striking strength is seen in the following quote:

> Women in the Union Church of Africans were given an opportunity very early to fill a role that was not so readily available to females in the A.M.E., A.M.E. Zion, and other black denominations. There is no record of the number of females who actually applied for a preaching license in the Union Church of Africans in the pre-Civil War years. . . . It is known that women such as "Mother" Ferreby Draper, Araminta Jenkins, and Annes Spencer did perform duties traditionally associated with ministry.[4]

2. Lewis V. Baldwin, *Invisible Strands of African Methodism* (Metuchen, N.J.: Scarecrow Press, 1983), pp. 51-55.

3. Baldwin, *Invisible Strands of African Methodism*, pp. 55-61.

4. Baldwin, *Invisible Strands of African Methodism*, p. 63.

Their organization never expanded beyond Delaware, New Jersey, Pennsylvania, and New York, missing entirely the vast opportunities of the West.

The A.M.E.'s

In contrast, the African Methodist Episcopal Church was aggressively expansionist. This was the vision of Richard Allen from the very beginning when, in 1786, he raised a society of forty-two African Americans and saw a great field of need and opportunity. The reticence of these forty-two to part from the whites at that time was the only reason Allen did not establish a separate body then and there. The majority readily agreed to withdraw after the abusive treatment they received in 1787; the church was legally recognized as a corporation in 1794; and title to their property was finally extricated from the control of St. George's in 1816. The African Methodists of Baltimore and other places were treated in similar manner. This constrained Allen to call a General Convention in April 1816 to form an "Ecclesiastical Compact."[5] Although held in Baltimore first, it is significant that no meeting was convened until the Philadelphia property was clear.

Daniel Coker, formerly of the African American Methodists at Baltimore's Sharp Street Church and next of the African American Bethel African Methodist Church, and Stephen Hill of the same Bethel, were very helpful in formulating the proper legal instruments. The following invited delegates were present and voting:

Philadelphia
The Revs. Richard Allen, Clayton Durham, Jacob Tapsico, and James Champion, and Mr. Thomas Webster
Baltimore
The Revs. Daniel Coker, Richard Williams, and Henry Harden, and Messrs Nicholas Gilliard, Stephen Hill, and Edward Williamson

---

5. *History of the African Methodist Episcopal Church,* vol. 1, ed. Daniel A. Payne (New York: Arno & The New York Times, 1969), pp. 6-8.

Attleborough (now Langhorne), Pennsylvania
 The Revs. William Anderson, Edward Jackson, and Jacob
 Marsh
Wilmington, Deleware
 Mr. Peter Spencer
Salem, New Jersey
 Mr. Reuben Cuff. He was elected to deacon's orders at the 1818
 meeting of the Philadelphia Conference, held in Richard Al-
 len's residence.

These sixteen adopted a resolution by which they became "one
body under the name and style of African Methodist Episcopal Church."
A Methodist type of Book of Discipline was adopted, and an election was
held. Daniel Coker was elected bishop, but declined (no doubt under cir-
cumstances that became the subject of charges at the 1818 Conference).
Richard Allen was then elected and consecrated bishop, having already
been ordained a deacon by Bishop Asbury in 1799, and an elder in that
same 1816 meeting. In the absence of any written record whatever, it must
be assumed that there was no Annual Conference held in 1817.[6]

Subsequent Annual Conference minutes document the amazingly small start of this fledgling denomination, only five of whose
first six represented congregations even stayed with the organization
past the first meeting in 1816. Nevertheless, in the minutes not written
or preserved, there must have been a decision to divide this General
Conference into two Annual or District Conferences, centered at Baltimore and Philadelphia, all under Bishop Allen.

The 1818 Baltimore Conference met April 7, in the residence of
Samuel Williams, opening with three delegates from Philadelphia and
seven from Baltimore. They confirmed charges against Daniel Coker,
and ordained two elders, one being later a bishop, Edward Waters. A
very capable layman, Don Carlos Hall, was appointed Book Steward,
and 1066 total members were reported. Bethel Church was made a separate charge or "station" from the Philadelphia Circuit. Richard Allen,
Jr., age 15, not a delegate, served as Secretary Pro Tem, author of the excellent minutes of that meeting. He served also in the 1819 conference
of the Baltimore District.

6. Payne, ed., *History of the African Methodist Episcopal Church*, vol. 1, pp. 13-18.

The 1818 Philadelphia Conference met May 9, in the residence of Richard Allen. Six clergy were admitted to full connection (ordained itinerant elders) including Morris Brown, and almost all of the original founding delegates were admitted to some level of ordination. Of the sixteen churches represented, the three largest were Philadelphia, with 3311 members; Baltimore, with 1066 members, and Charleston, South Carolina, with 1848 members. The total for the sixteen was 6748.

The 1819 Baltimore Conference met April 19, in the sanctuary of a church for the first time. The available record includes a total of 1388 members (300 more than the previous year), the addition of the Harrisburg (Pennsylvania) Circuit, and the reinstatement of Daniel Coker. Edward Waters was one of the three elders ordained.[7]

The 1820 Conference at Baltimore met with a total of twenty-one delegates. Bishop Allen presided, and made the assignments of elders to the various churches and circuits. There was, in addition, some discord, apparently concerning finances. At the first General Conference, held in Philadelphia in July of that year, a set of General Rules, first ratified in the Baltimore Conference, was adopted.

In 1821, the Eastern Shore of Maryland was added to the Baltimore Conference, giving them five circuits. In 1822, the vast territory west of the Allegheny Mountains was assigned to the Philadelphia Conference until it could become a district in its own right. This addition to the total membership was offset numerically by the loss of the Charleston church, which was ordered closed after the Denmark Vesey rebellion. In that same year, an annual conference was organized in New York City, based on the work of Henry Harden, who had only started his work there in 1819.

By this time the total number of communicants had grown to 7,257, and the rapid spread required the appointment of an assistant bishop.[8] Even so, the attendance at conferences was still very small, reflecting conditions of work, travel, and costs. The 1824 Baltimore Conference opened with six delegates and closed with twenty-six. The geographic spread was still impressive, with the 1824 New York Conference reporting churches as far afield as New Bedford, Massachusetts, with 22 members, and New York City's Bethel reporting 347 members.

7. Payne, ed., *History of the African Methodist Episcopal Church*, vol. 1, pp. 13-20.
8. Payne, ed., *History of the African Methodist Episcopal Church*, vol. 1, pp. 33-34.

The 1826 General Conference, at the close of the first decade, saw the election of a layman, Joseph M. Corr, as Secretary. He was a refugee from the closed church in Charleston. With the growing attendance at conference, lay stewards and exhorters were still permitted a seat but were now no longer permitted to vote. There were now twenty-nine clergy appointments in the Conference, but there were an abundance of charges brought against them, making the Secretary's work very demanding. This busy agenda was due largely to failure to understand the regulations in the Discipline. Most of the clergy were still illiterate, so they were not comfortable with the Discipline's alien culture of a multitude of rules.[9]

The 1827 Conference ordained a missionary to Haiti and elected delegates to the General Conference to be held the next year at Philadelphia. This Conference received a request for care of clergy from Canada, and referred it to the New York Conference. They elected a delegation with proportional representation from all districts, including the West (Cincinnati and Pittsburgh). The newly established New York Conference reported expansion into Buffalo, Rochester, Utica, Niagara, and Canada.

The 1828 General Conference elected and consecrated Morris Brown as Bishop. He then presided alone in the 1829 Annual Conference, without Bishop Allen, who was in declining health.[10]

This rather detailed sampling of the early years of the A.M.E. denomination reflects its amazingly small beginnings and impressive growth with the resources at hand. One major detail has been largely omitted: the awesome effort and expense required to hold all these meetings and coordinate these widespread efforts. One illustration is the bill for feed for the Bishop's horse between Philadelphia and Baltimore: $8.05.[11] This is to say nothing of the time and energy required to go from Philadelphia to Baltimore, much less from Philadelphia to Cincinnati. Just going from Philadelphia to Pittsburgh to General Conference required at least three days, "taking the cars to Harrisburg," where this mode of travel was exchanged for a boat.[12] To deal

---

9. Payne, ed., *History of the African Methodist Episcopal Church,* vol. 1, pp. 50-53.
10. Payne, ed., *History of the African Methodist Episcopal Church,* vol. 1, pp. 58-59.
11. Payne, ed., *History of the African Methodist Episcopal Church,* vol. 1, p. 41.
12. Payne, ed., *History of the African Methodist Episcopal Church,* vol. 1, p. 173.

with the challenge of far-flung administration, the Western or Ohio Conference was set apart from the Philadelphia Conference in 1830. The actual assignment was to minister to all the territory west of the Alleghenies.

No doubt the wear and tear of the work and travel contributed to the death of The Rt. Rev. Richard Allen on March 26, 1831, at age 71. Thus ended a most remarkable and productive career, as well as a highly significant period of A.M.E. history.

By the year 1865, the five congregations with which Allen started in 1816 had become at least 227. They stretched from New Orleans, Louisiana, to Ontario, Canada, and from Massachusetts to California. Much of this expansion had already taken place when Allen died. His vision was a continuing driving force, and there was not a hint of personal material gain as motive, although he openly clutched power. Financially, he almost completely subsidized his pastorate.

Bishop Allen would be called a civil rights leader today. He presided over the 1830 Convention of the Colored Men of the United States, which sponsored (with Quakers and others) a boycott of foods produced by the hands of slaves.[13] His wife and he were noted for an open purse to the poor and a never failing welcome to escaping slaves, as he participated in the Underground Railroad.[14] His labors during the great yellow fever epidemic of 1793 marked him a great humanitarian.[15] Although he was not apparently fully literate, he wrote many hymns for the A.M.E. hymnbook.

Not so well known is his sagacity in business and finance. He owned a boot and shoe store. He was known to have sums as great as 10,500 dollars to lend to Bethel for purchase of property, while serving as pastor for huge salary deferments. The church owed him as much as 11,700 dollars at one time.[16] The church promised him 500 dollars per year, but all he received for pastoral services was 80 dollars for the entire 35 years. All that the church owed he bequeathed to them. It may be assumed that he received at least some of the allotted twenty-five dol-

13. *Encyclopedia of African American Religions,* ed. Larry G. Murphy et al. (New York: Garland Publishing, Inc., 1993), p. 35.

14. Payne, ed., *History of the African Methodist Episcopal Church,* vol. 1, p. 85.

15. Richard Allen, *The Life Experience and Gospel Labors of Rt. Rev. Richard Allen,* ed. George A. Singleton (Nashville: Abingdon Press, 1960), pp. 48-68.

16. Payne, ed., *History of the African Methodist Episcopal Church,* vol. 1, pp. 84-85.

lars in fees for service as presiding prelate at conferences.[17] His support of his wife and six children came from a gifted and almost overlooked bi-vocationalism, which yielded an estate at his demise (including rental properties) estimated at 30,000 to 40,000 dollars.[18]

Still, Allen was not perfect. He was less than gracious in dealing with Jarena Lee, an A.M.E. preacher's widow called to preach. Even though he readily conceded that her preaching was as manifestly called of God as any man's, he justified his refusal to ordain her by citing the Discipline followed by the very whites from whom he had withdrawn in protest.[19]

A comparable self-contradiction occurred when the A.M.E. Zions of New York City approached him in August 1820. Having just broken away from the whites at John Street Church, they requested that he ordain their clergy, so that they wouldn't have to beseech it of a white bishop. Bishop Allen was understood to respond that "he was not a child — that he knew his business — that he had no intention to assist in ordination unless we put ourselves under his charge."[20] What, with some diplomacy and creativity, could have richly fulfilled Allen's expansionist vision by some form of cooperation, he turned aside with harsh, arbitrary demands. Ironically, at the same time of the A.M.E. Zion request, 1820, available records of the A.M.E. Conference in Baltimore showed ten people opening the 1818 session, and 21 opening in 1820.[21] In other words, at that stage they were not greatly different in strength, both being very small. They could graciously have found ways to help each other.

In 1884, the General Conference approved the licensing but not the ordination of preaching women, nor their appointment as pastors. But in 1882, Sarah Ann Hughes had already received an appointment to pastor a church in Fayetteville, North Carolina. Her preaching gifts were recognized as superior, and there was current a movement toward the liberalizing of restrictions against women. One of its outspoken leaders was Margaret Wilson of New Jersey. With the stirring up of the

17. Payne, ed., *History of the African Methodist Episcopal Church,* vol. 1, p. 32.

18. Payne, ed., *History of the African Methodist Episcopal Church,* vol. 1, p. 85.

19. Jarena Lee, *Religious Experiences and Journal* (self-published, 1849), p. 15.

20. William J. Walls, *The African Methodist Episcopal Zion Church* (Charlotte, N.C.: A.M.E. Zion Publishing House, 1885, 1974), p. 74.

21. Payne, ed., *History of the African Methodist Episcopal Church,* vol. 1, p. 19.

issue, the North Carolina Annual Conference of 1887 defrocked Sarah Ann Hughes, a move ratified by the General Conference of 1888.[22]

The A.M.E. Zions

James Varick was as important to the launching of the African Methodist Episcopal Zion denomination as Allen was to the A.M.E.'s, and the courses of development have many parallels.

In a sense, the formation of the denomination flows from the history of one church. Following the racial abuses leading up to the first separate worship organized by African Americans in New York City (1796), the building of their first edifice (1800) and the incorporation (1801) of the Zion congregation, Zion's freedom was compromised by corporate articles placing them under the white Methodist bishops, who still declined to ordain any African American as elder. Even the ordination of three African Americans to the order of deacon (1806) was kept secret, to avoid the opposition of Methodists in the slave-holding states.[23] However, there was also a New York residue of legal resistance to African Americans holding their own meetings, dating back to the bloody New York City Insurrection of 1712.[24] These civil restrictions on African American assemblies were more than matched by the rules of the first Methodist conference in 1784, which required all meetings of African Americans to have a white pastor over them.[25]

An odd arrangement allowed the trustees of the African American corporation to deal with all material matters, including real estate, but placed spiritual supervision, including choice of pastors, in the hands of the bishop or a senior white pastor. Complete control was further maintained by the whites' refusal to ordain elders into full itinerancy. It was this most crucial obstacle that delayed the start of a new denomination. Even the acceptance of a second African American "society" or congregation in 1816 was made contingent on the approval

22. Bettye Collier-Thomas, *Daughters of Thunder* (San Francisco: Jossey-Bass, 1998), pp. 26-27.

23. Walls, *The African Methodist Episcopal Zion Church*, p. 65.

24. Bracy, Meier, Rudwick, eds., *American Slavery: The Question of Resistance* (Belmont: Wadsworth Publishing, 1971), p. 26.

25. Walls, *The African Methodist Episcopal Zion Church*, p. 27.

of the first, Zion.[26] This amounted to a virtual chain of command, and affirmed the Episcopal order so essential to Methodism in the colonies. In contrast, the political order of the colonies matched the religious democracy of Baptists, Congregationalists, and, in some aspects, Presbyterians.

It was because of this ironclad denial of elder ordination by the bishopric that the Zion Methodists voted in 1820 to withdraw outright from the white Methodists. They took their chances on improvising an elder ordination until they could get a "proper" rite by an already ordained group of elders. It is noteworthy that 61 African Americans out of a total of 751 chose to remain in John Street Church and forfeited their right to African American elders.[27]

The official ordination of Varick, Abraham Thompson, and Leven Smith to the eldership on June 17, 1822, was accepted by William Stilwell, a kindly disposed and well-accepted former pastor who had himself withdrawn from the mother denomination, later to form the abolitionist Methodist Protestant denomination. Stilwell was joined by Sylvester Hutchison, a former presiding elder who also withdrew, and James Covell, who remained in the Methodist Episcopal Church. Varick, Thompson, and Smith politely declined the invitation to join Stilwell's anti-slavery denomination. A month later, at the Second Annual Conference, James Varick was elected full Superintendent,[28] having acted in that capacity since the first Annual Conference in 1821.[29] The title bishop was not adopted until 1864, and bishops were not tenured (elected for life, not just four years) until 1880.[30]

The 1822 conference then ordained six deacons, ordaining them elders on the same afternoon, to accommodate the new churches being so rapidly established.[31] Of these six, Christopher Rush was appointed missionary in 1823, and elected Superintendent in the General Conference of 1828. Both James Varick and Abraham Thompson cease to ap-

26. Walls, *The African Methodist Episcopal Zion Church*, p. 69.

27. Walls, *The African Methodist Episcopal Zion Church*, p. 71.

28. Walls, *The African Methodist Episcopal Zion Church*, p. 83.

29. David H. Bradley, *A History of the A.M.E.Z. Church, 1796-1872* (Nashville: Parthenon Press, 1956, 1972), vol. 1, p. 90.

30. Bradley, *A History of the A.M.E.Z. Church*, vol. 1, p. 156.

31. Bradley, *A History of the A.M.E.Z. Church*, vol. 1, p. 95.

pear in the minutes after 1826, both being in advanced age and failing health.[32]

In his few years of service, Varick was almost as productive as Richard Allen. Both were skilled cobblers (Varick was also a tobacco cutter) and excellent administrators, guiding their denominations' small beginnings through the connivings of key white Methodists. Both also supported large families. Varick was much more literate than Allen, and among his activities were the drafting of petitions and church legal papers, and the teaching of classes for African American children. He was impressive in the launching of many new churches in places like New Haven, in racial advocacy for freedom (he died just as slavery ended in New York) and the right to vote, and in his service as pastor of the Mother Zion Church in New York.[33] The A.M.E. Zion Church was blessed beyond measure to be led in its beginnings by a man of such great gifts.

This denomination was also greatly blessed by the gifts of Varick's successor, Christopher Rush, who served from 1828 to 1852.[34] Consecrated in 1856, the brilliant successor to Rush, and the youngest (less than thirty-three years old), was Joseph J. Clinton. He served twenty-five years and died in 1881, at age sixty. His record included organization of 13 annual conferences and reception into connection of 700 itinerant preachers. He was a champion of freedom and a peerless executive. His family included ten children.

James Walker Hood, who became a bishop in 1872, also deserves mention. He framed much of the post–Civil War Constitution of North Carolina in 1867, and was Assistant Superintendent of Education in North Carolina in 1870, all the while doing a prodigious work in the churches and elsewhere. He arranged to have 49,000 African American children in public schools in 1870.[35]

Careful reading of this account is bound to raise questions as to how eight bishops could be elected in the General Conference after Rush's retirement in 1852 when Clinton was consecrated as bishop in 1856. The answer is that there were, in effect, two sets of bishops in this

32. Bradley, *A History of the A.M.E.Z. Church*, vol. I, pp. 99-101.
33. Walls, *The African Methodist Episcopal Zion Church*, pp. 86-95.
34. Walls, *The African Methodist Episcopal Zion Church*, p. 566.
35. Carter G. Woodson, *The History of the Negro Church* (Washington, D.C.: Associated Publishers, 1972), p. 214.

rapidly growing denomination. But it wasn't size that created the two sets; they were sharply divided over petty issues from 1840 to 1860, with Clinton first elected by only one side in 1856. He was helpful in the 1860 reunion and managed to be elected by both sides, while some others had to step down. Until 1868, all A.M.E. Zion bishops were elected only for four-year terms, and every bishop always stood for reelection at General Conference. The surplus of bishops began with the contested election of 1840.

The divisive issues were begun when a second or assistant super-intendent was elected to assist or replace Rush. No established rule provided for this, and sides were chosen between the established offi-cers and a group bent on calling themselves Wesleyan rather than Afri-can, and on having as many as three more superintendents to replace Rush, who was feeble and blind. Of the three elected in 1848, one died in 1853. Subsequent moves by one side suspended the superintendent elected by the other, and two slates and different General Conferences evolved. The controversy became more and more complicated, even in-volving a new connectional name in an attempted transfer of deed to church property. Things neared resolution when S. T. Gray, an itiner-ant elder and medical doctor from New York, moved the elimination of all assistant superintendents in 1860. No elections were to be held until reunion was brought about, and a discipline crafted by S. T. Jones (later bishop). Three equal bishops were elected, of whom Peter Ross soon re-signed. William H. Bishop and Joseph J. Clinton were the other two elected, as peace reigned. The storm died before the great opportunities offered by the Civil War. The true greatness of this denomination and the stands it took could now come forth; the smoke of internal contro-versy had blown away.[36]

The A.M.E. Zions began early to show some interest in recogni-tion of the laity, a position not shared by Methodists, white or African American, except for Stilwell and his Methodist Protestants. As early as 1796, the Zionites recognized the democratic rights of laity. In 1852, they "tried and expelled a superintendent who dared to ignore his lay people in annual and quarterly conference."[37] At the close of the A.M.E.Z. schism, in 1860, the laity, who so greatly influenced the re-

36. Walls, *The African Methodist Episcopal Zion Church*, pp. 172-83.
37. Bradley, *A History of the A.M.E.Z. Church*, vol. 1, p. 7.

union, were given nine votes in General Conference. This trend grew until 1928, when full equality between laity and clergy prevailed.[38]

Similar leadership was evidenced on the position of women. The A.M.E.Z. Discipline was altered in 1876 to allow women to vote on the office of trustee. The first duly elected female delegate to General Conference was in 1896. The first A.M.E. Zion women to be ordained deacon were Mary J. Small in 1892 and Julia A. J. Foote in 1894. Mary Small was the first woman in any Methodist denomination to be ordained elder, in 1898.[39] The ordination of Florence Spearing Randolph in 1901 was already so accepted that she served one church, Wallace Chapel A.M.E. Zion Church of Summit, New Jersey, from 1925 to 1946.[40]

The A.M.E. Zions' outstanding leadership was perhaps most evident among the abolitionists, both as orator-advocates and as Underground Railroad operators. The list of great A.M.E.Z. orators included not only Frederick Douglass, Sojourner Truth, and Bishops Varick and Rush, but also Jehiel Beman, Hosea Easton, Eliza Ann Gardner, and many other well-known pastors.[41]

Their anti-slavery commitment extended beyond that of A.M.E.'s and African American Baptists in the South, some of whose own members and/or pastors owned slaves, and whose very church buildings and land were donated by African American owners of slaves. A.M.E. Zions, who were concentrated in the North, opposed any slave owners who did not free their slaves immediately. Their reputation in the South caused Bishop Clinton and his group to be jailed just for being seen in Alexandria, Virginia. And the churches briefly begun there and in Richmond were destroyed by local authorities, as was the A.M.E. church in Charleston, South Carolina.[42]

The Underground Railroad flourished in the regions where the A.M.E. Zions were strong: New York and New England. Bishop Germaine Loguen was an important leader in the days when he served in Syracuse. Harriet Tubman, the most successful of all Underground Railroad conductors, was a staunch Zionite. Strategic Underground Railroad stations were in many Zion-affiliated locations, such as

38. Walls, *The African Methodist Episcopal Zion Church,* p. 110.
39. Walls, *The African Methodist Episcopal Zion Church,* p. 111.
40. Collier-Thomas, *Daughters of Thunder,* pp. 101-5.
41. Walls, *The African Methodist Episcopal Zion Church,* pp. 144-68.
42. Walls, *The African Methodist Episcopal Zion Church,* p. 170.

Tubman's home in Auburn, New York, and the A.M.E. Zion parsonage at Jamestown, New York. The operation of the Underground Railroad was as much a part of the church's ministry as any other part.[43]

The closing years of the Civil War and the period of Reconstruction saw the A.M.E.Z.'s on the heels of the Union Army, going up the Atlantic coast from New Bern, North Carolina, starting churches and schools for the newly freed. This occupied area for the Lord and Zion widened out as the Union troops advanced.

The Baptists

The history of the various African American Baptists, as members of African American denominational bodies, is a scattered account indeed. Both in the South and in the East, African Americans were either not encouraged to organize independently, or they were supposedly already full members in the white Baptist associations. Indeed, some of the white-controlled associations were numerically African American. In 1818, the Savannah River Association divided along racial lines, but the almost all African American Sunbury Association found themselves voteless and still run by a handful of whites.[44] African Americans outnumbered the whites, often out-preached the whites, and yet were not privileged to vote in the business of either congregation or association. When the pastor of First African Baptist Church in Philadelphia was elected Preacher for the 1876 Philadelphia Baptist Association, and Moderator in 1894-95,[45] these were proud, rare exceptions for African Americans, not the rule.

Yet the first African American associations in the Midwest had been organized and self-governing since the 1830s. One such association began at Providence Baptist Church, at Burlington Crossroads, Jackson County, Ohio, in 1834. The name given the new body was "Providence Anti-Slavery Missionary Baptist Association." The gathered ministers "had been driven out of the Tees Valley Association, in

---

43. Walls, *The African Methodist Episcopal Zion Church*, pp. 141-69.

44. Mechal Sobel, *Trabelin' On: The Slave Journey to an Afro-Baptist Faith* (Westport, Conn.: Greenwood Press, 1979), pp. 214-15.

45. Local church history, p. 27.

and around Cincinnati, over the slavery question,"[46] according to the association's publication. James M. Washington reports that the group was gathered by an African American minister named Robert Townsend, who had been "appointed by the white Ohio Baptist State Convention in 1833-1834 to work five months as a missionary" in four counties of southeastern Ohio.[47] Mechal Sobel reports their starting year as 1835,[48] but the association celebrated its 100th anniversary at Tried Stone Baptist Church in Ironton, Ohio, in 1934. The six churches represented at the time of organization were from considerably east of Cincinnati, and close to the north shore of the Ohio River. They were almost all freed ex-slaves and illiterate but gifted and focused opponents of slavery. They were small churches, but many of them still engage in an active ministry. The association's first written history was lost, but a currently published oral tradition lists churches in settlements like Rendville, Athens, Nelsonville, Tabler Town, Piketon, Blackfork, Glouster, Bidwell, Greenville, Jackson, Ironton, and Gallipolis.[49]

The Providence Association was concentrated in the southeast corner of the state of Ohio, but the Union Association, which was organized in 1836,[50] included Columbus, Chillicothe, Brush Creek, and Cincinnati. It ultimately "spread its beneficial influence throughout Ohio." At first the Union Association's churches maintained dual affiliation with the white associations, but in 1840 they withdrew and changed their name to the Union Baptist Anti-Slavery Association. However, Union Baptist Church in Cincinnati and Second Baptist Church in Columbus maintained both memberships, to keep close ties with several anti-slavery white Baptist congregations in the association.[51]

The Union Baptist Association soon developed a denominational missionary thrust, reaching throughout Ohio and into Indiana and Illinois. Missionary leaders were Wallace Shelton, Peter Farley Fossett, and Charles Satchell, who alone launched churches as far away as Loui-

---

46. Local church history.

47. James M. Washington, *Frustrated Fellowship* (Macon, Ga.: Mercer University Press, 1986), p. 28.

48. Sobel, *Trabelin' On*, p. 216.

49. Local church history.

50. C. Eric Lincoln and Lawrence H. Mamiya, *The Black Church in the African American Experience* (Durham: Duke University Press, 1990), p. 26.

51. Washington, *Frustrated Fellowship*, p. 30.

siana and California, while also representing the American Baptist Free Mission Society. Between 1855 and 1857 the Union Baptist Association grew from twenty-two churches to twenty-seven churches. In 1864 they "provided the most influential leadership in the formation of the Northwestern and Southern Baptist Convention."[52] In the early 1900s, the Union Association reorganized as the Ohio Baptist General Convention, and divided into five district associations, one of which was the Providence Association.[53]

The third African American Baptist association, the Wood River, was formed in 1839 in Southwestern Illinois. It included three churches in St. Clair and Madison Counties under the care of a free African American preacher named John Livingston. He had founded one of them as early as the 1820s, with the help of a white missionary named James Lemen, who was also founder and Moderator of the local (white) Illinois Union Baptist Association and Friends of Humanity. Lemen presided when the African American association was set aside by its own request. Originally named the Colored Baptist Association and Friends of Humanity, it was better known as the Wood River. Its first Moderator was Livingston, but the first Clerk, Alfred Richardson, a layman, was the chief instigator of both the Upper Alton church and the Wood River Association. He had found a less than warm welcome in the white church he visited after he and his wife had left Tennessee. Already free, they came seeking better life in the North. Once committed to separate African American groups, he and his colleagues labored vigorously. In twenty years the association added churches as far away as Racine, Wisconsin, and Leavenworth, Kansas, and grew to a total of ten churches.[54]

The fourth of the early African American associations was the Amherstburg, formed in 1841. Its name came from a community of escaped slaves across the Detroit River in Ontario, Canada, but some of its charter churches were in Michigan. The leading church, in fact, was Second Baptist Church of Detroit, founded in 1835. The first meeting was held at Amherstburg, Ontario, and there were African American churches from Niagara, New York, to Windsor, Canada. George French

52. Washington, *Frustrated Fellowship*, pp. 30-31.
53. Local church history.
54. Washington, *Frustrated Fellowship*, pp. 32-33.

and Madison Lightfoot and their wives, noted for the heroic rescue of an escaping couple, were the unanimous choices for moderator and clerk, both being from Second Baptist, Detroit.

This choice reveals the understandably heavy anti-slavery emphasis of this association, gathered, as in Southeastern Ohio, by the rivers of escape. Their supply of good preachers from the South was excellent, and they grew to ten churches in five years. Among the preachers was Anthony Binga, who surfaced after the Civil War as pastor of First Baptist Church of South Richmond, Virginia. One of the Association's preachers, Samuel Davis, gave a speech as blazing as Henry Highland Garnet's at the 1843 National Colored Convention at Buffalo.[55]

A fifth association will doubtless belong in this series, in the minds of many, although it has not appeared in other works. In 1837, the widely known ex-slave Father Willis organized the first association in Louisiana. This historic event is worthy of record because of the African American man who led it, but this association does not belong in this series by definition. It was a racially mixed body, and, in keeping with the times, dominated legally by whites.[56] African American churches across the South were similarly governed, as already noted in the Sunbury Association in Georgia.

Beyond the level of the Baptist association there developed the "convention," a body covering a state, region, or whole nation, and devoted to only one or two limited purposes, such as missions and/or education. Prior to the Civil War, African American church leaders had formed two such quasi-national conventions: the American Baptist Missionary Convention (1840), and the Western Colored Baptist Convention (1853), which became the Northwestern and Southern Baptist Convention (1863-64).[57] In August 1863, during the war, President Lincoln authorized the A.B.M.C. to "go within the military lines and minister to their brethren there."[58] After the Civil War (1866), fully aware of the task before them, these two merged to form the "Consolidated American Baptist Missionary Convention." This complicated series of

55. Washington, *Frustrated Fellowship*, pp. 36-37.

56. William Hicks, *History of Louisiana Negro Baptists from 1804 to 1914* (Nashville: National Baptist Publishing Board, 1914), p. 31.

57. Washington, *Frustrated Fellowship*, pp. 38-39, 44.

58. Washington, *Frustrated Fellowship*, p. 61.

emerging conventions, named and renamed, is perhaps best understood when listed chronologically.

In 1840, at New York's Abyssinian Baptist Church, the American Baptist Missionary Convention was organized. Unlike a Baptist association, this convention's primary concern was missions (overseas), and it had no state or regional boundaries. Triggered by Sampson White, host pastor of the first meeting, its other charter congregations were Zion Baptist in New York City and Union Baptist in Philadelphia.[59] Churches in a total of ten different cities hosted their nineteen annual meetings in 1841-1860. Jordan's history records minutes as late as 1865. Their president from 1848 to 1858 was a layman, Hon. George N. Briggs.[60]

With the exception of a few prominent churches in St. Louis, Missouri and other border states, most of the member churches of the American Baptist Missionary Convention, being in the East, retained association-level affiliation with the white Baptists. However, there was no white assistance in the development of this new group. They represented something of a protest in favor of emphasis on African missions and a more outspoken opposition to slavery in what the whites called their Triennial Convention. This Convention attempted to speak softly about slavery and thus not alienate the churches of the South, while still refusing appointment to slave-holding missionaries. Still, by 1845 the Triennial Convention saw a regional split which led to the Southern Baptist Convention of today.[61] Meanwhile, since the Northern Baptists did lose the South because of their stand on missionary staff, the A.B.M.C. saw no reason to withdraw because of the weak public stance on slavery. The issue of more concern to them was African missions, which served as sufficient basis to form a separate African American organization.

Consequently, it was 1853 before the American Baptist Missionary Convention itself made its first outspoken witness against slavery. They too had to be careful about the sensitivity of their own slave-owning members in churches in border states. Mission work in Africa was a safe issue, even though their outspokenly anti-slavery convention

---

59. Washington, *Frustrated Fellowship*, p. 39.

60. Lewis G. Jordan, *Negro Baptist History, USA, 1750-1930* (Nashville: Townsend Press, 1930, 1995), p. 373.

61. Washington, *Frustrated Fellowship*, p. 39.

never met in a slave state. Their actual "mission" work consisted of some help to struggling new churches in the United States, and to member ministers' widows,[62] plus a barely existing mission at Waterloo, Sierra Leone, launched in 1858.[63]

In 1858, led by Leonard Grimes, Theodore Doughty Miller, William Spellman, and Sampson White, the African American members of the white convention were urged to withdraw outright. They voted also to have no fellowship with slave-holding ministers, although their strong churches in the slave-holding states of Missouri, Kentucky, Tennessee, Maryland, and Virginia were opposed to the resolution for practical reasons. While these churches were firmly opposed to slavery in principle, some of their best African American lay supporters owned slaves. The 1858 session reported forty-eight churches in mission support. In addition they had mailed in individual memberships for a dollar, drawn from far and wide. This made possible, at last, their sending a missionary to Sierra Leone.[64] But in 1859, when the missionary, William J. Barnett, was to return to the field, the Convention had to borrow both the 25 dollars for his ship ticket and the entire 200 dollars for his salary.[65] Such were the limitations on a most sincere vision.

The full commitment against slavery, which the A.B.M.C. had requested and the Triennial Baptist Convention had failed to make, was enthusiastically made by the radically anti-slavery American Baptist Free Mission Society, formed in 1843. Predominantly white, it was wide open to African American members and leaders, even to a merger with an African American missionary convention. Sampson White of New York and Wallace Shelton of Ohio were among its early members. Charles Satchell of Cincinnati was their partly supported staffer in church plantings in New Orleans, two of which are still known as First and Second Free Mission Baptist Churches. When this A.B.F.M.S. met its end in 1872, it turned its Canadian and Haitian works over to African American Baptist missionary bodies.

An earlier merger had been impossible because of technicalities such as the white Free Missioners' staunch opposition to Freemasonry,

---

62. Washington, *Frustrated Fellowship*, p. 40; Sobel, *Trabelin' On*, p. 217.
63. Jordan, *Negro Baptist History*, pp. 53-59.
64. Henry H. Mitchell, *Black Belief* (New York: Harper & Row, 1975), pp. 41-42.
65. Jordan, *Negro Baptist History*, p. 57.

a secret society to which African Americans were heavily committed. Even so, before their demise in 1872, the distinguished white Baptist leaders of the American Baptist Free Mission Society "played an important role in focusing Baptist opinion favorable to Radical Reconstruction,"[66] especially in the military occupation policy for the distribution of church property in the South.

In 1853, the Wood River Association called a meeting in St. Louis and formed the Western Colored Baptist Convention, which included several churches from other states west of the Mississippi. They met regularly between 1853 and 1859, but ceased to meet from 1859 to 1864 because of the Civil War. In 1864 the Wood River Association took the initiative to recall and rename the convention, again at St. Louis. This time there were representatives from Illinois, Indiana, Ohio, Missouri, Tennessee, Louisiana, Mississippi, and Arkansas. The earlier Western Convention had been limited to the "northerly banks of the Mississippi and the free states and territories west of St. Louis," places where they could operate and minister according to their conscience and convictions.[67] Now an entirely different prospect resulted from the Emancipation Proclamation of the previous year. The attendance at this resumption of meetings reflected the new situation. The South was now legally open, where the Union prevailed, to mission work among thousands of veterans of the worst forms of slavery. Organizational opposition to slavery was now possible without reservation, and was forcefully expressed in their new constitution and new name: Northwestern and Southern Baptist Convention.

Their new President was William Newman, fresh from four years of mission work in Haiti and Jamaica.[68] The militant Richard DeBaptiste, main instigator of the new convention and pastor of Chicago's Olivet Baptist Church, was elected Corresponding Secretary.[69] William Troy, formerly of Canada West, was elected Agent, a combination executive and promoter. It was a historic configuration of commitment and awesome need. The previous year, President Lincoln had already granted the American Baptist Missionary Convention permis-

---

66. Washington, *Frustrated Fellowship*, p. 43.

67. Washington, *Frustrated Fellowship*, p. 44.

68. Washington, *Frustrated Fellowship*, p. 44.

69. *Encyclopedia of African American Religions*, p. 229.

sion to follow fast on the heels of the Union troops.[70] This fully opened a mission field so long closed and so greatly desired.

A second task was their desired influence on the distribution of abandoned church property in the South. The huge problem lay in the fact that the American Baptist Home Mission Society was given temporary custody of abandoned Baptist church properties. A.B.H.M.S. seemed to be at great pains to see that ex-Confederate whites were easily classified as loyal to the Union, so that they could be eligible to regain their sanctuaries. Churches with huge African American majorities had their property awarded to a tiny white minority. The rights of ex-slaves were ignored while the A.B.H.M.S. tried to curry favor with the Southern whites, in hopes of bringing about a reunion of the Southern Baptists with the Northern Baptists. Rather than giving some empty buildings to their deserving African American members, the buildings were given to the Southern Baptists. Some were even left empty.

Free Missionists (white) and both African American conventions, the American Baptist Missionary Society and the Northwestern and Southern Baptist Convention, all lodged strong protests with the American Baptist Home Mission Society. Other societies of the Northern Baptists joined the protest, but to no avail. Such a miscarriage of justice could well have caused a permanent break of the African American conventions with the A.B.H.M.S. Fortunately for the overall needs of the newly freed, especially the educational needs, this atrocity didn't cause lasting separation. The outspokenly radical president of the Northwestern and Southern Baptist Convention, William P. Newman, wrote the A.B.H.M.S., expressing the hope that they were penitent for their injustice. However, should they fail to repent, his black missionary society would "forgive and work with them when they do right."[71]

The most important task before the American Baptist Missionary Convention and the Northwestern and Southern Baptist Convention was the education of the newly freed, especially their pastors. In August 1866, a critically important decision was made concerning who should assist in this task. They would accept the help of the Free Missionists, the American Baptist Home Mission Society, and the American Baptist

---

70. Washington, *Frustrated Fellowship,* p. 61.
71. Washington, *Frustrated Fellowship,* pp. 69-70.

Publication Society. But they would not accept the help eagerly offered by the Southern Baptists, in the certain knowledge of the control this would concede.[72] African American convention leaders obviously knew there would be some paternalism in working with any white convention besides the Free Missionists. But the Southern Baptist brethren sought outright to perpetuate Southern racial customs by keeping the Northern missionaries out. This would have been even worse. The results of the choice, in the founding of schools and colleges, are described in Chapter Eight.

In June of 1865, the members of the N.S.B.C. sensed a need to be more closely allied with the white, anti-caste Free Mission Baptists, who felt the same way about postwar federal policies towards African Americans. In his dream of union with whites, President Newman of the N.S.B.C. had the support of other leaders such as Charles Satchell and Richard DeBaptiste. The convention voted to authorize overtures to the Free Missionists and exchange of delegates.

In August of the same year, the American Baptist Missionary Society passed a resolution to fraternize more closely with the Free Missionists. Their resolution was amended to include the A.B.H.M.S., but neither of the African American conventions ever amended its resolutions to include its sister in specific terms. They spoke, rather, of the need for allies of both races, and sent a fraternal delegate to the meeting of the 1866 convention of the N.S.B.C. The common goal expressed was to establish the pre-eminence of African Americans in the Southern mission field.[73]

James M. Washington, whose excellent research is so frequently cited here, is hesitant to say it directly, but it is obvious that except for Newman himself, the leaders in both conventions were using these discussions of union for another purpose. They sought the union of the *African Americans* of the Eastern and Southeastern-oriented American Baptist Missionary Society with the Northwestern and Southern Baptist Convention. Their loyalty to Freemasonry would never have permitted them to join with the rigidly anti-Masonic Free Missionists. In fact, "most of those who spearheaded the drive for an all-black Baptist union were Masons themselves, or at least supportive of Masons."

---

72. Washington, *Frustrated Fellowship*, pp. 64-65.
73. Washington, *Frustrated Fellowship*, p. 75.

These included from the A.B.M.C. its President, Leonard Grimes, Nelson G. Merry, Edmund Kelly, and Duke William Anderson. These veterans were supported by younger ministers later well known, such as William Thomas Dixon, Theodore Doughty Miller, and Rufus Lewis Perry.

In the interim between the two annual meetings, Newman had originally drawn up a proposed name change and other details in the direction of a Free Missionist merger. But he became totally disillusioned by the "State of the Country," with its Black Codes and Ku Klux Klan, and the way he saw his Radical Republicans failing to stand up for the right. Then he also became aware of the A.B.M.C. movement for an African American Baptist union on the missionary field. He became convinced of the need for an African American union before the June 4, 1866, annual meeting of the N.S.B.C. in Nashville.

Newman led the N.S.B.C. to adopt a resolution affirming the union, and appointing three commissioners to attend the next meeting of the A.B.M.C. "at Richmond, Va., on Friday before the third Lord's Day in August 1866, to consummate a union upon these principles." Newman was so committed to this new conception that he appointed himself one of the commissioners. However, he died of cholera August 3, 1866, and it fell to his fellow appointees to carry forward the plan.[74]

To Nelson G. Merry of Nashville, who had been active in both African American conventions, fell Newman's lot to serve as head of the committee. He was ably assisted by the literate and articulate Richard DeBaptiste of Chicago's Olivet,[75] as well as William Troy, Emanuel Cartwright, and Jesse Freeman Boulden, formerly of Olivet, later of Natchez, Mississippi.[76] The Plan of Union Committees of the two conventions met as scheduled in August 1866 in Richmond, Virginia.

The name adopted was the Consolidated American Baptist Missionary Convention, and the structure adopted was traditionally Baptist. It had churches reporting to district associations, associations making up state conventions, which in turn comprised the C.A.B.M.C. All of this was confirmed in the official session of the new body, held in Nashville in August 1867. DeBaptiste of Chicago was elected President;

74. Washington, *Frustrated Fellowship*, p. 78.

75. William J. Simmons, *Men of Mark* (Chicago: Johnson Publishers, 1887, 1970), pp. 229-33.

76. Simmons, *Men of Mark*, pp. 491-94.

host pastor Merry, Vice President; and Perry of Brooklyn, Corresponding Secretary.[77] In the thirteen years that the C.A.B.M.C. survived, it was plagued with problems, many of which grew out of their relations with white Northern Baptists.[78]

As denominational histories go, the C.A.B.M.C. had one of the very stormiest, in both internal and external relations. A blow-by-blow chronicle would serve no real purpose. But the issues were clear, and deserving of analysis, especially since the same issues exist today among African American Baptists, in one form or another.

First of all, there was an extreme difference of culture and styles of communication between the clergy and churches of the North and South. Those in the North were direct, forthright, confident, and confrontational clergy and missionaries. In order to survive, however, the clergy and congregations of the South were far more adaptive to the existing harsh realities. The two were poles apart, and the Southerners did not take kindly to the Northerners' obvious sense of call to save those whom slavery had handicapped. The tested methods of the South, many predating the Civil War, were not respected or considered in many cases. It was a form of not-so-subtle insult.

The South was not asleep, however; they just gave misleading appearances. The conservative activist pastor at Paducah, G. W. Dupee, learned just how alert his own congregants were when many of them arose in a virtual riot protesting his published opposition to the proposed Civil Rights Bill of 1874.[79] This position, in which Dupee was joined by Nelson Merry of Nashville, divided the Convention's Northern and Southern leadership all the more. For the C.A.B.M.C., whose corresponding secretary and editorial mouthpiece was Rufus Perry, the missionary agenda included great emphasis on voting, as well as support of the bill. This implied support of the Radical Republican ticket.[80] Here again was a sectional cleavage based on the great aversion of the Southerners to politics.

Again, in an attitude of black-on-black paternalism, the C.A.B.M.C. leadership was critical of Southern culture in matters of

77. Simmons, *Men of Mark,* pp. 425-29.
78. Washington, *Frustrated Fellowship,* pp. 78-79.
79. Washington, *Frustrated Fellowship,* pp. 119-21.
80. Washington, *Frustrated Fellowship,* p. 119.

worship. Missionaries who were former fugitives from slavery them-selves viewed its inevitable cultural survivals as excessive and unre-strained. From Louisiana, an 1868 sample from Charles Satchell says it well: "In addition to the vices and irregularities inseparably attendant upon the state of slavery. . . . Then, again, there are bad men under the garb of preachers, who go around imposing on the ignorance of peo-ple."[81] Such bitter criticism of popular but uneducated African Ameri-can preachers could only breed a resentment greater than the resent-ment against the white missionaries who felt so superior to African Americans.

This North/South schism was further exacerbated by issues aris-ing out of the C.A.B.M.C.'s relations with the American Baptist Home Mission Society. As has already been noted in connection with their brief handling of Baptist church properties, the A.B.H.M.S. was loathe to act against the wishes of white Southern Baptists, in hopes of a North/South Baptist reunion. When finally convinced of the validity of a greatly increased mission to the African Americans of the South, the A.B.H.M.S. was determined to do it their way. They had two African Americans on their board, and they had some African American mis-sionary staff, but none of these were chosen in consultation with the C.A.B.M.C., the presumably logical group to know what was best. Yet even the C.A.B.M.C. was at odds with African Americans in the South. This division was exploited by the A.B.H.M.S.

Not only did the C.A.B.M.C. claim deserved hegemony over key personnel; they believed they should be charged with disbursing the money to support it. In other words, all money invested in the field should be entrusted by A.B.H.M.S. to the administration of the C.A.B.M.C., which in turn would render a report of how it was effec-tively employed. In hindsight, it is obvious that neither group had ade-quate insights and right attitudes for the union. It can only be assumed that the Southern mission might have been better accomplished if they had pooled both insights and resources.

Meanwhile, many of the Southern churches of C.A.B.M.C. were actually more comfortable with the A.B.H.M.S.'s style of mission. It seemed they found the A.B.H.M.S.'s paternalism more agreeable. The result was withdrawal of support for the C.A.B.M.C.'s program of mis-

81. Washington, *Frustrated Fellowship,* p. 109.

sions, and even less support for its officers and administrative staff of Perry and Co. In 1872, in desperation, Perry offered a summary of the work done in the C.A.B.M.C.'s first six years: "Perry claimed that C.A.B.M.C. had hired 209 missionaries, who had worked in twenty-four states. They had traveled 102,489 miles, preached 15,000 sermons, baptized 12,012 converts, formed ninety-five new congregations, and forty-six new schools."[82] As impressive as this may have sounded, it did not address the issues driving the inexorably growing division among African Americans.

In an effort to overcome the huge problems of geographic distribution and distance, the C.A.B.M.C. Board established on paper a system of regional bodies. However, it was again without consultation. It was also largely staffed by former colleagues, mostly from the North. The move enraged the Southern leaders and precipitated a series of withdrawals to form their own area conventions. Even the Northeast, discontent with ineffectiveness and with the proposed reorganization, joined the movement in 1874, forming the New England Baptist Missionary Convention,[83] a body which, unlike the other new regional conventions, survived until modern times.

In 1879 came complete dissolution of the Consolidated American Baptist Missionary Convention.[84] In the following year, at Montgomery, Alabama, the Baptist Foreign Mission Convention, U.S.A. was organized.[85] This was one of the three African American Baptist conventions that united in 1895 to form the National Baptist Convention, U.S.A. And out of it have grown at least three more African American national Baptist conventions.

Before moving on to the crucial topic of activism in the next chapter, the question that has lurked in the back of my mind has been what to do with the unreported hundreds, even thousands, of African Americans in majority white denominations. The easily chosen answer was that this was *African American* denominational history. No mostly white denomination had enough African Americans to constitute an African American body within the white body and thus fit into this type of cov-

---

82. Washington, *Frustrated Fellowship,* p. 123.
83. Washington, *Frustrated Fellowship,* p. 126.
84. Washington, *Frustrated Fellowship,* pp. 124-31.
85. Local church history.

erage. However, there is one glaring exception to my easy answer: the African Americans of the Methodist Episcopal Church, South.

The C.M.E.'s

The Methodist Church, South, mother church of the Colored (now Christian) Methodist Episcopal Church (C.M.E.), kept good records on its serious efforts to teach its brand of gospel to the slaves. Ever since the 1785 reversal of the 1784 position on slavery, Methodist Bishop Francis Asbury had been at great pains to avoid appearing to encroach on masters' control of slaves. His written instructions to missionaries were very explicit about getting masters' permission before seeking to preach the gospel to the slaves.[86] A sample of a resolution from an 1839 Mississippi Conference illustrates the approach of the Methodist Church, South: "The preachers in charge of circuits . . . be required to take into their regular pastoral care all colored societies within their bounds as far as practicable and preach to them and meet with them in class apart from the white congregation, as often as possible."[87] By the beginning of the Civil War, the total membership of African Americans in the Methodist Church, South, had risen to 207,766.

One year after the close of the Civil War (1866), the ranks of African Americans in the Methodist Church, South, had shrunk to 78,742. Those who had departed had joined in with the A.M.E.'s, the A.M.E. Zions, and the Methodist Church, North. The latter had developed a strong appeal to African Americans in the South. They had stood by and ministered well to African Americans during and after the Civil War. For example, they had stayed in Charleston when it was under siege, and the local ministry had fled. Also, Northern Methodists established Claflin College to train pastors for the influx of African Americans.

We have this report of movements toward an African American denomination, starting at the first General Conference of the Methodists, South, after the Civil War in 1866:

86. McTyeire, *A History of Methodism*, pp. 282-87.
87. Othal H. Lakey, *History of the C.M.E. Church* (Memphis: C.M.E. Publishing House, 1983), p. 96.

The remnant that clave to the Church which ministered to them in slavery were set off into circuits, districts, and Annual Conferences; and at their request were constituted an independent body under the name chosen by themselves — "The Colored Methodist Episcopal Church of America." The Discipline of the parent body was adopted, without material alterations, and two bishops, of their own selection, were ordained. The General Conference, which authorized this proceeding, also ordered that all Church property that had been acquired, held, and used for Methodist negroes in the past be turned over to them by Quarterly Conferences and trustees. Now was seen the fruit of a hundred years of Christian labor and influence bestowed upon the servile population.[88]

A note on the same page informs us that the denomination's establishment was completed with the ordination of W. H. Miles and R. H. Vanderhorst, December 16, 1870, at Jackson, Tennessee. The Organizing Conference had eight annual conferences throughout the South, with forty-one African American men as delegates. They spread beyond the South, and in 1954 changed their name to the Christian Methodist Episcopal Church.

88. McTyeire, *A History of Methodism*, pp. 670-71.

Chapter 7

Social Activism in the
Early Black Church

From the frequent appearance of "anti-slavery" in the titles of African American religious groups in free states, it might appear that they had one concern only: the end of chattel slavery. Since this account has dealt with the broader total development of church bodies, we will need now to examine what was behind the use of that militant term, anti-slavery. We will need also to examine the charge that early African American religion was used by masters to make better working slaves. An accurate record would have to report early African American churches as striving both for people to be saved from sin and to be set free. However, this former end was far more simply achieved than the release sought from earthly shackles. And so we now examine in some detail the early Black Church's wider concerns and its social activist struggles.

The variety and magnitude of the efforts put forth by the early Black Church command attention and respect. The most apparent evidence of the Black Church's concern for its people in shackles has already been seen in the name anti-slavery. This term readily bespoke association with social action groups by that name, and a great tradition of oratory at public gatherings to rally support for the abolitionist cause. Related to oratory was the persuasion sought by pamphleteering and other publications. The Black Church supplied great speakers and powerful authors. The second area of activity was the opposite of publication and communication: the secret Underground Railroad. A third and somewhat unusual area to consider as activism was the Black Church's ways of cooperation with a military involved in liberating action. Extended family mutual assistance, plus aid to all humanity in personal and public disasters, is undeniably a fourth form of social activism. And the fifth and final form of social activism for consideration here is the extent to which African American religion played a part in slave rebellions.

The Anti-Slavery Movement

The anti-slavery or abolitionist movement, primarily in the North, was led by liberal whites without whose resources and influence coherent struggle by effective agencies would have been almost impossible to sustain. Yet their greatest resources of mass meeting oratory undoubtedly came from African American preachers and laity, who often also served as staff. The list of famous abolitionist African American preacher/orators includes Amos G. Beman (Congregational), Hosea Easton (A.M.E.Z.), Henry Highland Garnet (Presbyterian), Leonard Grimes (Baptist), Nathaniel Paul and Thomas Paul (Baptist), J. W. C. Pennington (Congregational/Presbyterian), and Samuel Ringgold Ward and Theodore S. Wright (Presbyterian).

Virtually every African American church pulpit was an abolition- ist platform, and every preacher, as well as gifted laity, orators for the cause. Even so there were a variety of intensities. In the Second Baptist Church of Columbus, Ohio, a split occurred in 1847 over radical abolitionism. In 1858, the schism was healed, as Second Baptist Church called the activist pastor of the Anti-Slavery Baptist Church, and the congregations merged. The pastor was James Poindexter.[1]

Among the powerfully gifted laity enlisted in the abolitionist cause, and well known in history were Frances E. W. Harper, Sarah and her brother Charles L. Remond, Lunsford Lane, and William Wells Brown.[2] Most noted of all, along with Frederick Douglass, was Sojourner Truth, ex-slave and stinging orator. Douglass, best known as an

---

1. Local church history.

2. John Hope Franklin, *From Slavery to Freedom,* 3rd ed. (New York: Alfred A. Knopf, 1967), p. 251.

abolitionist orator and publisher, was licensed as a local preacher in the A.M.E. Zion Church.

Nearly every ex-slave in a pulpit in the North was also an effective witness against the diabolical system of slavery, not to mention the thousands of laity whose formal and informal testimony, along with their labors, was supportive of the cause. James Forten, a wealthy African American Episcopal layman, sail-maker, and supplier of ships, was an important leader (alongside Richard Allen and Absalom Jones) in many efforts put forth in Philadelphia, especially the 1831 boycott of slave-raised foods.

The ultimate anti-slavery orator, of course, was Frederick Douglass, original preaching product of the A.M.E. Zion Church in New Bedford, Massachusetts. On arrival there (1833) from his former bondage, he served every role all the way from sexton to class leader to preacher. His first public utterances were in this role, and his rise to unequalled excellence as an orator was meteoric.

Douglass became one of the great preacher-publishers of anti-slavery news organs, publishing *The North Star* in Rochester in 1847. Others included Samuel Cornish and John Russworm, who began publishing *Freedom's Journal* in New York in 1827. Among other papers published were short-lived organs in Pittsburgh and San Francisco.[3]

Douglass also authored a slave narrative of his life. This popular genre was an effective abolitionist tool, used by Rev. Josiah Henson and other clergy including J. W. Loguen, and J. W. C. Pennington. William Wells "Box" Brown's popular tale was one of many hair-raising slave narratives delivered by laity.[4]

The most noted of all the publications was *Walker's Appeal in Four Articles Together with a Preamble. . . ."* It was released in 1829 by David Walker, African American Boston shopkeeper and Methodist lay theologian. Citing strong biblical support, and calling it the very will of God, he urged all slaves to rise up and shake off their chains, by force if necessary.[5] The *Appeal* was widely circulated, even in parts of the South, and struck such fear in the minds of slave masters that rewards were offered for him, dead or alive.[6] The slave-owning establishment was no

---

3. Franklin, *From Slavery to Freedom*, pp. 233-34.

4. Franklin, *From Slavery to Freedom*, p. 232.

5. Franklin, *From Slavery to Freedom*, p. 243.

6. *Encyclopedia of African American Religions*, ed. Larry G. Murphy et al. (New York: Garland Publishing, Inc., 1993), pp. 812-13.

doubt responsible for the cowardly scheme by which Walker came to an early death in 1830, presumably by poisoning.

The Underground Railroad

All the while African American pastors and church members were be- ing publicly seen and heard and read in the anti-slavery movement, they were also covertly engaged wherever possible in assisting escaping slaves. It was a foregone conclusion that any church in the Providence Association north of the Ohio River was a stop or station on the Underground Railroad. The very locations of those churches told what they were about. The members themselves were free, so they could remain in sight. But instead of moving on further North to better country, they stayed near the border, to assist those not yet free, who fled the clutches of the Fugitive Slave Act.[7]

Richard Allen's Bethel A.M.E. Church in Philadelphia, and many other Bethels, had concealed quarters that still can be observed. The faithful Christians there were adept at misleading slave-catchers from the South. And Bishop and Mrs. Allen, who were noted for personal generosity to escapees, were imitated by many other members, by the church itself, and throughout much of the Black Church in the North.

Jermaine W. Loguen, later a bishop of the A.M.E. Zion Church, was a major figure in the Underground Railroad, operating out of Syracuse. His motivation was readily understandable. His mother had been born free in the North and kidnapped into slavery and carried to Tennessee, where her son Jermaine was born. After he escaped, he became a powerful anti-slavery orator. But his chief activity was off the public record, coordinating the traffic of a complicated and invisible network of African Americans, Quakers, and other supporters of freedom.

The greatest Underground Railroad conductor of them all was Harriet Tubman, a faithful and supportive member of the A.M.E.Z. Church. She supported her trips through domestic service. On the "road," she carried and used a pistol when necessary, and she led some 300 souls to freedom in the North. She suffered spells of dizziness from a head injury, but she prayed and persevered. Her greatest ambi-

---

7. Providence Missionary Baptist Association 150th Anniversary Souvenir, 1984.

tion in later life was to establish in her personal residence a home for the homeless, to be A.M.E.Z. owned and operated at her death.[8]

The Black Church and the Military

Harriet Tubman was small but brave. She served the Union troops in the Civil War as a very effective spy behind the Confederate lines. While selling chickens and eggs, she guided a very successful Union invasion up the Combahee River in South Carolina. She later served as a nurse in a freedman's hospital. Her work was sufficiently effective that she was finally granted a small military pension in her later years.[9]

The Black Church was never devoted to war. But as early as 1814, at the request of the United States Government, Richard Allen, Absalom Jones, and James Forten recruited an African American brigade for the defense of Philadelphia. It was never mustered into active service, because the war ended before the soldiers could be trained for service.[10]

The Black Church was hardly a reality at the time of the Revolutionary War; African Americans integrated into the regular troops and the African American brigades were recruited by the usual means. However, African American laity were anxious to take part with the Union Army from the very start of the Civil War, because they foresaw freedom. Their offer was not accepted at first. The reasons given were flimsy. Abraham Lincoln was known to have expressed the opinion that slaves had been too easy about forgiving their oppressors for African Americans to make good soldiers. Another reason was the rebel vow to take no African American prisoners; they would kill them all, in other words, and their white officers with them. A rumor circulated among African Americans that Northern whites didn't want African Americans killing whites from anywhere, even the South.

Another widespread idea in African American thinking has been that the final acceptance of African Americans was of military neces-

8. Franklin, *From Slavery to Freedom*, p. 259.

9. *Encyclopedia of African American Religions*, pp. 765-66; William J. Walls, *The African Methodist Episcopal Zion Church* (Charlotte, N.C.: A.M.E. Zion Publishing House, 1885, 1974), pp. 151, 156-59.

10. Philip Foner, *History of Black Americans* (Westport, Conn.: Greenwood Press, 1910), p. 486.

sity in 1863, and the Emancipation Proclamation was part of the plan. Rebel pressure was indeed high at that time, but somewhat earlier, Gen. David Hunter's African American regiment had been mustered in and then out of active service in a few months, and without pay. Apparently with better authorization, the First Regiment of South Carolina Volunteers was launched in November 1862, also prior to the Emancipation Proclamation. They were under a newly appointed Colonel, Thomas Wentworth Higginson. A theologically trained white clergyman and abolitionist, and already commissioned captain, he was an ideal person to command the First Regiment of South Carolina Volunteers. Being sensitive to religion, he provided rare, detailed descriptions of religious spontaneity among African American soldiers:

> that strange festival, half pow-wow, half prayer meeting, which they know only as a "shout." . . . This hut is now crammed with men, singing at the top of their voices in one of their quaint, monotonous, endless, negro-Methodist chants, with obscure syllables . . . accompanied with regular drumming of the feet and clapping of the hands. Men begin to quiver and dance . . . a circle forms, winding monotonously round someone in the center.[11]

Other samples were less African and less dramatic: "Then there are quieter prayer-meetings, with pious invocations and slow psalms 'deacon'd out.'"[12]

Higginson also believed the African American soldiers' amazingly good manners and habit of deference came at least in part from "their strongly religious temperament."[13] This would also account for a refusal to be vengeful and less than professionally military with formerly cruel masters. One of Higginson's "best sergeants pointed out to me the very place where one of his brothers had been hanged by the whites. . . . He spoke of it as a historic matter . . ."[14] They literally referred to themselves as "the gospel army."

11. Thomas W. Higginson, *Army Life in a Black Regiment* (Boston: Beacon Press, 1962), p. 17.
12. Higginson, *Army Life in a Black Regiment*, p. 24.
13. Higginson, *Army Life in a Black Regiment*, p. 254.
14. Higginson, *Army Life in a Black Regiment*, pp. 249-50.

African American clergy, who had struggled to get African Americans admitted to the armed forces, worked hard and effectively to enlist them once recruitment was authorized. The Fifty-Fourth Massachusetts was a product of preacher recruitment. Such was the case in large African American communities across the North. They once again showed themselves to be model citizens of the nation, regardless of the injustices heaped on them.

Civic and Social Responsibility

From the beginning, African American pastors and congregations rose to the occasion in times of disaster and need. In 1792 Philadelphia was hit with a disastrous yellow fever epidemic. A rumor spread that African Americans were immune, and the care of the sick, dying, and dead fell on their small community. Many healthy whites fled the city, abandoning their own sick. Richard Allen and Absalom Jones took over the organizing of the ministries of compassion rendered by their members, often at their own expense, and always at their own risk of infection, since they were not in fact immune. When the scourge was over, Philadelphia's mayor paid Jones and Allen and their members a great public tribute.[15] This was important not only as proper gratitude, but also to offset another rumor that had African Americans stripping the dead of their valuables.

Whatever social action African American churches did by way of political or economic responsibility was only as much as they were permitted. Even in most Northern states, African Americans were not permitted to vote until after the Fifteenth Amendment was passed. The two programs of activity where African Americans were best received were where the public at large was least accepting and the movement least powerful: temperance and women's suffrage. However, especially in the field of temperance and alcohol addiction, African American pastors and churches were outstanding. And one of the most powerful voices in women's suffrage was the already mentioned Sojourner Truth (1797-1883). A later powerful voice for women's suffrage was Amanda

---

15. Richard Allen, *The Life Experience and Gospel Labors of Rt. Rev. Richard Allen,* ed. George A. Singleton (Nashville: Abingdon Press, 1960), pp. 48-68.

Berry Smith (1837-1915), whose advocacy was set in the context of tent meetings and Holiness evangelism.

The Holiness movement was more open to African Americans, especially women, than any other part of the American church. And Holiness concerns about such issues as gambling, temperance, and family support provided a strategic platform and validation for the exercise of African American women's gifts of oratory and charisma, whether preaching or teaching. From Jarena Lee to Julia Foote to Amanda Berry Smith and other African American women, these gifts opened doors for both the persons and the prophetic concerns of suffrage and temperance.[16]

Activist options were greatest for the African American churches where needs were simple and resources, such as they had, were most accessible: food for the hungry, clothing, shelter, training, and burial. Even before African American congregations were formally organized in Philadelphia, there was an African Society whose task was to meet these visible and concrete needs of their sisters and brothers in the family, race, and faith.

Harriet A. Baker (1829-1913) was an example of both the meeting of needs and the opening of doors for women. When her career in tent meetings and evangelism was winding down, and women couldn't be appointed to parishes, she established a "mission" in Allentown, Pennsylvania. It was for feeding the hungry and clothing those in need, but her preaching to the needy drew hearers from most of the Northeast.[17]

The African American belief system supporting this ready reception of responsibility for the needy was traceable to ethnic and religious roots, as opposed to popular social theories. The call to which they responded was from the church as extended family. The common pattern of using familial titles such as brother and sister came from the ethnic roots in those same extended family communities in Africa. There they had no formal titles like mister; everybody was a relative, near or distant. Indeed, all the anti-slavery activity and other crusades were based, ultimately, on deep-seated belief in justice, going back to both African and Christian roots.

16. Bettye Collier-Thomas, *Daughters of Thunder* (San Francisco: Jossey-Bass, 1998), pp. xvii, 17, 33.

17. Collier-Thomas, *Daughters of Thunder,* pp. 71-72.

Slave Insurrections

For many African Americans, the concept of biblical mandates included the plans for violent uprisings for the liberation of the cruelly enslaved, as seen in Walker's *Appeal*. In the root culture of African Americans, nothing is excludable from the design and will of God. Surely efforts to eliminate the shackles of people made in God's image could be considered God's delivery from bondage, especially in the mind of the enshackled.

Bloody violence is a topic rarely associated with the Black Church. Nevertheless the three best-known violent slave insurrections had strong religious bases. These bear closer examination: the Gabriel Prosser conspiracy, 1800; the Denmark Vesey rebellion, 1822; and the Nat Turner insurrection, 1831.

Prosser's conspiracy, one of the most widely supported, was launched in Richmond, Virginia. The preparatory religious meetings featured "exposition of Scripture, bearing upon the perilous theme." The Israelites were used as models of successful resistance to tyranny. "Now, as in the time of the Israelites, God would stretch forth his arm to save, and would strengthen a hundred to overthrow a thousand."[18] This was not a program of a church, but Prosser obviously felt it helpful to show the approval of God. Reports indicated that "the insurgents could easily have passed for saints" in appearance (*Black Rebellion*, p. 1). The "plotters" included were too many and too valuable to be lost by execution, and the legislature in closed session considered colonization as an alternative.

The scheme was thwarted only by floodwaters too massive to allow the mobilization. But the city of Richmond was aware of how close it had come to defeat and destruction, and a force of perhaps 1100 men. The city stayed on alert for the rest of the slave era. Subsequently, Prosser and ten of his associates were hung on the gallows, on October 7, 1800 (pp. 80-99).

The uprising closest to being church-related was the Denmark Vesey Rebellion in Charleston in 1822. As late as the 1950s the local folklore had it that the officers of Emmanuel A.M.E. Church had been con-

18. Thomas W. Higginson, *Black Rebellion* (New York: Arno Press, 1969), p. 77. Subsequent references to this book will be given parenthetically in the text.

victed of complicity and hung on a huge oak tree in the center of Ashley Avenue. As late as the 1920s, that tree was avoided by children in Charleston, because it was rumored to be haunted.[19] There is some truth to the rumor of church connection; "Rolla" was the only prominent conspirator who was not an active church member. A correspondent of the day held that the ringleaders were rulers or class-leaders of the African Society, "and were considered faithful, honest fellows." Many masters found it hard to believe that their slaves would do a thing like this, because they felt that they had treated them so well (p. 128).

Vesey himself was free, having won 1,500 dollars in a lottery and bought his own freedom. But his wife and children were still slaves, and his religious principles obligated him to seek freedom for all enslaved people (p. 115). For several years before, he had engaged in strategic planning. This had yielded the "most elaborate insurrectionary project ever formed by American slaves, and came the nearest to a terrible success" (p. 109).

The military mastermind of the project was Peter Poyas. He was sure God's hand was in their planning, because it had managed to stay secret for four years. Estimates of the final force ran as high as 6600 to 9000 (p. 133). One theory has it that the one leak that defeated them all came about when a trusted busybody sought to engage in some unauthorized recruitment (p. 149). A recent book and television series holds that Vesey himself made an unwise choice of a recruit to trust. He in turn confided in a spiritual leader who, failing to convince Vesey's forces to call it off, turned them in along with all the facts he had been given.[20]

It is noteworthy that in the last call to arms there were white conspirators as well (p. 137). When Vesey found that the plot was uncovered, he moved the date up one month from the second Sunday in July 1822. Meanwhile whites began to round up every known suspect. At least 139 were arrested, and 47 of these were condemned, including four whites.[21] A total of thirty-five were executed in groups, at different times and at different places. The place where a group of twenty-two were hanged is not reported in the source quoted here (*Black Rebellion,*

---

19. According to Ella Pearson Mitchell.

20. Juan Williams and Quinton Dixie, *This Far by Faith* (New York: Harper Collins, 2003), pp. 34-38.

21. Franklin, *From Slavery to Freedom,* p. 212.

p. 47), making room for the Ashley Avenue execution story referred to above (p. 161).

Many free African Americans immediately migrated North, and some have already been noted previously, in their new situations. Chief among these was the pastor of Charleston's "African Society" (later Emmanuel A.M.E. Church), Rev. Morris Brown. He had been away on the appointed date of the Vesey insurrection, and when he slipped into town afterward, he was warned to turn back immediately. He became the second bishop of the A.M.E. denomination, and has a college named in his honor in Atlanta.

The only insurrection to take human life was the one with by far the smallest starting number of conspirators: the Nat Turner insurrection. This occurred on Sunday, August 21, 1831, in Southampton, Virginia.

Turner was known as a prophet, and assumed to have had impressive spiritual visions and gifts. But he was not an ordained preacher and had no known connections with a church as such. He was known as a Baptist and thought of widely as a man of prayer. He was also a careful student of the Scriptures. His orders to take all life, including women and children, were designed only for the first stage, for purposes of terror. The killing was seen to be part of the total plan ordered by God. Turner and his men held to this view even while they stood trial and endured execution.

His colleagues numbered only six or seven, and this limited number may be why he succeeded in starting without being exposed and stopped. The terror he spread throughout the slaveholding states was virtually limitless. It spawned overwhelming efforts at security until the close of the Civil War and the end of slavery.

This whole gamut of social activism related to African American religion and largely to the organized church is a fitting preview to the burst of activity noted in the concluding chapter. Starting from nothing, as it were, African American churches accomplished miracles under unspeakable handicaps but with great visions. The next thirty-five years of this account cover the Golden Era of Black Church history when, with fewer but still many obstacles, the Black Church inaugurated churches, schools, and businesses. Church leaders had political impact for major good, and succeeded in an array of other previously unthinkable accomplishments.

Chapter 8

African American Schools and Churches: New Roles in Reconstruction

Reconstruction began in the schoolhouses, not the statehouses. . . . The missionary teacher was at work in the South long before it was known how the war would end.

CARTER G. WOODSON[1]

The final chapter of this work covers the most interesting and productive period in Black Church history. I call it the "Golden Age," for reasons that will become apparent. We begin with the foundational educational labors of white denominations, followed in course by the educational crusade of the African American churches and denominations. We move on into the Black Church's other labors, accomplished concurrently, or as soon as they were educationally equipped. Marvels of progress sponsored or assisted by the Black Church followed, and they are covered here under the headings "Post–Civil War Black Churches and Family LIfe" and "Reconstruction Government: Black Churches and Politics."

---

1. Carter G. Woodson and Charles H. Wesley, *The Negro in Our History* (Washington, D.C.: Associated Publishers, 1962, 1966), p. 382.

White-Sponsored Colleges

We turn now to the great educational mission to the four million African Americans now freed. After the South was opened up to missionaries, under protection of military occupation, the Protestant churches of the North launched a veritable crusade to bring literacy to the huge host of the newly freed.

My most moving personal response to this crusade came when I was scanning some annual reports of the American Baptist Home Mission Society (A.B.H.M.S.), a group I have both criticized and praised in the following pages. I was actually looking for my grandfather's name, H. H. Mitchell. I knew that he, like me, had served years with the A.B.H.M.S. I was aware of the many groups they sought to serve: African Americans, Native Americans, and even recently arrived European immigrants. I couldn't deny the official report that the A.B.H.M.S.'s funds were stretched thin. They were stretched even thinner when confronting the needs of four million African Americans. So I was stunned to see whole pages of names of people who had been sent south to do mission work. There were hundreds of these names, in tiny print, on page after page. For example, Grandpa had served as a missionary to the "Colored People" three different years, for stints of 12, 26, and 52 weeks, in the latter of which he made 1139 visits![2]

It would have taken millions of dollars to place and keep those listed in the field, yet the board reported what seemed to me like very small amounts expended. Then suddenly I paid more attention to the columns noting the terms of service. These short terms seemed to suggest that people may have been volunteering their leaves or vacations to teach in the South. Many obviously had gone south several times because of the tremendous joy and satisfaction of teaching people of all ages who were so eager to learn.

Regardless of paternalism and hazards to African American self-esteem, it was this huge crew of volunteer and minimally paid instructors, of not just Baptist but all denominations, who laid the foundation for all the secondary and college work reported in the pages that

---

2. *Annual Report(s) of the American Baptist Home Mission Society,* 1889, 108; 1890, 98; 1891, 98.

follow. There may have been only a log cabin church to teach in at first; it may have been by firelight, but these volunteers taught their very hearts out. There simply isn't room to begin to cover the host of primary reading classes that were begun in churches and elsewhere soon after the Union troops took over.

We begin our white denominational coverage with the American Missionary Association (A.M.A.), later merged into the Congregational denomination (now United Church of Christ), and conclude with the American Baptist Home Mission Society (A.B.H.M.S.). There were, of course, some educated African Americans from the North hastening south to lift their sisters and brothers. But this vast number of newly freed African Americans required this white host at the outset, followed later by a vastly greater host of African American teachers, trained in the South, in primary, secondary, normal (two-year teacher training) schools, and then in colleges. The first Southern generation of locally educated African American instructors was first trained in schools planted by white missionaries.

The A.M.A. was unequaled in the founding of schools of quality. This superiority was due, possibly, to a historic interest in the welfare of African Americans, dating all the way back to the A.M.A.'s successful defense of the Africans in the Amistad Affair in 1839. They were also likely possessed of greater average wealth, and superior New England school backgrounds. And they were free of any inner division from former slave-owners in their constituency, since they all lived in New England, where slavery was long since illegal. Their greatest contribution was that of excellently educated, devoted teachers, some of whom remained at their posts well into the twentieth century.

In 1944, when I joined a college staff in the South, there were only four nationally accredited African American colleges in the South. Two were A.M.A.-founded, Fisk and Talladega; plus Howard, which A.M.A. had originally launched with federal funds. Other colleges founded by A.M.A. are listed later. There must have been other African American colleges, A.M.A. and otherwise, which surely deserved full accreditation, but it is at least notable that those few recognized were predominantly founded by the A.M.A.

The following excellent secondary and normal schools, in the locations indicated, were founded by the A.M.A. in the years noted. A great many of these school facilities have since been donated or sold to the local public schools, in an A.M.A. effort to avoid the trend, in the middle 1900s, for church-related missionary schools to become private and elitist, socially as well as academically. There was also a trend for schools to require more and more missionary funding. Lincoln School at Marion, Alabama, is an example. Founded in 1869, it is now a public school. It is widely known as the high school alma mater of Mrs. Coretta Scott King.

The secondary/normal schools founded by A.M.A. are listed here chronologically:

1865-66 Avery Institute, Charleston, South Carolina; Ballard Normal, Macon, Georgia; Washburn Normal, Beaufort, North Carolina; Trinity School, Athens, Alabama; Gregory Normal, Wilmington, North Carolina

1867 Emerson Institute, Mobile, Alabama; Storrs School, Atlanta, Georgia; Beach Institute, Savannah, Georgia

1868 Burrell Normal, Florence, Alabama; Ely Normal, Louisville, Kentucky

1869 Lincoln School, Marion, Alabama

1870 Albany Normal, Albany, Georgia

These "normal" schools and "institutes" granted teaching certificates, and were the standard two years of college required for teaching in the public schools. These schools all had high school curriculum, of course, and, in addition, elementary classes until the arrival of tax-based public schools. The same grade school provisions were offered, at first, at the four-year colleges the A.M.A. founded. Many started at elementary level and worked their way up, but listed the college's beginning as the date it began primary instruction.

When public grade schools were finally provided, they were able to hire the teachers now fully trained in A.M.A. and other schools. The A.M.A.-founded colleges were

1866 Fisk University, Nashville, Tennessee; Talladega College, Talladega, Alabama

1867 Howard University was launched in 1867 by the A.M.A., utilizing Freedman's Fund money, none of which could be applied to religious training. The A.M.A. paid the salary of the very first teacher, but gradually withdrew from liberal arts. They support only the Divinity School at Howard University today.[3]

1868   Hampton Institute, Hampton Roads, Virginia (later independent)

1869   LeMoyne College in Memphis, Tennessee, now part of LeMoyne-Owen College; Straight University, New Orleans, Louisiana, now part of Dillard University; Tougaloo School and College, Jackson, Mississippi

1877   Tillotson College, Austin, Texas, now part of Huston-Tillotson College

The "flaw" mentioned above is the way successful teachers tended to become too effective as models of white, middle-class culture (which they sincerely believed superior). Instead of being molded into bicultural African Americans, the students were trained to be more and more alienated from their indigenous culture and, with it, from African American identity and self-esteem. The great need for the affirmation of African American culture and African American identity had not yet occurred to some.

The Congregational churches that blossomed on every campus drew many students into this new affiliation for life. When they moved North for greater opportunities, the home churches near the campuses dwindled and died, because they were based on a culture not native to the area and incapable of growing and ministering without a school context. This same problem prevailed wherever white teachers gave their all and fully related to their students, while failing to affirm more than "Negro Spirituals" from African American culture. This flaw prevailed regardless of denomination, and these A.M.A. churches dwindled and often died, except in large cities or near surviving schools.

The Methodist Church, North, also planted many secondary/normal schools and eight colleges, beginning in 1865 with what became Walden University. This school expanded greatly, but was destroyed by fire and subsequent lawsuits, forcing closure in 1935 of all but the health science professional schools, known today as Meharry Medical

---

3. *Encyclopedia of African American Religions,* ed. Larry G. Murphy et al. (New York: Garland Publishing, Inc., 1993), p. 362.

College.[4] The other colleges to the credit of the Methodist Church, North, are:

1866   Rust College, Holly Springs, Mississippi

1867   Morgan College, Baltimore, Maryland, which became Morgan State University in 1939

1869   Claflin College, Orangeburg, South Carolina

1870   Clark College, Atlanta, Georgia, which became Clark Atlanta University by merger in 1988; Wiley College, Marshall, Texas; and New Orleans University, Louisiana, now part of Dillard University

1873   Bennett College, Greensboro, North Carolina (became a women's college in 1926)

1900   Samuel Huston College (Huston-Tillotson College in 1952) was founded at Austin, Texas, by the West Texas Conference (African American) of the Methodist Episcopal Church.

The three predominantly white denominations that failed to take strong stands against slavery did less in colleges also, comparatively, for the newly freed. Presbyterians finally stood against the Fugitive Slave Law in 1857, causing a North/South split, twelve years after the 1845 split of the Baptists and Methodists.[5] But the Episcopalians never did come out against slavery in any way, protecting their historic ties with the slaveholding Anglicans of Virginia. Lutherans were fewer and later, but also had Southern slaveholding connections.[6] Later Lutheran schools and missions were begun in Alabama (1916) by the later-arriving Missouri Synod.[7]

The following are the schools these denominations founded:

1854   Ashman Institute, later Lincoln University, was founded in Chester County, Pennsylvania, near Philadelphia, by the Presbyterians. It was the first institution for the higher educa-

4. *Encyclopedia of African American Religions*, p. 811.

5. Carter G. Woodson, *The History of the Negro Church* (Washington, D.C.: Associated Publishers, 1972), p. 115.

6. Jeff G. Johnson, *Black Christians* (St. Louis: Concordia Publishing, 1991), pp. 58-60.

7. Johnson, *Black Christians*, p. 168.

tion of African American men in the United States (and did not become coed until the 1950s).

1867   Biddle Memorial Institute was founded at Charlotte, North Carolina, with Presbyterians North and South involved, though the latter withdrew. In 1921, with five new buildings, the name was changed to Johnson C. Smith University.[8]

1867   Episcopalians founded St. Augustine Normal & Collegiate Institute at Raleigh, North Carolina, with four-year curriculum and large student body growth in the 1920s.

1875   Knoxville College (Tennessee) opened under the auspices of the United Presbyterians.

1876   Stillman Institute was launched by the Presbyterians of the South, at Tuscaloosa, Alabama. It had opened as Tuscaloosa Institute, but changed its name to that of its founder, and grew to a full four-year curriculum as Stillman College in 1924.[9]

1878   The Virginia Theological Seminary of the Episcopal Church opened what became Bishop Payne Divinity School at Petersburg, Virginia, for the training of African American priests. It closed in 1948.[10]

1888   St. Paul's Normal and Industrial School (now a four-year college) was opened by the Episcopalians at Lawrenceville, Virginia.[11]

1903   Immanuel Seminary and College opened at Concord, North Carolina, but was moved by the Lutheran Synodical Conference to Greensboro, North Carolina, in 1905. It served for 56 years.

1903   Luther College, modeled on the pattern of Immanuel College, was opened as St. Paul's Lutheran Church in New Orleans. It closed in 1925.

1925   Concordia College was opened as Alabama Lutheran College at Selma, with secondary curriculum. The Concordia name signifies inclusion in the Missouri Synod system of colleges called Concordia.[12]

8. *Encyclopedia of African American Religions*, p. 403.

9. *Encyclopedia of African American Religions*, pp. 728-29.

10. *Encyclopedia of African American Religions*, p. 88.

11. *Encyclopedia of African American Religions*, p. 672.

12. *Encyclopedia of African American Religions*, p. 205; Johnson, *Black Christians*, pp. 151-81.

*   *   *

The Northern Baptists (A.B.H.M.S.) likewise were involved in the founding of several colleges and many secondary/normal schools. However, the statistics on secondary schools are hard to differentiate, because of the varying levels of local African American initiative, which was always higher among Baptists than in other denominations. This was and is due to a far larger African American Baptist membership base and the Baptist principle of local congregational autonomy, which caused an equally local sense of responsibility for educational improvement. It seems most secondary schools were more locally sponsored and owned (and A.B.H.M.S.-assisted), while a few were A.B.H.M.S.-owned and sponsored (and locally assisted).

A quote out of the *American Baptist Quarterly*'s survey of the related schools exemplifies the mind of the local partners. Concerning Waters Normal Institute at Winton, North Carolina, it said, "Although supported by the American Baptists, it was established by the 'Colored' Baptists of Hertford, Bertie, and Northampton Counties, North Carolina." In the *Quarterly* article there follows an all–African American list of trustees from these counties.

This raises the issue mentioned above of a second flaw in all mission work. The first flaw had to do with self-esteem and culture; this second deals with contests for control. The truth is that when the A.B.H.M.S. held land title, they yielded their virtually absolute control only after they could no longer contribute what they saw as substantial funds. African American colleges then appointed their first African American presidents, and made their own decisions with their own mostly African American boards of trustees, because they had to raise their own funds. It was in awareness of this flaw that a number of African American–initiated and controlled schools and colleges were attempted. These "independent" Baptist colleges are listed separately at the end of the A.B.H.M.S. colleges, but they almost all resorted to the A.B.H.M.S. because of the enormous resources required. In the list of secondary schools that follows the colleges, it is virtually impossible to determine if any were launched by the A.B.H.M.S. Certainly almost all were launched locally and then assisted to a limited extent.

A chronological list of A.B.H.M.S.-founded colleges follows, with the further understanding that, with very rare exceptions, there has been no *major* support given to any A.B.H.M.S. or A.B.B.E.P. (American Baptist Board of Education and Publication) colleges, African American or white, since the Great Depression. The only colleges claiming American Baptist affiliation today are Benedict, Shaw, Virginia Union, and Florida Memorial (which received a $50,000 emergency grant in 1946 and a $450,000 loan guarantee in 1976).[13]

1865   Raleigh Institute (North Carolina) was founded. In 1875 it became Shaw University, with the term "University" later supported by an accredited medical school. Along with the schools of pharmacy and law, Leonard Medical School was closed in 1914, but not before it had produced over 300 physicians.[14] It had depended for faculty on the state university's medical school, which had to move to Greensboro to meet a legal requirement that the medical school be associated with a teaching hospital. Shaw still has an accredited divinity school.[15] It might be conjectured that the absence of an African American Baptist "independent" college in North Carolina suggests a better than typical relationship between the African American Baptist state convention and the A.B.H.M.S.

1867   Roger Williams University was founded at Nashville, Tennessee. The school accepted Native American students, and thrived until a major fire in 1905. In 1908 it reopened under the control of the local African American Baptists, and it closed in the early 1930s.[16]

1867   Morehouse College opened as Augusta (Georgia) Institute, moving in 1879 to Atlanta, as Atlanta Baptist Seminary. It was named Morehouse College in 1913, after the longtime Secretary of the A.B.H.M.S., which figured greatly in the launching and relocation. In 1906 they installed their first African American president, John Hope, who served twenty-five years, beginning a meteoric rise in collegiate education. Today it is fully accredited and hosts one of the first African American college chap-

---

13. *American Baptist Quarterly* 11 (December 1992): 321, 323.
14. *Encyclopedia of African American Religions,* p. 691.
15. *Encyclopedia of African American Religions,* pp. 690-91.
16. *Encyclopedia of African American Religions,* pp. 653-54.

ters of Phi Beta Kappa. It was the alma mater of Martin Luther King, Jr.[17]

1867   Storer College was founded at Harpers Ferry, West Virginia, by the Freewill Baptists. It closed in 1955, and merged its assets with A.B.H.M.S.-affiliated Virginia Union University in 1964.[18]

1867   The A.B.H.M.S. took over what became Richmond Theological Seminary (Virginia) and merged it in 1898 with Wayland Seminary from Washington, D.C., to form what is now Virginia Union University. Hartshorn Memorial College, a school for women, merged with the university in 1932, and Storer College merged in 1964.

1870   Benedict Institute was founded by the A.B.H.M.S. at Columbia, South Carolina. Blessed with major gifts from Stephen and Bathsheba Benedict (American Baptist deacon and his wife, of Pawtucket, Rhode Island), it became Benedict College in 1890, and amassed a million-dollar endowment.[19]

1871   Leland College was founded at New Orleans, Louisiana, by a combination of American Baptist Free Mission and A.B.H.M.S. representatives, with local support. It closed in the 1950s.

1881   Spelman College (for women) was founded in Atlanta, in the basement of Friendship Baptist Church. Founders were supported by the Women's American Baptist Home Mission Society, with later support (from 1884 on) also from the John D. Rockefeller family.[20] The name was changed from Atlanta Baptist Female Seminary to Spelman Seminary, in honor of Mrs. Rockefeller's parents.

1881   Bishop College was founded at Marshall, Texas, with a rare combination of support from A.B.H.M.S. and local conventions of both African American Baptists and white Southern Baptists. Joseph H. Rhoads, their first African American president, was installed in 1929, serving until 1951. He was succeeded by M. K. Curry, under whom the college was moved to Dallas in 1961. Bishop received full accreditation from the Southern

17. *American Baptist Quarterly* 12 (March 1993): 34-35.
18. *Encyclopedia of African American Religions,* p. 803.
19. *American Baptist Quarterly* 11 (December 1992): 346-47.
20. History of the college, pp. 13, 24.

Association when they first accepted African American colleges, in 1957.[21] The college encountered financial difficulties due to over extension of facilities and loss of support. The college was closed and the magnificent campus sold in 1990. Among its host of great preacher alumni are Caesar A. W. Clark and William J. Shaw, current President of the National Baptist Convention, U.S.A., Inc.

1883   Hartshorn Memorial College (for women) was established in Richmond, Virginia. It was later included in the Virginia Union University campus.

Independently Launched Four-Year Colleges

All African American–sponsored Methodist colleges were independently launched, with the exception of the help given C.M.E.'s by the Methodist Church, South.[22]

*   *   *

1863   Bishop Payne of the A.M.E. Church purchased the property of a former Methodist Episcopal–sponsored school for African Americans and launched Wilberforce University. In 1887 the State of Ohio established the University's Normal and Industrial Departments, and in 1895 the Payne Theological Seminary was founded. In 1947, the State of Ohio withdrew its budget support and the buildings owned by the state. Wilberforce has increased its adjacent facilities and rebounded with its own Colleges of Education and Business Administration.

1870   Allen University opened as Payne Institute, in Columbia, South Carolina. It moved to college level in 1880, adding the Dickerson Theological Seminary, named for the college's founding bishop. In its early years the school was known for teacher training. It still serves as an accredited four-year college.

21. *Encyclopedia of African American Religions,* pp. 87-88.

22. Othal H. Lakey, *History of the C.M.E. Church* (Memphis: C.M.E. Publishing House, 1983), pp. 444-45.

1881   Morris Brown University was founded at Atlanta, Georgia, by the North Georgia Conference of the A.M.E. Church. It was actually opened in 1885, with Turner Theological Seminary, a current component of the Interdenominational Theological Seminary (I.T.C.), opening in 1894. Payne College, which opened in 1879, at Cuthbert, Georgia, was absorbed by what became Morris Brown College. The college's accreditation was withdrawn in 2003 because of financial problems.

1881   Paul Quinn College was opened by the A.M.E.'s of Texas at Waco. In 1991 it moved to the former campus of Bishop College in Dallas.

1883   After a failed effort at Live Oak, Florida, from 1872 to 1875, Edward Waters College was opened in 1883 at Jacksonville. A theological department was opened in 1904. The accredited four-year college program is still in operation.

*   *   *

1877   Livingstone College was opened at Salisbury, North Carolina, by the A.M.E. Zions, under the leadership of Joseph C. Price. Hood Theological Seminary was added in 1903.

*   *   *

1882   Lane College was opened as The High School in Jackson, Tennessee, by the Tennessee Conference of the Colored (now Christian) Methodist Episcopal Church. In 1903 Lane Institute named its first African American president. It was funded largely by the Methodist Episcopal Church, South.

1883   On the initiative and long-term commitment of support from the Methodist Episcopal Church, South, C.M.E. Bishops Holsey, Miles, Beebe, and Lane agreed to launch Paine Institute at Augusta, Georgia. M.E.C.S. support continues today through the United Methodist Church, into which M.E.C.S. was merged. Renamed Paine College in 1903, it did not have its first African American president until 1971.

1894   Texas College was opened at Tyler, Texas, with support of three Texas C.M.E. Conferences.

1907   The two Alabama C.M.E. Conferences voted to combine Booker City High School and Thomasville High School into Miles Memorial College in Birmingham. In the 1960s Miles College was an organizing center for the civil rights demonstrations led by Martin Luther King, Jr.

*   *   *

1876   Florida Institute (later Florida Memorial College) was established by the "Education Board of Florida Bethlehem Association," at Live Oak, Florida. It soon appealed for help from A.B.H.M.S. and received it. Its second move carried it to St. Augustine, after racial hostilities at Live Oak, and its third move to Miami (1968), where it once again was rescued by the American Baptists' Board of Education. Meanwhile there had been a split and a reunion, involving a "Florida Baptist Academy" (1892) at Jacksonville, and in 1894 there was an effort to involve the Southern Baptist Convention in a three-way plan of support. Today, it is a strong, accredited four-year school.

1877   Natchez Seminary (Mississippi) opened, culminating efforts of the Baptist Missionary Convention to establish a school beginning in 1873. The A.B.H.M.S. came to the rescue in 1875, offering help. Since there was no state-provided teacher training in the state until 1940, the school's goals were widened to include teacher training. In 1882, the location was changed to centrally located Jackson, and the name changed to Jackson College. In 1911 the first African American president and board took charge. In 1934, the A.B.H.M.S. withdrew all support and ordered the school closed. A local board rallied interim support, and teachers taught as many as forty class hours per week. Six years later, in 1940, the State Legislature voted to add "Mississippi Negro Training School" (now Jackson State University) to the state college system. Margaret Walker, famous author of the American classic *Jubilee,* taught there for many years. The first Bachelor of Arts degree was awarded in 1924. Joseph Harrison Jackson, longtime President of the National Baptist Convention, U.S.A., Inc., graduated in 1927.

1879   Kentucky Normal and Theological School was founded at

Louisville by the General Association of Colored Baptists of Kentucky. In 1884 they took the name of Baptist State University, and most recently Simmons Bible College. At its peak in the 1920's it had schools of medicine, pharmacy, law, and business, as well as religion. In 1880, President William J. Simmons led in the formation of the Baptist Foreign Mission Convention, U.S.A., the first constituent group of those forming the National Baptist Convention in 1895.

1884   Arkansas Ministers Institute was launched, and soon incorporated as Arkansas Baptist College, with the aid of the A.B.H.M.S., who paid the first teachers. The college also operated Griggs Industrial Farm. The college survived a devastating fire in 1893.

1890   Virginia Seminary, incorporated in 1888, opened for classes at Lynchburg. After many ups and downs, this college today has a four-year curriculum and includes the title "University" in its name. The quality of studies at the turn of the twentieth century was such that many students graduated fluent in German and with a serious commitment to academic excellence and further study.

1890   A group of African American Baptist ministers established Western College and Industrial Institute at Independence, Missouri, moving two years later to Macon, Missouri. This school, renamed Western Baptist College, still exists in Kansas City, Missouri.

A tendency of African Americans to fight over the terms of A.B.H.M.S. cooperation ran through some states where the A.B.H.M.S. established an African American college, exposing the second flaw mentioned above. It involved a contest between African American demand for control of ministries directed to African Americans, on the one hand, and, on the other, white insistence on control, because the whites involved did not consider the African Americans ready for leadership. Both sides failed to come to a middle ground and utilize African Americans' cultural insights and available financial and personnel resources alongside white financial, personnel, and professional resources. Instead, with rigidity on both sides, the gap between them has been so great that only recently have American (Northern) Baptists and an African American national convention joined in shared administration of joint projects.

After the Civil War, African American Baptist conventions rightly charged the A.B.H.M.S. with paternalism and refusal to respect the talents of the available African American leaders. The A.B.H.M.S. answer always was that there were African Americans on their board. The African American response was that the African Americans were too few in number, and carefully chosen by the whites for their own purposes. A second white response to the charges can be seen in the trend to reduce support for colleges of *all* races equally. In the process, African American college boards of trustees and state Baptist conventions inherited both control and ultimate financial responsibility for keeping colleges alive and state convention ministries operating.[23]

To sum up the case of the African American Baptist colleges, they eventually organized and controlled colleges of their own, but in doing so inaugurated obligations far beyond their support bases, as seen above. The result has been that only one such locally launched college has survived and progressed to full current accreditation, without at least some A.B.H.M.S. assistance: Morris College, Sumter, South Carolina, founded in 1908 by the Baptist Educational and Missionary Convention of South Carolina, affiliated with the National Baptist Convention, U.S.A., Inc.

Some African Americans accommodated and cooperated with the A.B.H.M.S. for their own benefit. Others were utterly insulted and broke ranks with their African American brethren. This is apparent even now in the fact that African American Baptists in several states (including Texas and Virginia) still have two conventions, as originally divided on this issue of A.B.H.M.S. terms of cooperation, which is long since moot.

African American–Sponsored Secondary and Normal Schools

Another response of self-determined African Americans can be seen in the dates when the independent African American secondary schools

23. James M. Washington, *Frustrated Fellowship* (Macon, Ga.: Mercer University Press, 1986), pp. 84-104.

were founded. They waited until African American teachers had been trained, and then launched their own schools as soon as they could raise the money. In the case of both primary and secondary schools, their church-based schools bridged the gap the white-sponsored schools could not close until the day of public schools. A.M.E.'s, A.M.E.Z.'s, and C.M.E.'s, as well as African American Baptists, all boldly took on this more reachable goal of primary and then secondary education. This inventory of the Black Church's greatest single area of achievement concludes with a rather comprehensive list of Baptist schools, drawn from articles in the *Quarterly* of the American Baptist Historical Society, and the published dissertation of Lester F. Russell, *African American Baptist Secondary Schools in Virginia, 1887-1957*.

*　　*　　*

The list begins with the African American Methodist schools, by the three connections, A.M.E.Z., A.M.E., and C.M.E.:

1879　Pettey High School was opened by Charles C. Pettey, A.M.E.Z. pastor at Lancaster Court House, South Carolina. It was accepted as a connectional school in 1880, renamed Lancaster High School, then Lancaster Normal and Industrial Institute. It survived until 1924.

1887　Greenville, Tennessee, High School was established by the East Tennessee Conference of the A.M.E. Zion Church. It served for a period as Greenville College, but failed to survive the Depression and leased its property to the public schools.

1889　Atkinson College was established by the Kentucky Conference of the A.M.E. Zion Church, at Madisonville, Kentucky, as Madisonville High School. In 1896, in honor of a major donor, it was renamed Atkinson Literary and Industrial College. It closed in 1936.

1891　Bishop C. R. Harris founded Ashley County High School, at Wilmot, Arkansas. The name was changed to Walters Institute, and the school was moved in 1906 to Warren, Arkansas. Following a merger (1936) with a Masonic-sponsored school and another relocation, Walters-Southland Institute closed down sometime after 1948.

1892   Jones University was launched at Tuscaloosa, Alabama, by the West Alabama Conference of the A.M.E.Z. Church. It was merged into Lomax-Hannon High School in 1900.

1893   Lomax-Hannon Junior College was founded as Greenville High School. Under Bishop Alstork, who died in 1920, it was raised to the level of junior college.

1894   Clinton Junior College was founded as Clinton Institute, in the Yorkville District of the A.M.E.Z. Church, at Rock Hill, South Carolina. Accredited for high school and two years of junior college, it had 207 students and 21 faculty in 1976.

1900   Zion Institute was accepted as a connectional college, but supported by the A.M.E.Z. Churches of the Mobile, Alabama area.

1904   Pastor William H. Sutton founded the Eastern North Carolina Academy, at New Bern, with the patronage of the North Carolina Conference. The school closed in 1932.

1910   Dinwiddie Agricultural and Industrial School was opened by the Albemarle Conference at a location north of Petersburg, Virginia. It became inoperative in 1944.

1919   A. J. Johnson, wealthy A.M.E.Z. layman, provided for the West Tennessee Conference to found Johnson Rural High School, at Batesville, Mississippi. Closed around 1960, the school property is still used for Head Start and community as well as denominational needs.

This admirable list of A.M.E. Zion secondary schools is not complete, however. The A.M.E.Z. denominational history describes eleven,[24] but lists nine more closed (by the Depression) in 1932, after brief but often impressive records: Carr Academy, Norwood, North Carolina; Edenton High School, Edenton, North Carolina; Hemphill High School, Crockett, Georgia; Lloyd Academy, Elizabethtown, North Carolina; Lomax-Rutledge Academy, Tampa, Florida; Macon Industrial School, Macon, Georgia; Palmetto Institute, Union, South Carolina; Pettey Institute, Calvert, Texas; and Zion High School (which "once registered several hundred students"), Norfolk, Virginia.

---

24. William J. Walls, *The African Methodist Episcopal Zion Church* (Charlotte, N.C.: A.M.E. Zion Publishing House, 1885, 1974), pp. 319-30.

*　　*　　*

1880　Payne Institute was opened by the A.M.E.'s at Selma, Alabama.

1886　Kittrell College was opened at Kittrell, North Carolina, with the backing of the North Carolina Conference of the A.M.E. Church. In 1888, the support of the Virginia Conference was added. Closed 1934-1937, its junior college program was revived for a time with the help of the Duke Foundation. It is now closed and under lease.

1887　Campbell College (A.M.E.) was opened on two campuses, with the two united in 1898 in Jackson, Mississippi. Between the two World Wars it absorbed Lampton College. Today the well-kept campus is used for denominational and community purposes.[25]

1887　Turner Normal Institute was opened in Shelbyville, Tennessee, by the Tennessee Conference of the A.M.E. Church. It closed in 1935.

1887　Shorter College was founded at North Little Rock, supported by three Arkansas A.M.E. Conferences. An attempt to operate a second campus at Arkadelphia failed.

1889　Flagler High School was opened at Marion, South Carolina.

1890　Delhi Institute (A.M.E.), later known as Lampton College, was opened in Delhi, Louisiana. After a fire in 1907, the school was moved to Alexandria, Louisiana. Some time after World War I it was absorbed by Campbell College in Jackson, Mississippi.

1891　Wayman Institute was opened at Harrodsburg, Kentucky.

1917　Flipper-Key-Davis College was opened in Tullahassee, Oklahoma.

The A.M.E. Budget of 1904 also lists Sisson High School, Indian Territory. The latter was named for J. F. A. Sisson, a white man who spent his entire career as a member and missionary of the A.M.E. Church.[26]

*　　*　　*

25. *Encyclopedia of African American Religions*, p. 145.

26. *A History of the African Methodist Episcopal Church*, vol. 2, ed. Charles Spencer Smith (New York: Johnson Reprint Company, 1968), pp. 93, 347-69.

1880   Homer Seminary was independently launched by C.M.E. leaders at Homer, Louisiana, and taken under care of the Louisiana Conference in 1893, and under the C.M.E. General Conference the next year. The name was changed to Homer College in 1910. Since only ten or twelve students were at college level, and the public schools had improved, the school was closed in 1918.[27]

1887   Union Academy was opened by C.M.E.'s at Lumber City, Georgia.

1892   Holsey Normal and Industrial Academy was opened by the C.M.E. Georgia Conference at Dublin, Georgia, and moved to Cordele, Georgia, in 1906.

1903-1908 Short-lived Williams Industrial College operated in Little Rock, Arkansas.

1906   "Indian Mission" High School for African Americans at Boley, Oklahoma, was accepted into the General Conference of the C.M.E. Church.

1907   The two Alabama C.M.E. conferences voted to combine Booker City High School and Thomasville High School into Miles Memorial College, which opened in Birmingham. In the 1960s Miles College was an organizing center for the civil rights demonstrations led by Martin Luther King, Jr.

1908   Helen B. Cobb Institute for girls was opened at Barnesville, Georgia, under C.M.E. care.

1909   Harriet E. Holsey Normal and Industrial Institute was opened by the Central Georgia Conference of C.M.E.'s, at Dublin, Georgia.

1909   Hartwell Institute was opened by the Georgia Conference of C.M.E.'s.

1903   Mississippi Theological and Industrial Seminary was opened at Holly Springs, Mississippi, and chartered as Mississippi Industrial College in 1906. By 1908 it had 450 students from elementary and secondary levels to agricultural and industrial programs. Local C.M.E. initiative was supplemented by a Carnegie Grant.

27. *Encyclopedia of African American Religions*, p. 357.

In an effort to serve the entire South, the C.M.E. General and Annual Conferences launched secondary schools beyond those listed above. They included People's High School, Covington, Mississippi; Edwards High School, Salem, Alabama; Jackson Colored High School, Corsicana, Texas; and South Boston High School, South Boston, Virginia.[28]

*   *   *

As previously stated, the African American Baptists of the South were so active in the founding of secondary schools that all are accounted for by local churches and associations. A possible exception is the Mather Industrial School for Girls, founded in 1867 by the newly formed Women's American Baptist Home Mission Society.

The following list comes from two issues of the *American Baptist Quarterly*, in which some assistance is implied to virtually all. The greater details on the Virginia schools come from the study by Lester F. Russell.

1867 Mather Industrial Academy was opened at Beaufort, South Carolina, by the Women's A.B.M.S.

1886 Waters Normal Institute was opened at Winton, North Carolina (mentioned above).

1886 Jeruel Academy (last named Union High School) was founded in Athens, Georgia, by an association including seven counties apparently organized for the major purpose of education. By 1927 it had gained the combined support of many more associations whose schools had failed, while Union High School was accredited.[29]

1887 Coleman Academy was opened in Gibsland, Louisiana.

1888 Howe Bible and Normal Institute was founded in Memphis, Tennessee.

1891 Spiller Academy was founded at Hampton, Virginia, and moved to Cheriton, on the Eastern Shore of Virginia, with its

28. Lakey, *History of the C.M.E. Church,* pp. 437-75.
29. *American Baptist Quarterly* 12 (March 1993): 28-30.

name changed to Tidewater Collegiate Institute. It went public in 1934.[30]

1892 Walker Baptist Institute was founded at Augusta, Georgia. It was named for the veteran pastor of the Franklin Covenant Church, Rev. Joseph Walker. He had served even before the Civil War, and had been the only African American pastor in his white association.

1894 Ruffin Academy, later King and Queen Industrial High School (Virginia), was launched single-handedly by James Robert Ruffin as the only African American secondary school in five counties. It became a public high school in 1922.[31]

1897 Americus Institute was opened in Americus, Georgia.

1898-1934 Northen Neck Industrial Academy (rural location in Virginia, central to four counties) was founded by Northern Neck Baptist Association.[32]

1898-1957 Keysville Mission Industrial Academy was founded by the Bluestone Harmony Baptist Association at Keysville, Virginia. It was closed when the 1954 Supreme Court ordered integration of Charlotte County High School, which charged no tuition.[33]

1900 Thompson Institute was started at Lumberton, North Carolina.

1902 New Bern Collegiate Institute was started at New Bern, North Carolina.

Subsequently, after 1900, eight more secondary schools were launched, all of them by an African American Baptist association, with one exception consisting of a civilian board of directors, all Baptists. These include Virginia schools Corey Memorial and Rappahannock in Essex County, Pittsylvania in Gretna County, Northern Neck in Ivondale County, and Halifax in Houston County. Most of them were closed in the 1930s, one as early as 1914, and others in 1945 and 1955.[34]

30. Lester Russell, *Black Baptist Secondary Schools in Virginia* (Metuchen, N.J.: Scarecrow Press, 1981), pp. 60-64.

31. Russell, *Black Baptist Secondary Schools in Virginia*, pp. 65-69.

32. Russell, *Black Baptist Secondary Schools in Virginia*, pp. 70-74.

33. Russell, *Black Baptist Secondary Schools in Virginia*, pp. 75-77.

34. Russell, *Black Baptist Secondary Schools in Virginia*, pp. 5-6.

The audacity and dedication of these semi-rural associations, with small churches and tiny communities, were awesome. Their motives, in story after story, were to remove illiteracy and build up from there. What they lacked in modern conveniences and educational technology was more than compensated for by the person-to-person impact of dedicated teachers and the ambition of the students. Even now a highly disproportionate number of the leaders in African American communities are graduates of such church-sponsored schools. They are from areas where public school education stopped in grade school, but student, parent and teacher motivation remained to further education. The phenomenal success of the educational crusade of the African American churches during the Reconstruction Era surpasses anything before or since, including the Civil Rights campaigns of the 1960s and 1970s. The level of commitment and sacrifice was, and remains, unsurpassed.

Post–Civil War Black Churches and Family Life

Firmly undergirding this powerful educational crusade was a stable family and church base. Despite all the horrible assaults previously made on slave family life and structure, the mass deterioration of the African American family did not begin until the mass migrations of African Americans to the Northern cities in the early years of the twentieth century. During the years following the Civil War, the African American family made a surprising recovery. At the heart of this awesome reclamation was the Black Church and its efforts to assist the thousands of couples brutally separated by the system of heartless slave sale, or denied solemn and legally binding marriage. For many, this desire for a legally proper and religiously recognized marriage was as great as the desire to learn to read. And the African American churches fostered both reading and family ties, once congregations were established by the host of missionaries, both white and African American, from "up North."

The personnel and approaches to the establishment of churches varied with particular denominations. Methodist and Baptist churches in the South evolved from visible as well as invisible congregations, which were now free to surface. The already visible churches were now able to cast loose from white supervision. Churches which were already Methodist accepted advice and direction from African American bishops and missionaries. Churches already Baptist, visible and invisible, were organized as congregations, and then recognized by associations and conventions. Other Protestant churches slowly moved their African American members into closely supervised mission congregations. This amazing organizational growth is manifest in part by the statistics of total membership in the major groups as compared to the total African American population.

The number of African Americans set free in the South is generally accepted to be well over four million. On the face of it, this would seem an impossible total of people to integrate into a working society or functioning communities. This would appear especially true since so many were illiterate and unskilled. After five years of concentrated efforts at instruction, the illiteracy rate had only been reduced to 79.9 percent in 1870.[35] As late as the 1890 census, 90 percent of African Americans lived in the South, and 80 percent of those lived still in rural areas. All of which added lengthy distances to the already great difficulties hampering the teaching of needed skills and the forming of needed organizations.[36]

Yet, with all these handicaps, the membership of African American congregations grew explosively. African American Baptists in the South totaled 150,000 in 1850, and 500,000 in 1870.[37] Although the census of 1900 took no account of the African American churches, the U.S. Bureau of the Census took a special census of religious institutions in 1906. At that time, six African American Baptist bodies reported 2,354,789 communicants.[38]

A.M.E.'s reported 20,000 members in 1856, 75,000 in 1866, and 200,000 in 1876.[39] In the 1906 study by the Census Bureau, ten combined African American Methodist groups numbered 1,182,131 adherents. All African American bodies in that study had a total of 3,685,097

35. Woodson and Wesley, *The Negro in Our History,* p. 382.

36. C. Eric Lincoln and Lawrence H. Mamiya, *The Black Church in the African American Experience* (Durham: Duke University Press, 1990), p. 95.

37. John Hope Franklin, *From Slavery to Freedom,* 3rd ed. (New York: Alfred A. Knopf, 1967), p. 310.

38. Woodson, *The History of the Negro Church,* p. 265.

39. Franklin, *From Slavery to Freedom,* p. 309.

members.[40] Although only 80 percent of these church members were in the South and among the newly freed, their hopes for meaningful assistance were greatly enhanced by the strength inherent in their very size and percentage of total church membership.

In addition to the tremendous number of primary schools in churches, and the secondary schools sponsored by local conferences and associations (often taught by pastors), the newly formed African American congregations of the South made a crucially important contribution to African American family structure. In other words, the African American churches supported and facilitated the deep desire of the ex-slaves to embrace the old African and Christian traditions of the sanctity of marriage. The gross under-estimation of slave family ties is clearly documented in Herbert Gutman's authoritative work on *The Black Family in Slavery and Freedom*. The censuses of 1850 and 1860 suggest that a "larger percentage of adult slaves as compared to adult southern free whites were (or had been) married at the time of death."[41] It was the task of the African American churches not so much to "sell" marriage as to make it possible and firmly binding, and to give the ceremony itself an aura of holiness. For the now "really married," this was cause for great gratitude.

While it was clearly understood that marriage was a legal contract, and the Freedman's Bureau had to be involved in the paperwork, it is interesting to note that civil marriages were few and far between. Even mass marriages required the blessing of a preacher: "Families were re-united, nevertheless; husbands and wives, separated for years, along with those who had been able to remain together, legalized their vows in mass ceremonies before Black ministers and Freedman's Bureau officials in 1865 and 1866."[42]

However, it was not always that simple. Many family reunions were severely complicated both before and after 1865, and there had been examples and precedents already set among the African American members of white churches. In Georgia, "whites worried about remarriage that followed the sale of a slave spouse. Dispute over this issue . . .

40. Woodson, *The History of the Negro Church*, pp. 261-65.

41. Herbert Gutman, *The Black Family in Slavery and Freedom, 1750-1925* (New York: Random House, 1977), pp. 269ff.

42. Peter Rachleff, *Black Labor in Richmond, 1865-1890* (Urbana: University of Illinois Press, 1989), p. 15.

caused a regional body to recommend that married slaves 'separated by force' be allowed to 'stay in the Church if they . . . take another companion.' The Savannah River Baptist Association . . . finally decided that separation by sale was the civil equivalent of death and 'would be so viewed . . . in the sight of God.'"[43] This matter was far from settled when an ex-slave, now free to move about, confronted a former mate, as in the classic novel *Jubilee*. The protagonist, Viry, a slave spouse, had a credible report that her first husband's dead body had been seen on a wagon in the midst of a Civil War battle. She had remarried, only to be faced years later with two husbands.[44] The solution in cases like this required deeply spiritual insights and mediation — in short, the ministry of the church.

The greater number of unions, however, were easier to deal with. They began as early as 1861, the minute the Union Army took over a section of ex-slave territory. At Fortress Monroe, in Virginia, Louis Lockwood, an A.M.A. missionary, asked his New York office to send him 100 engraved marriage certificates. "More than half of the married 'contrabands'" he had met had been married only in slave fashion, taking up together in agreement. Lockwood married thirty-two couples in one week.[45]

The establishment of schools and the legal clarification and solemnization of marriages, however, were only part of the Black Church's "Golden Age" of ministry. Families had to be stabilized and supported, and communities and whole governments needed wisdom and high principles far beyond the old slaveowning hierarchy of systemic injustice. The needs were dire and numerous, and the Black Church was the main institution to which white workers, as well as African Americans as a whole, could look for solution.

Research of the City of Richmond yielded this appraisal:

> The church was the most important extrafamilial institution in African American Richmond. In critical ways, the church and the family were interrelated, reinforcing each other ideologically and socially. Families more than individuals joined specific churches,

43. Gutman, *The Black Family in Slavery and Freedom*, p. 287.
44. Margaret Walker, *Jubilee* (New York: Bantam Books, 1972), pp. 391-410.
45. Gutman, *The Black Family in Slavery and Freedom*, p. 412.

with the Baptist church holding an overwhelming attraction. The church promoted family values. Deacons adjudicated family disputes, and divorce was discouraged, becoming a rarity among church members.

. . . The physical structure accommodated public mass meetings, day school, night classes, and the like. The church also provided skills in self government from the deacons who managed the church on a daily basis to the men who elected them. . . . Sermons, lectures, classrooms, folk tales, and secret societies echoed and reechoed the sacred world view that had been created by slaves, confirmed by emancipation, and transmitted to their offspring.[46]

The church became, for all intents and purposes, a reincarnation of the African extended-family community. The nostalgia that drove it was not recognized for more than a century, but the lodge-like secret societies and the advocacy and mutual-aid functions were clear evidence of a continuing heritage. Blood kinship ties were helped economically by members of the church family. For instance, the relatively early death rate of the day left many widows with young families. It was common for skilled former slave craftsmen to seek the young sons of widows for apprenticeship. Thus Samuel Mayo, a member of Second African Baptist Church in Richmond, had been taught plastering as a means of helping him help his mother and sisters. His father had been lost from his family in the 1850s by sale to a slaveowner in the deep South.[47]

Churches and the communities at large were proud of their capacity to care for the aged, widowed, crippled, homeless, and destitute. Churches had auxiliary organizations with names like "The Good Samaritans," whose ministry was to aid those in need even to the point of such tasks as the regular and sustained care of bedridden invalids. "While little surplus capital among Negroes could be channeled into philanthropic and charitable undertakings, a surprising amount of effort was devoted to helping the unfortunate and underprivileged. Orphanages, homes for the aged, hospitals, and sanitariums were established in many communities."[48]

46. Rachleff, *Black Labor in Richmond*, pp. 23-24.
47. Rachleff, *Black Labor in Richmond*, p. 17.
48. Franklin, *From Slavery to Freedom*, p. 407.

Societies like the Good Samaritans had some of the mystique of secret orders, but were undoubtedly related to a specific church. In fact, many churches had numerous societies. One member often belonged to several societies, and might hold office in more than one of them. Humphrey Osborn, member and sexton of Richmond's First African Baptist Church, served at one time or another as an officer of the Soldiers of the Cross, the First Star of Jacob, and the United Sons of Adam. He was also a trustee for the Poor Saints' Fund and the Foreign Mission Society. His wife Margaret was an officer of many of the same groups or their female counterparts, such as the Female Star of Jacob.[49] Not all churches were as advanced as First African, but the point is that the Black Church in the Reconstruction era was a devotedly giving and serving institution — this despite, for most, the recent horrors of enslavement and the handicap of enforced illiteracy.

There was immense personal satisfaction and pride in this plethora of offices held. But this very pride was, in itself, a ministry to the long-battered ego of the ex-slave, and even the socially brutalized free African American. There can be no better basis for improved self-esteem than such generosity and self-giving.

The spontaneous family formation already seen in the slave community and in the extended family above continued in full bloom after the Civil War. What had been mostly a means of emotional and spiritual support could now become more nearly a replica of the African extended-family society, even without blood ties. No detached female or male, young or old, need be an orphan in a relational vacuum. And instant "kin" now had resources, though meager, which could be shared to meet real needs. One didn't have to wait years for the tie to become binding enough to involve a sense of familial obligation. "The extended family, the church, and [its] rapidly growing network of secret societies provided institutions by which new residents integrated themselves into the African American community. Material and emotional survival was often too great a struggle for the isolated individual. Single men and women shared lodging or boarded with African American families." And odds and ends from several generations of grandparents, parents, aunts, uncles, and orphaned cousins or children were frequently gathered together to create a functional house-

49. Rachleff, *Black Labor in Richmond,* pp. 25-26.

hold.[50] This pattern is alive and well even today in some African American communities.

Reconstruction Government: Black Church and Politics

The Black Church, with all its contributions in education and family life in the Reconstruction Era, was equally distinguished in government and politics. Nor was this involvement in politics a spur-of-the-moment act of opportunism. Some based their political ministry on solid theological grounds, such as Pastor James Poindexter, of the Second Baptist Church of Columbus, Ohio, who explained his purposes at a pastor's union meeting in the 1870s:

> Nor can the preacher more than any other citizen plead his religious work or the sacredness of that work as an exemption from duty. Going to the Bible to learn the relation of the pulpit to politics, and accepting the prophets, Christ, and the apostles, and the pulpit of their time, and their precepts and examples as the guide of the pulpit today, I think that their conclusion will be that wherever there is a sin to be rebuked, no matter by whom committed, and ill to be averted or good to be achieved by our country or mankind, there is a place for the pulpit to make itself felt and heard. The truth is, all the help the preachers and all other good and worthy citizens can give by taking hold of politics is needed in order to keep the government out of bad hands and secure the ends for which governments are formed.[51]

This powerful theology comes from a man born in Richmond, Virginia, in 1817, and trained as a barber. His grasp of the English language came from tutoring by a kind English gentleman, and from carefully listening to his aristocratic and powerful white clientele as they chatted in his barbershop in Columbus. Poindexter's life story is typical of the way the Black Church bred preachers and other leaders of the Reconstruction Era, despite the earlier restrictions against their learn-

---

50. Rachleff, *Black Labor in Richmond,* p. 16.
51. Woodson, *The History of the Negro Church,* p. 202.

ing.[52] Poindexter held many public offices, but always maintained an unwavering commitment to what he saw to be justice and the very will of God.

Through its preachers and laity in the South, with similar theological foundations, the Black Church wielded great political influence for the good of the South in rebirth. J. W. Hood, later A.M.E. Zion bishop, publicly declared to an African American convention in 1865, at Raleigh, North Carolina, that "The Negro was among those who came from one blood [Acts 17:26], and among those whom the Declaration of Independence included as endowed with inalienable rights."[53] This credo of equality prevailed until the withdrawal of the federal troops in 1877 stripped African Americans of their proper political place and power. They left a lasting contribution, nevertheless, in the states where they held office.

At the close of the Civil War, states that had seceded from the Union were dissolved and had to be reconstituted and readmitted to the Union. Their white citizens had been disfranchised until they were willing to pledge allegiance to the Union, which many were slow to do. Meanwhile, African Americans were voting and sending representatives to the conventions that drafted the new state constitutions. Though they held a majority in South Carolina only, their contributions to all the states were an everlasting credit to African Americans, their churches, and their clergy, many of whom were the best leaders and legislative representatives available for taking part in these constituting conventions.

Historian John Hope Franklin said of their influence in these formative assemblies:

> The state constitutions drawn up in 1867 and 1868 were the most progressive the South had ever known. Most of them abolished property qualifications for voting and holding office; some of them abolished imprisonment for debt. All of them abolished slavery, and several sought to eliminate race distinction in the possession or inheritance of property. . . . The conservative element of the

---

52. William J. Simmons, *Men of Mark* (Chicago: Johnson Publishers, 1887, 1970), pp. 259-61.

53. Simmons, *Men of Mark*, p. 71.

South almost unanimously denounced the new constitutions and fought to defeat their ratification. When they gained power . . . they seemed anxious to rewrite only those clauses which enfranchised Negroes.[54]

Other constitutional goals included rights for women to inherit property and to vote. The first tax-supported "relief," now known as public welfare, was also adopted during this period.

The first public schools in the South were written into state constitutions by African Americans, even though they did not share the long-term benefits of high school in some areas until the 1940s and 1950s, eighty years later. Best known for a state's public educational advance was J. W. Hood. Hood had been sent by the A.M.E.Z's to New Bern, North Carolina, in 1864 on invitation from General Butler of the Union Army. In addition to his prodigious activities starting new churches, Hood was elected a delegate to the Constitutional Convention of the State of North Carolina. He rose so quickly to leadership that his Democratic Party opponents labeled the document adopted as "Hood's Constitution," because it included Hood's provisions for homesteads and public schools. This school law included no racial restrictions. When the new state government was organized in 1868, Hood was appointed by the white governor and cabinet as Assistant Superintendent of Public Instruction. This appointment was a complete surprise to Hood. By 1870, he had 49,000 African American children enrolled in public schools, and had established departments for African Americans who were deaf and blind, an unprecedentedly humanitarian provision. He had hoped to establish a state university, but when the Democrats got control of the legislature, they removed him from office and ended his visionary achievements. It is important to note that he considered all of his educational and humanitarian accomplishments as part of his sacred calling, and worked as hard in his ecclesiastical role as in his political role.[55]

From 1872 to 1874, Florida's Superintendent of Public Instruction was a highly educated African American Presbyterian, Jonathan C.

54. Franklin, *From Slavery to Freedom*, pp. 316-17.

55. Simmons, *Men of Mark*, pp. 71-75; Woodson, *The History of the Negro Church*, pp. 213-15.

Gibbs. He was well respected for his crusading for relief and suffrage. Gibbs left his superintendency to become Secretary of State.[56] Other states with highly placed educational officials included Mississippi, where James D. Lynch, an A.M.E. pastor, was Assistant Superintendent (1873).

A large number of African Americans held other offices at state level and below. And they too included many pastors, as well as dedicated laity from the Black Church. Among the best-known state legislators was B. W. Arnett, later an A.M.E. bishop, who succeeded in getting the legislature of the State of Ohio to abolish its despicable Black Laws in 1887.[57] However, South Carolina's first legislature, with eighty-seven African Americans and forty whites, was the only African American–controlled legislature in the South for the entire Reconstruction period.[58]

At the national level, Carter Woodson reports a total of twenty-three African American members of Congress, of whom only two were clergy,[59] a much lower percentage than prevailed in local governments. Of the two African Americans in the Senate, Hiram Revels, an A.M.E. clergyman, served only a partial term. Of the twenty-one in the House of Representatives, Richard Cain of South Carolina was the only clergyman known to the author. He served two two-year terms and was later elected an A.M.E. bishop.

John M. Langston, who practiced law and held local office in Ohio, was admitted to practice before the Supreme Court, and served as Dean of the Law School at Howard University. He then was appointed Minister to Haiti, followed by many years as President of what is now Virginia State University. Much earlier, while searching for acceptance into law school, he completed a seminary degree at Oberlin. However, he never practiced ministry, except to officiate at a funeral.[60]

William J. Simmons's personal description of Robert Smalls from South Carolina includes extremely detailed data of his heroic feats in the Civil War. It goes so far as to report also his high spiritual life and

56. Franklin, *From Slavery to Freedom,* p. 319; *Encyclopedia of African American Religions,* p. 299.

57. Simmons, *Men of Mark,* pp. 628-30.

58. Franklin, *From Slavery to Freedom,* p. 318.

59. Woodson and Wesley, *The Negro in Our History,* pp. 405-7.

60. Simmons, *Men of Mark,* pp. 345-56.

regular attendance as a member of Berean Baptist Church in Washington while he served in Congress.[61] This is an example of the church commitment of African American laity in public office.

This trend of piety among the politically active laity of the Black Church was frequently matched by a concern to clean up the corrupt local governments so common in the South. Oscar J. Dunn of Louisiana, as Lieutenant Governor, led the fight against corruption and extravagance in 1874. Similarly, "the Negro members of the [Georgia] legislature introduced many bills on education, the jury system, city government reform, and women's suffrage. Two able Negro legislators, Jefferson Long [who served a part of a term in Congress] and H. M. Turner, sought better wages for Negro workers."[62]

This H. M. Turner is the same Henry McNeal Turner who later became a bishop of the A.M.E. Church and a leader of both African American religious thought and African missions.[63] His greatest contribution was his organization of the A.M.E. Conferences of Sierra Leone in 1891, Liberia in 1891, and the Transvaal Annual of the South African Conference in 1898.[64]

Turner's second most lasting contribution may well have been his much-needed emphasis on African American pride, including his idea of God as black. His prolific writing led to many publications of church-related books and periodicals. This focus on publications was shared by most African American churches and communities, and was a major part of their impact on political and economic life. Just as there was so much faith and hope vested in education, there was hope and pride in knowing they could express themselves in print. Churches readily aided in the launch of African American newspapers, while African American conventions and conferences supported African American printers with their own news organs, annuals, and literature.

The Black Church, as implied in Poindexter's statement, considered no area of life so sacred as to exempt itself from righteous service. Thus the Reconstruction-era Black Church had every reason to support the economic enterprises designed to support its members. "Cler-

61. Simmons, *Men of Mark*, p. 104.

62. Franklin, *From Slavery to Freedom*, p. 319.

63. Franklin, *From Slavery to Freedom*, pp. 318-19.

64. *A History of the African Methodist Episcopal Church*, vol. 2, ed. Charles Spencer Smith (New York: Johnson Reprint Company, 1968), pp. 175, 179, 183.

gymen often played a prominent role in organizing insurance societies and banks. . . . The True Reformers Bank, the Galilean Fishermen's Bank, and the St. Luke's Bank were either founded by clergy or closely connected to the churches." The historical museum in the basement of the Sixteenth Street Baptist Church in Birmingham, Alabama, has records of the Penny Saver Bank, which was established by that church for its members in the late nineteenth century. The bank's first president was the pastor.[65]

It is probable that the trust needed to launch banks was slow in coming because of the failure of the Freedman's Savings and Trust Company, chartered by Congress in 1864 and closed in 1874 because of incompetent officials and a great economic depression. There was not a single African American–owned bank in 1887, but there were forty-seven in operation in 1905.[66]

In the late 1880s and 1890s, African American insurance companies began to appear, evolving from the quasi-religious mutual aid societies and fraternal orders as well as the churches. "The Afro-American Industrial Insurance Society of Jacksonville, founded in 1901, began as a mutual benefit society in the Baptist church pastored by Rev. J. Milton Waldron."[67] Still another economic offshoot of the African American churches was influenced by the African cultural emphasis on proper burial. Funeral homes had close ties to churches and specialized insurance to guarantee a grand exit from this life for even the poorest.

The effort to establish a secure and supportive community life involved the churches in the finding of employment, a role quite common today. No business was launched in the African American community without seeking the support of the nearby churches. A few churches entered into cooperation to launch grocery and clothing stores, new or used. Even barbershops and later beauty parlors sought and easily received the blessing and publicity of the worshiping church. Craftsmen, from carpenters to plasterers and plumbers, were given the church's reference whenever possible. References were supplied for those who cared for infants and the aged, or who had a room to rent.

65. Lincoln and Mamiya, *The Black Church in the African American Experience*, p. 246.

66. Lincoln and Mamiya, *The Black Church in the African American Experience*, p. 245.

67. Lincoln and Mamiya, *The Black Church in the African American Experience*, p. 245.

The doctors, dentists, and lawyers in the membership of every African American church were publicly bragged about and loyally supported. Reconstruction-era churches built not only sanctuaries, but also people and communities.

*   *   *

The Black Church of the Reconstruction era was incredibly committed to and active in the life and welfare of its people and communities. No phase of need or challenge to action was overlooked. If the Black Church of the twenty-first century were to be half as energetic, sacrificial, and visionary, with all its unprecedented advantages, the condition of African Americans would be immeasurably improved.

Epilogue

The dream that drove the writing of this book was, as such dreams often are, beyond all realistic possibility. Not that it was a wild dream, but simply that almost every book proposal has hidden in its goals innumerable unanticipated or overlooked details that cry for coverage. Among the topics that call out to me for more attention are overseas missions, the place of women in the history of the Black Church, and the pivotal place of African Americans in the development of Pentecostalism. Time definitions prevent other words on African American Adventists and Muslims. My response, though too brief, to each of the above urgent topics is presented in the paragraphs following.

One of the strangest anomalies of the African American churches is the "missionary" in so many Baptist churches' names, and the frequent rhetoric about overseas missionary work in the abstract. All of this is to be compared with the actual missionary work and workers, along with the necessary budget, or the lack thereof. In the period that has just been covered, actual mission work across the ocean seems all but ignored. The truth is that this was a period in which the immediate "home mission" work was much more needed and quite visibly demanding. These new congregations had to get "up and running" before they had strength enough to reach across oceans. Once they had launched the churches and schools, the resources remaining were very limited. Stable denominational overseas work did not really begin until the twentieth century. In fact, even the great white campaign to win the world for Christ, the Student Volunteer Movement, had only begun at the turn of the century.

It is interesting to note the one great by-product of the irresistible urge of African American churches and denominations to idealize about overseas missions. It has been the assignment of the support of missions to otherwise under-recognized and under-utilized women. It may be hard to think of churches without "women's missionary societies," but there was such a time prior to the catalytic influence of the mission ideal. It must not be forgotten that there were no programs run by women at the national level among whites as well as African Americans, until the dawn of the missions vision — after the American colony had come of age, so to speak.

The history of missions in the A.M.E. Church is instructive. "A Missionary Department" was created in 1844. It was staffed with a male secretary/director in 1864. But the serious support began in 1896, when the General Conference established the Women's Home and Foreign Missionary Society.[1]

Other denominations followed roughly the same pattern. Among the A.M.E. Zions, the Ladies' Home and Foreign Missionary Society was established by the General Conference of 1880.[2] The C.M.E.'s established an all-male General Missionary Board in 1873, and set up the General Women's Missionary Society in 1886.[3] The Baptists had sent six missionaries to Liberia in 1883 before organizing the Baptist Women's Missionary League in 1900.[4]

In all these four denominations, it becomes strikingly clear that the overseas missionary enterprise was rescued from a very low place in the priorities, if not from virtual oblivion, by being assigned to the women. Women were thus focused away from the central circles of authority, like overseas missions; they were thus kept relatively low in the

1. *A History of the African Methodist Episcopal Church*, vol. 2, ed. Charles Spencer Smith (New York: Johnson Reprint Company, 1968), pp. 342-43.

2. William J. Walls, *The African Methodist Episcopal Zion Church* (Charlotte, N.C.: A.M.E. Zion Publishing House, 1885, 1974), pp. 388-89.

3. Othal H. Lakey, *History of the C.M.E. Church* (Memphis: C.M.E. Publishing House, 1983), p. 303.

4. Lewis G. Jordan, *Negro Baptist History, U.S.A., 1750-1930* (Nashville: Townsend Press, 1930, 1995), pp. 283-84.

budget priorities and the places of power. Their task was to raise missionary money, but even now the top administration of that overseas missions money is still in the hands of male bishops and other clergy, with the exception of one female bishop in an A.M.E. episcopal district on the continent of Africa, the Rt. Rev. Vashti Murphy McKenzie. And she will likely stay there no more than four years.

More and more African American congregations and denominations accept the full ordination of women to the itinerant ministry, or senior pastorate, though far from a majority. Seminaries today often have student bodies more than half comprised of women. But talented women are all too often assigned or called to the smallest churches in a denomination. In other words they are forced to be bi-vocational, and subsidize and even resurrect the weakest congregations. Only within the past few years has an A.M.E. bishop assigned a woman to a congregation of 1300 members or more. All the rest start much lower, and Bishop McKenzie had to build her last flock up to that number. It may be that God will reverse the declining trend of all current denominations through women clergy. The kingdoms of this world do have to fall, and maybe God will use the gifted women who "sit on the bench" to breathe new life into the churches, or whatever God may design to replace churches and establish the Kingdom.

The idea of God engaged in definitive actions using people from powerless circles should pose no questions. The African American Christians of America made one of the three greatest and most lasting revival impacts on American religious life in a revival meeting that lasted three years, day and night, in downtown Los Angeles, beginning in 1906. Out of that meeting in a revised stable, led by a one-eyed African American man named William J. Seymour, grew nearly all the Pentecostal churches in the world.

The roots of that historic breakthrough go back to the decades following the Civil War, when a Holiness reform movement swept through camp meetings and revivals emphasizing John Wesley's doctrine of "entire sanctification." Many of the pastors involved were from the Methodist Episcopal Church, South, but there were Methodists from New Jersey and the rest of the North and West as well, along with some African American Baptists and others. When denominations failed to yield to Holiness pressures, whole new denominations were organized. Among them were the Church of God, Anderson, Indiana; the

Church of God, Cleveland, Tennessee; the Church of the Nazarene; and several groups with titles including the word "Holiness."

An African American congregation of Nazarenes was expelled from among the Baptists in Southeast Los Angeles and sent to Houston, Texas, for a revival preacher who had been working in the kitchen at a Bible college. He had gone there primarily to eavesdrop on classes with permission. Under the leadership of Charles Fox Parham, this school was advancing a doctrine of glossolalia (speaking in unknown tongues) as the sign of receiving the Holy Spirit. When Seymour preached this doctrine in his first sermon of the revival, it was promptly ended and he was locked out. He then started a prayer meeting in the home of Deacon Asberry at 214 Bonny Brae Street, in the East Hollywood area. There the meeting caught fire, and Seymour and others finally received the tongues gift of which he had preached. The meeting grew swiftly and had to move to the front porch, where crowds caused the porch to collapse. They then moved to a slightly remodeled stable at 312 Azusa Street in downtown Los Angeles, where First A.M.E. Church had met.

The meeting lasted, night and day nonstop, for three years, and the news spread across the U.S.A. and the world. People eventually came from England, Scandinavia, and Germany.[5] The San Francisco Earthquake of 1906 occurred not long after a Seymour prophecy of doom, and added to the spectacular news of ecstatic movements, tongues, and healing. A reporter from a major newspaper came expecting to scoff, only to be overcome himself by the Spirit. The fervor transcended racial difference, and at least briefly, the rules of the Kingdom seemed to prevail.[6]

There are other versions of this account that perhaps should be noted. A book by a German scholar of the Pentecostal movement attributed great credit for the revival to the former pastor of Los Angeles First Baptist Church. Still another account associated the former African American Baptists with a predominantly white ex-Baptist South-

5. Walter J. Hollenweger, *The Pentecostals* (Minneapolis: Augsburg Publishers, 1972), pp. xx-xxii.

6. I gathered this material from informal conversations with survivors of the Azusa Street Revival and subsequent meetings. I interviewed Miss Asberry, daughter of Deacon Asberry, in 1973, with the help of her former neighbor, Jack Catherill of Sacramento. She died a short time later.

ern California Holiness Association, and reported Seymour as called to be pastor, and preaching a whole week before being locked out of the church premises.[7] Yet respected scholars on the subject, such as Walter J. Hollenweger and Vinson Synan, do not share this version; they credit Seymour. After long interest and direct contact with survivors of the revival, I was surprised to encounter these twisted versions of the history in print. Suffice it to say that many nations and races came to be baptized in the Spirit under Seymour.

Among those attending in 1907, from Mississippi, was C. H. Mason. He was co-leader with C. P. Jones of a rapidly spreading African American Holiness movement. When Mason returned, having been baptized in the Spirit and anointed with the gift of tongues, he and Jones failed to find agreement on tongues. Each went his own way in 1907. Mason became head of the Church of God in Christ, and Jones became head of the Church of Christ (Holiness) U.S.A.

Because the Church of God in Christ had been incorporated in Memphis in 1897, and was one of few church bodies with such legal standing, hundreds of white as well as African American Pentecostals sought its ordination. This gave legal recognition to the marriages they performed, and qualified them for greatly reduced train fares. When the Assemblies of God formed in 1914, they drew whites away from the Church of God in Christ, half of whose listed congregations were white. "At least ten other [white] church bodies owed their origins to Mason's church,"[8] to say nothing of the Black Pentecostal Assemblies of the World (1913) and dozens of other African American Pentecostal groups across the face of America. The C.O.G.I.C. is the largest African American Pentecostal group and the fastest growing denomination of any name or race today.

*   *   *

Many years ago, I heard the great philosopher of history Arnold J. Toynbee lecture on the role in history of what he called the "internal

---

7. *Encyclopedia of African American Religions,* ed. Larry G. Murphy et al. (New York: Garland Publishing, Inc., 1993), p. 685.

8. *Dictionary of Pentecostal and Charismatic Movements,* ed. Stanley M. Burgess and Gary B. McGee (Grand Rapids: Regency Reference Library, 1988), p. 587.

proletariat." He brought forth from that Stanford University audience a kind of startled awe at the powerful influence of the proletarian subcultures at the socioeconomic bottom of a society. He pointed out the authenticity and psychic attraction common to supposedly primitive practices. Far from the fads they often became, these practices had evolved from efforts, conscious or not, to meet the real existential needs of a people.

Toynbee's most memorable example was that of America's widespread, expensive, and dangerous habit of smoking tobacco, taken from a powerless, oppressed people mislabeled "Indians." Here were billions spent by millions, bringing death to thousands, from misuse or overdose of a plant and practice introduced to the world from the bottom.

Needless to say, my mind immediately ran to all the African American popular as well as spiritual practices that wield influence in America's worlds of athletics, entertainment, religious music, and worship. I thought of the blues, jazz, pop, and soul. The cultural debt to African Americans in the popular vein is widely acknowledged.

In the field of classical and religious music, the face of the race is prominent. The only music indigenous to America is the Spiritual. The cry of all humanity is summed up here, again, with no contest, and with acknowledgement of cultural debt. Few hearers fail to be moved by a sincere rendition of "Were You There?" regardless of the race of the singer.

The subtleties of great preaching, to which America's declining churches look for fresh life, are, knowingly or not, heavily dependent on the pulpit tradition of the Black Church. At its best, this art has for centuries been healing and empowering to a people at the bottom.

Given the power of traditions like these, this study of Black Church beginnings has many meanings. Among the most important is surely the fact that the African American proletariat, or masses, bear a future responsibility for the spiritual welfare of the entire nation, commensurate with the awesome influence already wielded. In other words, we are accountable for the impact we have had, now have, and will have on religious America, as well as on our own black extended family. This responsibility is as great as it is only because this heritage is so amazingly rich and powerful.

The challenge is for African American believers to reclaim and refine the spirit and the powerful commitment that uplifted so many illiterate ex-slaves, built schools for them, briefly shaped government for them, and encouraged the newly freed as they launched out into the deep of private enterprise. The starting place is in the resurrection of our own self-image, to look at our great-great grandparents and rediscover who we really are, and what in fact is our potential. This we must do for the good of our own larger family, and for the world in which we are so inextricably bound. It appears beyond question that this is our providential place in history, the role for which we were divinely chosen, and from which we dare not default. The hope is that we who are African American in the twenty-first century will be later looked upon as having had still the vision, courage, commitment, and wisdom of our enslaved ancestors of the eighteenth century and our emancipated ancestors of the latter nineteenth century. It may be that the sharing of our heritage will not be as materially profitable as it is in the entertainment world. But that which we possess is better in abundant living than all the riches we could acquire (Psalm 37:16). It was this reality that caused African American ancestors to rejoice so fully as they labored so diligently and sacrificed so much.

Black Church Growth
in the North: 1801-1840

1802#   Mt. Pisgah Church was founded in Salem, New Jersey, becoming A.M.E. in 1816.

1805   Joy Street Baptist Church, Boston, was founded by Thomas Paul.[1]

1807   John Gloucester founded First African Presbyterian Church, Philadelphia.[2]

1807#   Campbell A.M.E. Church of Philadelphia was founded.

1807   Macedonia Baptist Church was founded at Burlington, Ohio, near the Ohio River.[3] Now meets twice a year.

1808#   Bethel A.M.E. Church of Pittsburgh was founded.

1808   New York City's Abyssinian Baptist Church was founded by Thomas Paul.[4]

1809*   First African Baptist Church of Philadelphia was founded and received by the Philadelphia Baptist Association.

1809#   Bethlehem Church of Langhorne, Pennsylvania, was founded, becoming A.M.E. later.

---

1. *Encyclopedia of African American Religions,* ed. Larry G. Murphy et al. (New York: Garland Publishing, Inc., 1993), p. 574.

2. *Encyclopedia of African American Religions,* pp. 301-2.

3. Beverley Gray, Chillicothe, Ohio, history website, www.angelfire.com/oh/chillicothe.

4. Carter G. Woodson, *The History of the Negro Church* (Washington, D.C.: Associated Publishers, 1972), pp. 76-77.

1809# A.M.E. Union Church was founded in Philadelphia.

1809# Union (A.M.E.) Church of Allentown, Pennsylvania, was founded.

1811# Macedonia Church of Flushing, New York, was founded, later becoming A.M.E.

1811# "First Colored Church," now Mt. Zion A.M.E., was founded at Trenton, New Jersey. (Mechal Sobel and others list First Colored Church of Trenton as Baptist.[5])

1813 Macedonia Baptist Church was organized at South Point, Ohio.[7]

1814 African Asbury A.M.E. Zion Church was begun in New York City.[8]

1815 Black Methodist Church was founded at Deer Creek, Pennsylvania.[9]

1816 St. Philip's (African) Episcopal Church was organized in New York City.[10]

1816# Bethel Methodist Church, later A.M.E., was established in York, Pennsylvania.

1817# Bethel A.M.E. Church was established in Lancaster, Pennsylvania.

1817# Bethel A.M.E. Church was established in Woodbury, New Jersey.

1818# Bethel A.M.E. Church was established in Westchester, Pennsylvania.

1818# St. Paul A.M.E. Church was established in Washington, Pennsylvania.

1818 James Varick (later bishop) organized John Wesley Church in New Haven, Connecticut.[11]

5. Mechal Sobel, *Trabelin' On: The Slave Journey to an Afro-Baptist Faith* (Westport, Conn.: Greenwood Press, 1979), p. 269; Lewis G. Jordan, *Negro Baptist History, U.S.A., 1750-1930* (Nashville: Townsend Press, 1930, 1995), p. 25.

6. William Hicks, *History of Louisiana Negro Baptists from 1804 to 1914* (Nashville: National Baptist Publishing Board, 1914).

7. Providence Regular Missionary Baptist Association 150th Anniversary Souvenir Book, 1984.

8. William J. Walls, *The African Methodist Episcopal Zion Church* (Charlotte, N.C.: A.M.E. Zion Publishing House, 1885, 1974), p. 68.

9. Sobel, *Trabelin' On*, p. 406.

10. *Encyclopedia of African American Religions*, p. lxiii.

11. Walls, *The African Methodist Episcopal Zion Church*, p. 91.

1818   African Methodist Society organized in Williamsburgh, Brooklyn. Later A.M.E.Z.[12]

1818   First African Baptist Church organized in St. Louis, Missouri as a Sunday School for African Americans.[13]

1818#   John Gee A.M.E. Church was established on the Ohio River at Gallipolis.

1819   Union Baptist Church was established at Blackfork, Lawrence County, on Ohio River.[14]

1819#   Bethel A.M.E. Church was established in New York City.

1819#   New North Street A.M.E. Church was established in Springfield, Ohio.

1819   Salem/Wood River Baptist Church, Illinois, was organized by James E. Welsh, a white missionary.[15]

1820   Wesley A.M.E. Zion Church was organized in Philadelphia.[16]

1820#   Bethel A.M.E. Church was established in Carlisle, Pennsylvania.

1820   Second Baptist Church of Geneva, New York, was formally constituted.

1821   (or 1822) Nathaniel Paul founded Hamilton Street Baptist Church, Albany, New York.[17]

1821   Samuel Cornish established the first African American Presbyterian Church in New York City.[18]

1821#   Quinn Chapel A.M.E. Church established in Chillicothe, the first capital of Ohio.

1822#   Bethel A.M.E. Church was established in New Bedford, Massachusetts.

1822#   St. Paul A.M.E. Church was established in Uniontown, Pennsylvania.

1822   First A.M.E. Zion Church was established in Providence, Rhode Island, by Leven Smith.[19]

---

12. Walls, *The African Methodist Episcopal Zion Church*, p. 74.
13. Jordan, *Negro Baptist History*, p. 89.
14. Providence Assn. Anniversary Book.
15. Sobel, *Trabelin' On*, p. 280.
16. Walls, *The African Methodist Episcopal Zion Church*, p. 69.
17. *Encyclopedia of African American Religions*, p. 573.
18. *Encyclopedia of African American Religions*, p. 212.
19. Walls, *The African Methodist Episcopal Zion Church*, p. 128.

1823#   St. Paul A.M.E. Church was established in Columbus, Ohio.

1823#   Quinn Memorial A.M.E. Church was established in Steubenville, on the Ohio River.

1823*   Blockley African Baptist Church (now "Monumental") was founded in West Philadelphia.

1824#   Payne Chapel A.M.E. Church was established in Cannonsburg, Pennsylvania.

1824#   Allen A.M.E. Church was established in Cincinnati, Ohio.

1824*   First Baptist Church, Chillicothe, Ohio, was founded. It had 181 members by 1845.[20]

1824   Eden Baptist Church was founded in Ross County, Ohio.[21]

1825   Ebenezer Baptist Church in New York City was founded.

1826#   Ebenezer A.M.E. Church was established in Rahway, New Jersey.

1826#   Mt. Moriah A.M.E. Church was established in Mt. Holly, New Jersey.

1826#   Bethel A.M.E. Church was established in Bridgeport, Connecticut.

1826#   St. Paul A.M.E. Church was established in Zanesville, Ohio.

1827#   Mt. Olive A.M.E. Church was established in Philadelphia.

1827#   Mt. Zion A.M.E. Church was established in New Brunswick, New Jersey.

1827   Charles B. Satchell founded Union Colored Baptist Church of Cincinnati.[22]

1828#   Israel A.M.E. Church was established in Albany, New York.

1828#   Quinn Chapel A.M.E. Church was established in Wilmington, Ohio.

1829   Dixwell Avenue Congregational Church was founded at New Haven, Connecticut.[23]

1829   Fifth Street Baptist Church of Louisville, Kentucky, was founded.

1830#   Mt. Teman A.M.E. Church was established in Elizabeth, New Jersey.

20. Sobel, *Trabelin' On,* p. 215.

21. Beverley Gray, Chillicothe, Ohio, edited local church history.

22. James M. Washington, *Frustrated Fellowship* (Macon, Ga.: Mercer University Press, 1986), pp. 43, 58.

23. *Journal of Negro History,* 60 vols. (Washington, D.C.: Associated Publishers), vol. 7, p. 15.

1830# Bethlehem A.M.E. Church was established in Burlington, New Jersey.

1830# St. John A.M.E. Church was established in Cleveland. Ohio.

1831# Bethel A.M.E. Church was established in Buffalo, New York.

1832# Macedonia A.M.E. Church was established in Camden, New Jersey.

1832# Mt. Pisgah A.M.E. Church was established in Princeton, New Jersey.

1832# Bethel A.M.E. Church was established in Reading, Pennsylvania.[24]

1832 Zion Baptist Church, New York City, grew out of Abyssinian Baptist Church.

1832 Union Baptist Church of Philadelphia was founded.

1833 Paint Creek Regular Baptist Church was organized in Gallipolis, Ohio, on the Ohio River.[25]

1833# Charles Street A.M.E. Church was established in Boston, Massachusetts.

1833 The African Relief Society of Hartford, Connecticut, split. The Methodist branch became A.M.E. Zion in 1836.[26]

1833# Bethel A.M.E. Church was established in Monongahela, Pennsylvania.

1833# United A.M.E. Church was established in Xenia, Ohio.

1834# Thornbury A.M.E. Church was established in Cheyney, Pennsylvania.

1834# St. Paul A.M.E. Church was established in Circleville, Ohio.

1834* Allen A.M.E. Church founded in Jamaica, Long Island, New York.

1835 Zion Baptist Church, Cincinnati, was constituted by members from Union Baptist Church.

1835# Bethel A.M.E. Church was established in Harrisburg, Pennsylvania.

1835# Trinity A.M.E. Church was established in Newark, Ohio.

1835# Mt. Zion A.M.E. Church was established in Brownsville, Pennsylvania.

24. Cf. Chapter Four, pp. 75-77.
25. Providence Assn. Anniversary Book.
26. Walls, *The African Methodist Episcopal Zion Church*, p. 128.

1836#   Bethel A.M.E. Church was established in Indianapolis.

1836#   St. James A.M.E. Church was established in Hightstown, New Jersey.

1836*   Second Baptist Church, Columbus, Ohio, was founded with white help. It was incorporated in 1847.[27]

1836   The First Baptist Church of Baltimore, Maryland, was founded.

1837   First Baptist Church of Hartford, Connecticut, was founded; an African American branch withdrew in 1839.

1837#   Allen Chapel A.M.E. Church was established in Portsmouth, Ohio.

1837#   Bethel A.M.E. Church was established in New Haven, Connecticut.

1837#   An A.M.E. Church was established in Rochester, New York. It was reborn in the 1950s as Baber Chapel.

1837#   Allen A.M.E. Church was established in Terre Haute, Indiana.

1837   The Colored Baptist Church of Upper Alton, Illinois, was organized by John Livingston, the first African American ordained in Illinois.

1837#   Brown Chapel A.M.E. Church was established in Pittsburgh, Pennsylvania.

1837#   St. James A.M.E. Church was established in Troy, Ohio.

1838   Seventeen African American Methodists withdrew from a white Methodist church in Boston and established Columbus Ave. A.M.E. Zion Church.[28]

1839   John Livingston organized Jacksonville (Illinois) Baptist Church, the last of five African American churches he organized in Illinois.

1839   Nineteenth Street Baptist Church of Washington, D.C. was founded.[29]

1840#   Zion A.M.E. Church was established in Delaware, Ohio.

1840#   Payne Chapel A.M.E. was established in Hamilton, Ohio.

---

27. Local church history.

28. Walls, *The African Methodist Episcopal Zion Church*, p. 129.

29. Jordan, *Negro Baptist History*, p. 25; Woodson, *The History of the Negro Church*, p. 196.

1840   Meeting Street Church, Providence, became Baptist from non-denominational.

1840   Second Independent (12th Street) Baptist was organized in Boston; forty members withdrew from Joy Street Baptist Church.

Appendix II

Bishop Rush's A.M.E. Zion Report of Churches to 1843

New York City: Zion and Asbury Churches

Rochester, New York: Memorial Church

Ithaca, New York

Bath, New York

Binghamton, New York

Lockport, New York

Syracuse, New York

Buffalo, New York (in progress)

Troy, New York

Poughkeepsie, New York

Newburgh, New York

White Plains, New York

New Rochelle, New York

Harlem, New York (in progress)

Sag Harbor, New York

Lakeville, New York

Flushing, New York

Brooklyn, New York

Baltimore, Maryland (two churches)

Wilmington, Delaware

Boston, Massachusetts

Salem, Massachusetts

Nantucket, Massachusetts

Providence, Rhode Island

Hartford, Connecticut

Middletown, Connecticut

New Haven, Connecticut

Bridgeport, Connecticut

Newark, New Jersey

Elizabethtown, New Jersey

Shrewsbury, New Jersey

Philadelphia, Pennsylvania (two churches)

Harrisburg, Pennsylvania

York, Pennsylvania

Carlisle, Pennsylvania

Shippensburg, Pennsylvania (in progress)

Williamsport, Pennsylvania

Johnstown, Pennsylvania

Pittsburgh, Pennsylvania (two churches)

Lewisto(w)n, Pennsylvania

Washington, D.C.

Appendix III

Black Church Growth in the South

1802   Sharp Street Methodist Church was organized in Baltimore.[1]

1802   Second Colored Baptist Church of Savannah was organized by 200 ex-members of First African Baptist Church.

1803   Great Ogechee Colored Church was organized for slaves fourteen miles south of Savannah.

1803   The Colored Baptist Society of Alexandria, Virginia, was organized. It was later renamed Alfred Street Baptist Church.

1806   Stone Street Baptist Church was organized in Mobile, Alabama.

1810   Calvary Baptist Church was organized in Bayou Chicot, Louisiana, by Joseph Willis.

1810   The "African Church" was organized at Bayou Pierre, Louisiana.

1810*   Elam Church of Charles City, Virginia, was organized.

1812*   Fourteen slaves and nine owners organized Raleigh Baptist Church, later known as First Baptist Church.

1812   Calvary Baptist Church was organized in Louisiana.[2]

1. *Encyclopedia of African American Religions,* ed. Larry G. Murphy et al. (New York: Garland Publishing, 1993), p. 187.

2. Lewis G. Jordan, *Negro Baptist History, U.S.A., 1750-1930* (Nashville: Townsend Press, 1930, 1995), p. 25.

1817#   Emanuel A.M.E. Church was founded in Charleston, South
        Carolina, with Morris Brown as pastor.[3]

1820#   Metropolitan A.M.E. Church was founded in Washington,
        D.C.

1821*   The African Church of Manchester, Virginia, was organized by
        free African Americans. It is now known as First Baptist
        Church of South Richmond.

1821   Second African Baptist Church of Richmond was started by
        Second Baptist Church (white).

1826#   Union Bethel A.M.E. Church was founded in Randallstown,
        Maryland.

1828#   Third Street Bethel A.M.E. Church was founded in Richmond,
        Virginia.

1829   Fifth Street Baptist Church of Louisville, Kentucky, was orga-
        nized.[4]

1830   First Colored Baptist Church of Washington, D.C., first met.
        First Baptist Church released members to it in 1839.

1830   Harry Cowan set up five churches in Rowan and Davidson
        Counties, North Carolina. All five were closed in 1835.

1832#   St. Paul A.M.E. Church was founded in St. Louis, Missouri.

1834   A biracial Baptist church was organized in Darien, Georgia. It
        had all African American members by 1841. In 1860, it had 900
        African American members and 23 white members.

1836#   Ebenezer A.M.E. Church was founded in Baltimore, Maryland.

1836   First Colored Baptist Church of Baltimore was organized with
        an ex-slave African American pastor.

1837#   Metropolitan A.M.E. Church was founded in Cumberland,
        Maryland.

1838#   Quinn Chapel A.M.E. Church was founded in Louisville, Ken-
        tucky.

1838#   Ebenezer A.M.E. Church was founded in Hagerstown, Mary-
        land.

1838   First African Baptist Church of Richmond, Virginia, paid First
        Baptist Church of Richmond 6,500 dollars for its building.

---

3. Gayraud S. Wilmore, *Black Religion and Black Radicalism,* 2nd ed. (Maryknoll,
N.Y.: Orbis Books, 1983), p. 83.

4. Jordan, *Negro Baptist History,* p. 250.

1838   First Baptist Church was founded at Jacksonville, Florida.[5]

1840#   St. John A.M.E. Church was founded in Norfolk, Virginia.

1840   Huspah Mission organized near Beaufort, South Carolina, one
         of five missions of the First Baptist Church of Beaufort
         (white).

5. Jordan, *Negro Baptist History,* p. 25.

Black Church Beginnings
in Overseas Missions

Year	Missionary/Agent	Denom.	Country	Sponsorship
1791	George Liele 1750-1820	Baptist	Jamaica	Independent/self-supported. Some help came later from Britain.
1792	David George 1742-1810	Baptist	Sierra Leone	Independent
1820	Daniel Coker c. 1780–c. 1840	A.M.E.	Sierra Leone	A.M.E., helped by Maryland colonization; later independent Methodist
1821	Lott Carey 1780-1828 & Colin Teague	Baptist	Liberia/ Sierra Leone	Richmond Af. Bap. Foreign Mission Soc.; Bapt. Board of Foreign Missions (white); Am. Colonization Society
1853	Alexander Crummell 1819-1898	Episc	Liberia	Am. Colonization Society
1876	Andrew Cartwright	A.M.E.Z.	West Africa	Missions director for A.M.E. Zions in W. Af. — Liberia, Ghana, etc.
1883	"First six missionaries"	Baptist	Liberia	Baptist Foreign Mission Convention, org. 1880. Start of NBC, USA, Inc.
1891	Bishop Henry McNeal Turner	A.M.E	Sierra Leone	Org. conferences in Liberia, Sierra Leone & South Africa (1898)

Index